7/01

The Ornament of the World

The Ornament of the World

HOW MUSLIMS, JEWS, AND CHRISTIANS

CREATED A CULTURE OF TOLERANCE

IN MEDIEVAL SPAIN

María Rosa Menocal

LITTLE, BROWN AND COMPANY
BOSTON   NEW YORK   LONDON

First Edition

ISBN 0-316-56688-8
LCCN 2002090675

10 9 8 7 6 5 4 3 2 1

Q-FF

Text design by Meryl Sussman Levavi / Digitext
Maps by Jeffrey L. Ward

Printed in the United States of America

For *un hombre sincero de donde crece la palma* . . .
my father, the intrepid Enrique Menocal,
who has lived in lifelong exile
from his own land of the palm trees

Contents

List of Maps

Foreword

by
Harold Bloom

María Rosa Menocal begins this poignant story in Damascus in 750, and ends at Granada in 1492, the year of the expulsion of the Moors and the Jews from Spain. Menocal's epilogue, "Andalusian Shards," uncannily recounts the destruction, exactly five hundred years later, of the National Library in Sarajevo by Serbian artillery. Between the brutal disaster of 1492, the work of Spanish Catholicism, and the 1992 cultural atrocity, the deliberate achievement of Serbian Orthodox Christians, Menocal stations my favorite pages in this book, dealing with the publication of the first part of Cervantes' *Don Quixote* in 1605. That was also the year Shakespeare put on the first performance of *King Lear* at the Globe Theatre in London. Nothing in Western literature, in the four centuries since, is of the eminence of *Don Quixote,* greatest of comedies and of novels, or of *King Lear,* the ultimate tragic drama, and perhaps the limit of literary art.

Cervantes' Spain, a century after the expulsion, remained haunted by the cultural and economic traumas of that catastrophic happening. For the Jews and Moors it meant permanent exile from what had been "a first-rate place"; for the Old Christians it meant their triumph and their Golden Age. What it meant for Cervantes is an enigma that cannot be resolved. Sancho Panza rather too frequently protests his Old Christian lineage, and once gratuitously adds that he hates the Jews. Which Jews? He may mean the New Christian Conversos (converts), but the reader is unlikely to believe that the marvelously good-natured Sancho hates anyone. Don Quixote himself is finally defeated, abandons his knighthood, and goes home to die devoutly. Spain died devoutly, from the later seventeenth century until the death of Francisco Franco, and since then has become something else, not yet fully definable. Compared to the United States and Ireland, Spain no longer is obsessed with religion, though the cult of death still lingers in cultural recesses.

Menocal's Andalusia, where "Muslims, Jews, and Christians created a culture of tolerance," may to some degree represent an idealization, healthy and useful. The author herself refers to the terrible massacre of Jews in Granada in 1066, while ascribing it entirely to fundamentalist Berbers, which is not wholly convincing. Still, the central vision of *The Ornament of the World* is persuasive. The Jews and Christians of Muslim Andalusia flourished economically and culturally under the Umayyads, whose dynasty had been transplanted from Damascus to Cordoba by the audacious Abd al-Rahman. Indeed, of the Jewish exile cultures, from Babylon to the United States, the three later summits are Alexandria (from the second century B.C.E. to the second century C.E.), Muslim Andalusia, and Austria-Germany (from the 1890s through 1933). Compared to these three, American Jewry seems culturally pathetic, though the Babylonian Talmud and the Genesis-through-Kings creation by the Redactor probably outshine even the Jewish cultures of Alexandria, Cordoba-Granada-Toledo, and Vienna-Prague-Berlin.

Menocal's book is a love song addressed to the Jewish, Muslim, and Christian (mostly troubadour) poets of what once we called the High Middle Ages. I hesitate to nominate a single hero of the book (Menocal's heart seems to belong to the warrior-poet Samuel the Nagid, who reinvented Hebrew poetry), but I would vote for Ibn Hazm, also a warrior-poet, but in Arabic, whose *The Neck-Ring of the Dove,* a handbook on romantic love, is also a monument to a devastated Cordoba, its great era forever passed. Menocal presents Ibn Hazm as a Don Quixote, holding on to an aesthetics, an erotics, and a cultural tradition unrecoverable but unforgettable.

Menocal's book, as wise as it is poignant, studies such nostalgias, not altogether for their own sake, but also because of their current relevance. There are no Muslim Andalusians visible anywhere in the world today. The Iran of the ayatollahs and the Afghanistan of the Taliban may mark an extreme, but even Egypt is now not much of a culture of tolerance. The Israelis and Palestinians, even if they could achieve a workable peace, would still be surrounded by a Muslim world very remote from the Andalusia of Abd al-Rahman and his descendants. It is salutary to be reminded of what Cordoba and Granada once were, and yet it is also disquieting.

I come away from a reading of Menocal's book with a sense of loss, another tribute to her evocative power. Our current multiculturalism, the blight of our universities and of our media, is a parody of the culture of Cordoba and Granada in their lost prime. All the cultural achievements so passionately described by Menocal, from the Alhambra to the poetry of Judah Halevi, were *aesthetic* triumphs, strong in conception, exquisite in execution. As a contribution to cultural memory, in its best aspects, *The Ornament of the World* is an authentic and heartening gesture of the spirit.

A Note on Transliterations and Non-English Names

To make the significant number of foreign names and words in the text more accessible to the reader, I have generally followed these guidelines:

No diacritics or other accent marks are used on foreign names, and familiar English forms are given whenever possible: thus Cordoba rather than Córdova, Saragossa rather than Zaragoza, Quran rather than Qur'an (the former spelling being now preferable to the older Koran).

Foreign words with no conventional English equivalents appear in italics on first mention. Once translated or explained, however, such commonly used terms will appear without italics. Thus, *taifa* and *fitna* are written as conventional English words after they have been introduced. Most book titles are given only in English translation.

Arabic and Hebrew names that have familiar English equivalents are initially given in the original and thereafter in their more familiar form. Thus Musa ibn Maymun will be Maimonides. In most instances, I have also given anglicized versions of proper names of people not well known; thus the Archbishop Raymond (rather than Raimundo) of Toledo. Many of these, in any case, appear in variant forms in medieval documents.

Al-Andalus is typically referred to with the Arabic article *al-* assimilated into the proper name, whereas ha-Sefarad conventionally drops the article *ha-* and is called simply Sefarad.

The Ornament of the World

Beginnings

*O*NCE UPON A TIME IN THE MID-EIGHTH CENTURY, AN INTREPID young man named Abd al-Rahman abandoned his home in Damascus, the Near Eastern heartland of Islam, and set out across the North African desert in search of a place of refuge. Damascus had become a slaughterhouse for his family, the ruling Umayyads, who had first led the Muslims out of the desert of Arabia into the high cultures of the Fertile Crescent. With the exception of Abd al-Rahman, the Umayyads were eradicated by the rival Abbasids, who seized control of the great empire called the "House of Islam." This sole survivor was undoubtedly too young—he was in his late teens or early twenties—to be terrified at the odds against him, nor was his flight westward, toward what was the farthest frontier of the Islamic territories, as arbitrary or hopeless as it might have seemed. The prince's mother was a Berber tribeswoman from the environs of today's Morocco, which Arab conquerors had reached some years before. From this place, which the Muslims called the Maghrib, the "Far West," the descendants of the Prophet and his first followers had brought women such as Abd al-Rahman's mother back east as brides or concubines for the highest-ranking families, to expand and enrich the bloodlines.

The Abbasid massacre of the Umayyads in Syria took place in 750. Abd al-Rahman reappeared in the Far West five years later, and when he finally reached that distant land, he found that many of his Berber kinsmen had themselves emigrated from there. These non-Arab nomads, who in antiquity had settled between the Sahara and the Mediterranean west of the Nile, had been largely converted to Islam and partially Arabized with the westward expansion of Islam in the seventh century. Beginning in 711, the Muslims—here the Berbers under the leadership of the Syrian Arabs—had pushed across the small sliver of sea that separates Africa from Europe, the Strait of Gibraltar, to the place the Romans had called Hispania or Iberia. Unlike Abd al-Rahman, who crossed the formidable desert as a political refugee, the Berbers of the Maghrib, along with the Syrians who rode at the head of the troops, were driven by military expansiveness and ambition, as well as by that sense of adventure and the desire for a better life that have motivated pioneers throughout history.

Abd al-Rahman followed their trail and crossed the narrow strait at the western edge of the world. In Iberia, a place they were calling al-Andalus in Arabic, the language of the new Muslim colonizers, he found a thriving and expansive Islamic settlement. Its center was on the banks of a river that wound down to the Atlantic coast, the Big Wadi (today, in lightly touched-up Arabic, the Guadalquivir, or Wadi al-Kabir). The new capital was an old city that the former rulers, the Visigoths, had called Khordoba, after the Roman Corduba, who had ruled the city before the Germanic conquest. It was now pronounced

Qurtuba, in the new Arabic accents heard nearly everywhere. The governor of that amorphous and fairly detached frontier "province" was understandably taken aback by the unexpected apparition of this assumed-dead Umayyad prince. Out in these hinterlands, after all, so far from the center of the empire, the shift from Umayyad to Abbasid sovereignty had, until that moment, made little real difference in local politics.

The local politics had been shaped perhaps most of all by the often murderous rivalries between the majority Berber rank and file and the Arab leadership, rivalries within this community of Muslims whose animus would decisively dominate the politics of al-Andalus—the name used for the ever-shifting Muslim polities of Iberia, never quite the whole of the peninsula—for half a millennium. The emirs (*emir,* or *amir,* is the Arabic word for "governor") of these Andalusian frontier territories, the westernmost edge of an empire that in the east was then reaching China, had been "clients" of the Umayyads, fairly autonomous representatives of the rather remote central government. Recent word of the Umayyads' overthrow in Damascus was largely of symbolic importance to Muslims in the west. This was especially so for the majority Berbers, for whom all Arabs were overbearing and brash overlords. Granted, the Arabs had brought the Revelation of the True Faith to these southwestern reaches of the ruined Roman basin—but they had persisted in treating the Berbers as inferiors, even after most had proven to be enthusiastic converts.

With Abd al-Rahman's arrival in 755, the fate of the House of the Umayya was no longer a distant and abstract matter but the center of local political turmoil. The wild turn of events, and its consequences, can perhaps only be imagined by conjuring the image of Anastasia, and what might have happened if she really had reappeared one day in Paris and unambiguously claimed the survival of the Romanovs. Abd al-Rahman was in some ways the quintessential Arab, the heir and descendant of the desert warriors who were the companions of the Prophet himself, and yet he was no less a Berber, the child of one of their own tribeswomen. This made it easy for him to claim the loyalty of the soldiers and settlers in this fertile and promising new land. The vexed emir of al-Andalus saw at least some of the handwriting on the wall and offered the young man permanent refuge in the capital city as well as his daughter's hand in marriage. But the grandson of the caliph, the successor to the Prophet and the supreme temporal and spiritual leader of the Islamic world, could not be so easily bought off. Abd al-Rahman assembled forces loyal to him, Syrians and Berbers combined, and one day in May 756, a battle just outside the city walls of Cordoba decisively changed the face of European history and culture. Abd al-Rahman easily defeated his would-be father-in-law and became the new governor of this westernmost province of the Islamic world.

Technically Abd al-Rahman was nothing more than the governor of a frontierlike outpost at the edge of the caliphate, and the caliphate was now under the control of the Abbasids, the regime that had not only overthrown but also slaughtered Abd al-Rahman's family. But during those half-dozen years since the bloody coup, the Abbasids had moved the capital of the Islamic empire farther east, to Baghdad, away from any lingering traces of Umayyad legitimacy. Abd al-Rahman's improbable and triumphant resurrection as a viable leader was a disturbing loose end, since he was himself the living and vital memory of that legitimate past, with its direct links to the beginnings of Islam itself. Despite whatever dismay the Abbasids might have felt about the Umayyad who got away, they let him be, no doubt reckoning that in the permanent exile in that backwater to which he was condemned, Abd al-Rahman was as good as dead.

But this young man was, for nearly everyone in those outer provinces, the legitimate caliph, and he was not about to spend the rest of his life in embittered exile. He built his new

Andalusian estate, Rusafa, in part to memorialize the old Rusafa deep in the desert steppes northeast of Damascus, where he had last lived with his family, and also, no less, to proclaim that he had survived and that this was indeed the new and legitimate home of the Umayyads. Although it would be two more centuries before one of his descendants actually openly declared that Cordoba was the seat of *the* caliphate, al-Andalus was transformed and now anything but a mere provincial seat. Here, on the western shores of the Roman empire's great inland sea, and at the front door of what was not yet truly Europe, a real contender had arrived and settled in.

This book tells the story of how this remarkable turn of events, which actually had its origins in the heart of the seventh century in what we call the Near East, powerfully affected the course of European history and civilization. Many aspects of the story are largely unknown, and the extent of their continuing effects on the world around us is scarcely understood, for numerous and complex reasons. The conventional histories of the Arabic-speaking peoples follow the fork in the road taken by the Abbasids. At precisely the point at which the Umayyad prince sets up his all-but-declared caliphate in Europe, the story we are likely to be told continues with the achievements of the Abbasids, who did indeed make Baghdad the capital of an empire of material and cultural wealth and achievement.

Even the histories traditionally told within the Muslim world rarely take the Umayyad path, and they spend relatively little time in al-Andalus, despite the fact that al-Andalus represents, in one form or another, the presence of Islam in Europe for the subsequent seven-hundred-odd years, some three times the present duration of the American Republic. From the normative perspective of the history of Islam or of the Arabic-speaking peoples, al-Andalus is reckoned more a nostalgic curiosity than anything else—and mostly, in the end, a failure, because Islam did not survive as one of the religions of Europe and because by 1492, Granada, the last Islamic city-state in Europe, was quashed and the "Moors" (the disparaging Christian term for Muslims), along with the Jews, were driven out of Spain. Worse, for us, in the stories that constitute our European heritage, the chapters about the "Middle Ages," when all these events take place, typically describe a time that was dark and barbaric. In the popular imagination, and even in the vision of most well-educated people, the very adjective "medieval" (which itself comes from the expression "in the middle," thus signaling a placeholder between two legitimately freestanding eras, the classical and the modern) is often a synonym for an unenlightened, backward, and intolerant culture.

But if we retell the story beginning with the narrative of that intrepid young man who miraculously evaded the annihilation of his line and migrated from Damascus to Cordoba, which he then made over into his new homeland, we end up with an altogether different vision of the fundamental parameters of Europe during the Middle Ages. This is a vision still evident today, in the lasting influence of this complex, rich, and unique civilization. When one walks past synagogues on the Upper West Side of New York City, buildings created by devout German Jews in the nineteenth century, one notices their clear and intentional allusions to mosques—to take one conspicuous and lovely example among hundreds. Yet where are the stories in our education that reveal to us why this is so?

This book aims to follow the road from Damascus taken by Abd al-Rahman, who, Aeneas-like, escaped the devastation of his home to become the first, rather than the last, of his line. It is about a genuine, foundational European cultural moment that qualifies as "first-rate," in the sense of F. Scott Fitzgerald's wonderful formula (laid out in his essay "The Crack-Up")—namely, that "the test of a first-rate intelligence is the ability to hold two opposed ideas in the mind at the same time." In its moments of great achievement, medieval culture positively thrived on holding at least two, and often many more, contrary ideas at the same time. This was the chapter of Europe's culture when Jews, Christians, and Muslims lived side by side and, despite their intractable differences and enduring hostilities, nourished a complex culture of tolerance, and it is this difficult concept that my subtitle aims to convey. This only sometimes included guarantees of religious freedoms comparable to those we would expect in a modern "tolerant" state; rather, it found expression in the often unconscious acceptance that contradictions—within oneself, as well as within one's culture—could be positive and productive. Much that was characteristic of medieval culture was profoundly rooted in the cultivation of the complexities, charms, and challenges of contradictions—of the "yes and no," as it was put by Peter Abelard, the infamous twelfth-century Parisian intellectual and Christian theologian.

The very heart of culture as a series of contraries lay in al-Andalus, which requires us to reconfigure the map of Europe and put the Mediterranean at the center, and begin telling at least this part of our own story from an Andalusian perspective. It was there that the profoundly Arabized Jews rediscovered and reinvented Hebrew; there that Christians embraced nearly every aspect of Arabic style—from the intellectual style of philosophy to the architectural styles of mosques—not only while living in Islamic dominions but especially after wresting political control from them; there that men of unshakable faith, like Abelard and Maimonides and Averroes, saw no contradiction in pursuing the truth, whether philosophical or scientific or religious, across confessional lines. This vision of a culture of tolerance recognized that incongruity in the shaping of individuals as well as their cultures was enriching and productive. It was an approach to life and its artistic and intellectual and even religious pursuits that was contested by many—as it is today—and violently so at times—as it is today—and yet powerful and shaping neverthe-less, for hundreds of years. Whether it is because of our clichéd notions about the relative backwardness of the Middle Ages, or our own expectations that culture, religion, and political ideol-ogy will be roughly consistent, we are likely to be taken aback by many of the lasting testimonies of this Andalusian culture, mon-uments like the tomb of Saint Ferdinand in Seville. Ferdinand III is the king remembered as the Castilian conqueror of the last of all the Islamic territories save Granada, and yet his tomb is rather matter-of-factly inscribed in Arabic and Hebrew as well as in Latin and Castilian.

In the end, much of Europe far beyond the Andalusian world, and far beyond modern Spain's geographical borders, was shaped by the deep-seated vision of complex and contradic-tory identities that was first elevated to an art form by the Andalusians. "The ornament of the world" is the famous de-scription of Cordoba given to her readers by the tenth-century Saxon writer Hroswitha, who from her far-off convent at Gandersheim perceived the exceptional qualities and the cen-trality of the Cordoban caliphate. Tellingly, Hroswitha coined the expression even as she wrote an account of a Mozarab Christian martyr of the tenth century. For her, and eventually for most oth-ers who came to know Andalusian culture throughout the Middle Ages, whether at first hand or from afar—from reading a translation produced there or from hearing a poem sung by one of its renowned singers—the bright lights of that world, and their illumination of the rest of the universe, transcended differ-ences of religion. And I too use the expression generously; as this book's title, it means to describe the culture that long survived and transcended the destruction of the caliphate of Hroswitha's time, the culture that centuries later did produce the tomb of Saint Ferdinand, and did give a "Moorish" style to some of New York City's nineteenth-century synagogues.

Rather than retell the history of the Middle Ages, or even

that of medieval Spain, I have strung together a series of miniature portraits that range widely in time and place, and that are
focused on cultural rather than political events. They will, I
hope, lay bare the vast distance between what the conventional
histories and other general prejudices would have us expect
(that, for example, Christians saw the Muslim infidels as their
mortal enemy and spent seven hundred years trying to drive
them from Spain) and what we can learn from the many testimonies that survive in the songs people really sang or the buildings they really put up. These vignettes and profiles highlight
stories that in and of themselves seem to me worth knowing and
worth retelling as part of our common history. Beyond that, together, they point to some of the unknown depths of cultural tolerance and symbiosis in our heritage, and they may begin to suggest a very different overall portrait of this "middle" age. It
would be foolish to try to replace all the older clichés with another equally simplistic new one — to suggest that this was a
world devoid of all manner of intolerance and darkness. What
age, no matter how golden, is? But how many among us know
the stories that also make the Middle Ages a golden age, in fact
a whole series of golden ages?

Before these stories can make much sense, the larger scene
needs to be set. Before we can return to Cordoba in the spring of
756, we need to conjure up some vision of that strange land.
Who were the fellow Muslims Abd al-Rahman found in al-
Andalus, and how had they come to be there? What was that
place, Europe, where they lived? And just what did happen to
that Islamic polity in medieval Europe during the hundreds of
years before it disappeared altogether, leaving the world behind
it transfigured?

A Brief History
of a First-Rate Place

*T*HE MOMENTOUS EVENTS OF EIGHTH-CENTURY EUROPE WERE first set in train by the death of Muhammad, the Prophet who bore the Revelation of submission to God that is Islam. The story of Muhammad's transformation, from ordinary citizen of Mecca to charismatic military leader and radical founder of a religious and civil order, played itself out in a corner of our ancestral world about which we know precious little. The Arabs of the steppes and deserts of the Arabian peninsula were more or less settled in the oases that provided what scant water there was to be had. Some few were traders, serving as connections between one settlement and another. The most powerful were the nomads, the Bedouin. The desert culture of these peoples—who also had historic connections with the adjacent cultures of the Fertile Crescent—was itself strongly marked by two features that gave distinctive shape to the religion that Muhammad's revelations brought into existence. On the one hand, the pagan and idol-worshiping religions of the desert were the target for this new and utterly uncompromising monotheism, which begins with the starkest possible declaration on the matter: "There is no god but God."* On the other hand, not only conserved but fully appropriated from the culture whose ritual center was Mecca was the loving cultivation — some would say adoration — of language, and of poetry as the best that men did with the gift of language. Muhammad's revelation, preserved in the Quran, embraced the poetry-besotted universe of his ancestors and contemporaries, and thus ensured the survival of the pre-Islamic poetic universe, with its many blatant contradictions of what would become normative Islamic belief.

The vexed question at the heart of the story we are following, the one that will take us to Europe's remarkable transformations in the medieval period, lies not in Muhammad's life but in his death. (The Islamic calendar hinges neither on Muhammad's birth nor on his death, but on the turning point in the story, in 622, when Muhammad and his followers moved from Mecca to Medina, a journey known as the *hijra,* or hegira.) Muhammad had died in Mecca in 632 without an obvious successor. He had left behind, first and foremost, a powerful revelation, a combination of tradition and revolution. Islam was nothing less than the return to the pristine monotheism of Abraham — abandoned or misunderstood by Jews and Christians alike, the revelations asserted, and unknown altogether to the benighted pagans of the desert. All this came forth not in Muhammad's own words but through his transmission of the direct language of God, his

---

*One of the inappropriate and alienating ways we speak about Islam in English is to use the Arabic word *Allah,* God, as if it were a proper name, creating the false impression — ironic and horrifying for a Muslim — that this is some different god. I will invariably use the word "God" for the God of the three monotheistic religions, whose different languages use, of course, different words for the same Being.

"Recitation"—the word *Quran* means "recitation"—of what God was revealing and dictating to him.

Alongside that relatively straightforward revelation, however, and inextricably intertwined with the essentially spiritual reorientation he urged, Muhammad had also created a community with distinctive social-civil-moral values, one that was already a military and political empire in the making. But there were no clear guidelines for how that empire should be organized or ruled, and Muhammad's death left an inevitable vacuum. No question in Islam is more fundamental and shaping than this one, a source of political instability and violent dispute from the beginning, as it remains to this day. Who could, after all, succeed a prophet who was also a dominant statesman? In that highly contested succession lie the origins of many of the major shapes and terms of Islam that are mostly unknown or puzzling to non-Muslims: Shiites and Sunnis, caliphs and emirs, Umayyads and Abbasids, all of these crucial internal divisions. One of the earliest chapters of this struggle within Islam for legitimate authority was the one that transpired in 750, the bloody massacre of the Umayyad royal family that led to the foundation of a rival Islamic polity in southern Europe, and the origins of that story lie in the moment directly following the Prophet's death, over a century before.

The simplified version of the succession to the Prophet is that the initial four caliphs—from the Arabic *khalifa*, or "successor"—were chosen from among Muhammad's contemporaries, from the community of his companions and close relatives. The last of this foursome (called the Rightly Guided by many Muslims) was Ali, a cousin of Muhammad who was married to the Prophet's daughter Fatima. But Ali ruled for a mere five years before his caliphate came to a bloody end with his assassination in 661. This was barely thirty years after the Prophet's death, yet this fateful event began a new act in the drama of the ever-expanding Islamic empire. The Umayyads, the new dynasty that came to power, were both Arabs and Muslims, and they symbolized the original fusion of a culture—and especially a language—with a revelation, a fusion that was the very soul of a new religion and civilization. But they moved their capital from the provincial and dangerously factional Medina to the more open and friendly spaces of Damascus, and in coming out of the isolation of the Arabian desert and making Syria over into the new homeland, and in the conversions of people far removed from Mecca and Medina, the Umayyads' Islam forged a new culture that added generously to the Arab foundation. Transplanting the heart of the empire out of the Arabian peninsula and into Syria, which had its own mixed cultural legacy, was the first significant step in creating the ill-understood, crucial distinction between things Arab and things Islamic, a distinction that is particularly relevant to our story.

The Umayyads presided over this expansive period from their central and accessible caliphal seat in Damascus, a cosmopolitan and venerable city, in its previous lives Aramaean, Greek, Roman, and, most recently, Christian. There and elsewhere they began building new defining monuments in places where the remains of other cultures were still visible. The Great Mosque of Damascus was not built out of blank clay but with the bits and pieces of a Roman temple and a Christian church. The Dome of the Rock in Jerusalem was built on the ruins of the Temple Mount and around the natural rock where Abraham's sacrifice of his son was mercifully rejected by Abraham's God. The building was thus erected by the Umayyads as a monumental version of the Quranic understanding that this is the One God, and that the Muslims are also, and now preeminently, among the Children of Abraham.

The borders of the Islamic empire continued to spread, and by 711, armies of recently converted Berbers, led by Umayyads from Syria, moved into Europe. Within and around the Mediterranean basin, from the Taurus Mountains in the northeast (the border with Anatolia) to the Pyrenees in the northwest (the border with Gaul), the new empire filled almost exactly the bed left by the old Roman empire: a map of the Mediterranean territories of the nascent Islamic empire—the Umayyad caliphate—in the seventh and eighth centuries corresponds remarkably to the Mediterranean center of a map of the Roman world in the second century. In our casual acceptance of the notion that there is some critical or intrinsic division between Africa and Europe, we are likely to neglect just how central this southern shore of the Roman world was. But if we reexamine the stretch of North African coastline as it was plotted out geopolitically in the second- or third-century Roman world, and then in the eighth, we can see the relative inconsequence of small stretches of water such as the Strait of Gibraltar and the baylike line of blue between Carthage and Sicily, as well as the obvious underlying unities and orders.

The Islamic transformation began to remake the entire ancient Near East, including Persia and reaching as far, already at the time of the Umayyads, as northwestern India. The virtue of this Arab-Islamic civilization (in this as in other things not so unlike the Roman) lay precisely in its being able to assimilate and even revive the rich gifts of earlier and indigenous cultures, some crumbling, others crumbled, even as it was itself being crafted. The range of cultural yearning and osmosis of the Islamic empire in this expansive moment was as great as its territorial ambitions: from the Roman spolia that would appear as the distinctive capitals on the columns of countless mosques to the Persian stories that would be known as *The Thousand and One* (or *Arabian*) *Nights,* from the corpus of translated Greek philosophical texts to the spices and silks of the farthest East. Out of their acquisitive confrontation with a universe of languages, cultures, and people, the Umayyads, who had come pristine out of the Arabian desert, defined their version of Islam as one that loved its dialogues with other traditions. This was a

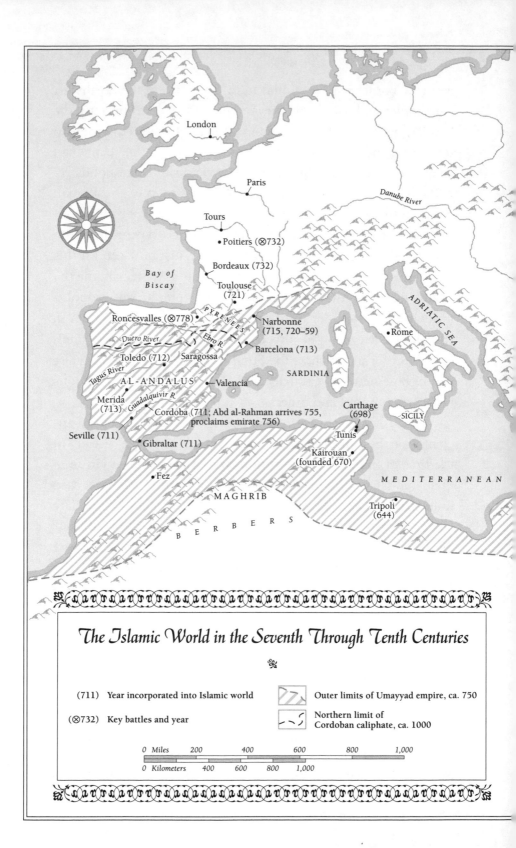

London

Paris

Danube River

Tours

Poitiers (⊗732)

Bordeaux (732)

Bay of Biscay

Toulouse (721)

P Y R E N E E S

Roncesvalles (⊗778)

Duero River

Narbonne (715, 720–59)

Ebro R.

Rome

A D R I A T I C   S E A

Toledo (712)

Saragossa

Barcelona (713)

Tagus River

AL-ANDALUS

Valencia

SARDINIA

Merida (713)

Guadalquivir R.

Cordoba (711; Abd al-Rahman arrives 755, proclaims emirate 756)

Carthage (698)

SICILY

Seville (711)

Gibraltar (711)

Tunis

Kairouan (founded 670)

Fez

M E D I T E R R A N E A N

MAGHRIB

Tripoli (644)

B E R B E R S

The Islamic World in the Seventh Through Tenth Centuries

(711)   Year incorporated into Islamic world

(⊗732)   Key battles and year

Outer limits of Umayyad empire, ca. 750

Northern limit of Cordoban caliphate, ca. 1000

| 0 | Miles | 200 | 400 | 600 | 800 | 1,000 |
| 0 | Kilometers | 400 | 600 | 800 | 1,000 | |

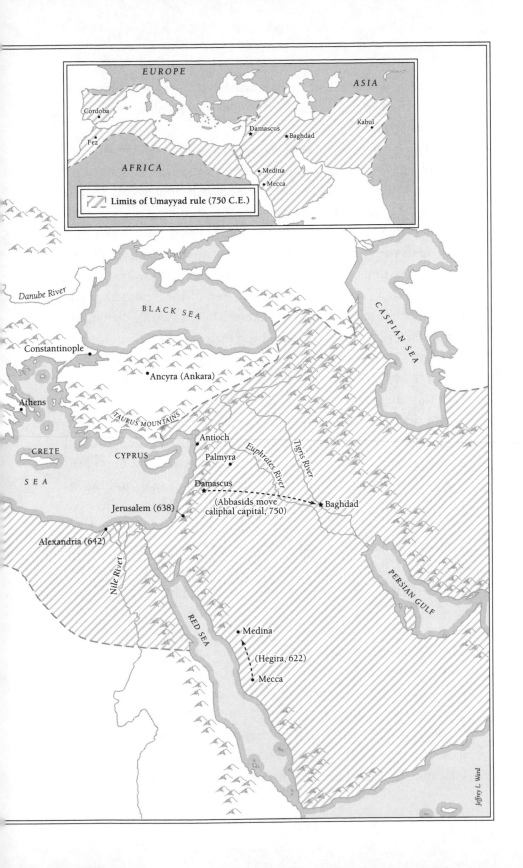

EUROPE

ASIA

Cordoba

Damascus

Kabul

Fez

Baghdad

AFRICA

Medina

Mecca

◩ Limits of Umayyad rule (750 C.E.)

Danube River

BLACK SEA

CASPIAN SEA

Constantinople

•Ancyra (Ankara)

Athens

TAURUS MOUNTAINS

CRETE

CYPRUS

Antioch

Palmyra

SEA

Damascus

Jerusalem (638)

(Abbasids move
caliphal capital, 750)

Baghdad

Euphrates River

Tigris River

Alexandria (642)

PERSIAN GULF

Nile River

RED SEA

Medina

(Hegira, 622)

Mecca

Jeffrey L. Ward

remarkable achievement, so remarkable in fact that some later Muslim historians accused the Umayyads of being lesser Muslims for it.

The Umayyads themselves did not survive to see the pattern of growth and acculturation they had established come to fruition, at least not in their adopted Syrian home. This change of leadership in the Islamic world is the beginning of our narrative of medieval European culture. The Abbasids, who overthrew the Umayyads in Damascus in 750, had different claims to caliphal legitimacy; indeed, they claimed something resembling direct descent from the Prophet, by way of the Prophet's uncle Abbas, whose name became their own. But, as with other ruling groups before and since, establishing their own authority seemed to require eliminating rival, and especially previous, claimants, which is why they massacred the Umayyads at their family estate in Rusafa and abandoned Damascus. The capital of the Abbasid Islamic empire was moved away from the Mediterranean basin to Iraq, which had been the center of the Abbasids' support and armies. Baghdad, the circular "City of Peace," resembling nothing so much as a fortress, was made the new capital, and the familiar setting of many of *The Arabian Nights*. The sole survivor of the massacre at Rusafa, Abd al-Rahman, went west and became the first of the Umayyads in a place we too often relegate to being a "corner" of Europe but which became Europe's veritable center for centuries thereafter.

The Iberian Peninsula, much like the rest of post-Roman Europe in the eighth century, was a culturally and materially dreary place. Rome had governed there for nearly six hundred years, beginning about 200 B.C.E., when it followed in a long line of Mediterranean settlers and cultures—Phoenicians, Carthaginians, and Greeks. During the years of both republic and empire, Hispania flourished from the material and cultural benefits of the

Romans and sent native sons to the centers of power and into the annals of Latin letters. But that became a distant memory—or, rather, something like no memory at all—forgotten during the long period that in European history is most paradigmatically the age of "barbarians." The cataclysmic upheavals, the pan-European migrations of the Germanic tribes, in the third and fourth centuries C.E., led to the decline and, if not the fall of the Roman empire, at least the loss of both the civil order and the long-term continuity from classical Greece that constituted the heart of our cultural heritage. Rome had replaced Greece in part by self-consciously absorbing Greek culture and history and by building its own civilization on the foundations of its ennobling predecessor, with whom it had a naturally rivalrous relationship.

The collapse of Rome's northern and eastern frontiers and the assumption of power by various Germanic tribes ruptured Europe's connection with its own cultural past, an event that would shape the West's consciousness of itself. Among the tribes that dismantled and then resettled what had once been the Roman empire, the Visigoths played a notorious role. This tribe, infamous for the sack of Rome in 410, eventually ended as the overlords of the former province of Hispania, although not with-out centuries of destructive battling over the territory with the Vandals and then among themselves. As elsewhere among the ruins of the Roman empire, and among the mobile Germanic tribes, Christianity was rather imperfectly adopted, from the per-spective of the Catholic ("Universal") Church. Not until 589 did the Visigoths join the Roman Church, disavowing their own de-viant version of Christianity. Although there were important Church seats in Visigothic Hispania, Toledo notable among them, paganism was far from unknown throughout the country-side, where the once Romanized rural population had little to do with either Visigoths or Christianity, and where the Jewish com-munities that had arrived with the Romans lived in nearly en-slaved squalor.

The bright lights during the long twilight that had begun in the fifth century were few and far between, and a lonely figure like Isidore of Seville stood out conspicuously: a notable church-man, he understood the extent to which some sort of Christian order had to fill the terrible vacuum left by the collapse of Roman civil institutions. His most revealing and influential po-litical work, *In Praise of Spain,* was an attempt to bring the rul-ing Visigoths into the fold of the cultural continuum that they had ruptured by conceiving their history as a continuation of the Romans' own. Much more famous is Isidore's still quite readable masterpiece, the *Etymologies,* an unrivaled intellectual effort during those centuries to preserve and transmit the tattered re-mains of the knowledge of the ancient world to the still uncer-tain future. Despite Isidore's brave attempts to make the Visigoths out to be a regime worthy of the Roman succession, they were not remotely up to it. As a result there was very little center to hold when, shortly after the turn of the eighth century, the next wave of conqueror-immigrants came knocking force-fully on the door.

Like the Romans long before and the Germanic tribes more recently, the Muslims were seduced by the fat and nearly round peninsula that hangs at the western end of the Mediterranean. Hispania was ripe for the picking, since the Visigothic kingdom that the newly minted Muslims from North Africa coveted, and then rather easily overran and settled, was all the things one might expect from hundreds of years of civil discontinuity: po-litically unstable, religiously and ethnically fragmented, cultur-ally debilitated. Even the Christian mythology surrounding the events of 711, stories elaborated many centuries later to tell how the old Christian Spain had been lost to the Muslims, hinged on the utter political disarray, moral corruption, and decadence of the last of the Visigothic kings. By time Abd al-Rahman ar-rived, less than fifty years after the first Muslim armies had ven-tured across the Strait of Gibraltar, nearly all the formerly

Visigothic territories as far north as Narbonne, in Aquitaine, had been taken over by Muslims. When the Umayyad prince surveyed this place where he was bound to live out his life in political exile, he must have known that there would be no returning to his native land. This land where he had ended up would be only what he managed to make of it. Yet he could feel sanguine that it had nowhere to go but up, and that he might well make its barren and ruined landscape thrive and bear new fruit.

Over the course of the subsequent three hundred years until roughly the turn of the first millennium as it was calculated in the Christian calendar, the sort of political order and cultural flourishing that had once graced Roman Hispania returned to the peninsula. The Muslims never took and held the entire peninsula, however, and Christian outposts clung to the mountainous regions of the northwest Atlantic coast and the Pyrenees. Yet although the scattered Christian settlements there led to occasional skirmishing along its frontiers, the political history of the Cordoban state is amazingly even. Its very stability might well make it boring to anyone other than an enthusiast: one emir ruling for decades after the next, one addition to the Great Mosque of Cordoba after the next, one damned thing after another, as someone once wittily defined history itself. But within the stability of the long reigns and orderly successions of Abd al-Rahman's sons, grandsons, and great-grandsons, other kinds of revolutions occurred. There was a vast economic revival: the population increased, not just in the invigorated and ever more cosmopolitan cities, but even in the once decimated countryside, where the introduction of new crops and new techniques, including irrigation, made agriculture a prosperous concern; and the pan-Mediterranean trade and travel routes that had helped maintain Roman prosperity, and which were vital for cultural contacts and continuities, were reconfigured and expanded.

Al-Andalus fattened and bloomed with a distinctive identity. The original armies, and the settlers they became or brought with them, had been relatively few compared with the peninsula's population at the time. The newcomers, with their new languages, new customs, and new religion, constituted perhaps one percent of the overall population in the first generation of conquest and settlement. Like Abd al-Rahman, they were already an ethnic mix, part Arab and mostly Berber. Within a few generations, a vigorous rate of conversion to Islam from among the great variety of older ethnic groups, and from the Christian and pagan populations, made the Andalusian Muslim community not only vastly larger, but one of thoroughly intermarried and intermixed ethnic and cultural origins. Whereas the Visigoths, distinguished primarily by their ethnicity, had remained a minority of outsiders during their several hundred years of dominance of Hispania, the Muslims were members of several different ethnic groups. As with the Christians before them, the Muslims' distinctive power and authority resided in a faith to which conversion was not only possible but desirable and encouraged, pragmatically coerced by the range of civil advantages to any Muslim, whether he had converted the day before or descended from the most prestigious Bedouin tribe, the Quraysh of the Prophet himself. And convert the population did, in droves.

The convergence of mixed ethnicity and a religion of converts meant that the ancestors of a Muslim from Cordoba in the year 900 (let alone another two hundred or four hundred years later) were as likely to be Hispano-Roman as Berber, or some measure of each, perhaps with smaller dollops of either Syrian-Arab or Visigothic, these latter two having always been the smaller but politically dominant groups. It was of course the height of prestige to be able to claim, as many would over the years, that one was descended from the original small group of desert Arabs who had first trekked out of the Arabian peninsula or from the Syrians who had led the earliest westward expeditions. Arabness was the most aristocratic feature of ancestry one could want, and Syrian-Arabness was the venerable paternal line of Andalusian culture, both literally and figuratively. But even the emirs, and then their children, the caliphs who were direct and linear descendants of Abd al-Rahman—himself half Berber and half Syrian—were nearly all children of once-Christian mothers from the north, and the pale skin and blue eyes of these Umayyads were regularly remarked on by eastern visitors.

By the same token, all that was Arab was not necessarily Islamic. The other foundation of Andalusian culture, the Arabic language, spilled over the banks of its original religious riverbed and roamed beyond the exclusively religious needs of the Muslim community. This was, after all, the esteemed and powerful language of an empire, and was marked by its vital links to the rest of civilization. As far as the eye could see, and beyond, Arabic was the lingua franca of all save the barbarians—if not the native tongue, at least the pidgin of traders and travelers. Throughout most of the invigorated peninsula, Arabic was adopted as the ultimate in classiness and distinction by the communities of the other two faiths. The new Islamic polity not only allowed Jews and Christians to survive but, following Quranic mandate, by and large protected them, and both the Jewish and Christian communities in al-Andalus became thoroughly Arabized within relatively few years of Abd al-Rahman's arrival in Cordoba. One of the most famous documents from this period is the lament of Alvarus of Cordoba in the mid-ninth century detailing the ways in which the young men of the Christian community couldn't so much as write a simple letter in Latin but wrote (or aspired to write) odes in classical Arabic to rival those of the Muslims.

Of course, one can see this adoption of Arabic by the *dhimmi*—the Arabic word for the protected "Peoples of the Book," Jews and Christians, who share Abrahamic monotheism and scripture—throughout the rest of the Islamic world. In principle, all Islamic polities were (and are) required by Quranic injunction not to harm the dhimmi, to tolerate the Christians and Jews living in their midst. But beyond that fundamental pre-scribed posture, al-Andalus was, from these beginnings, the site of memorable and distinctive interfaith relations. Here the Jewish community rose from the ashes of an abysmal existence under the Visigoths to the point that the emir who proclaimed himself caliph in the tenth century had a Jew as his foreign min-ister. Fruitful intermarriage among the various cultures and the quality of cultural relations with the dhimmi were vital aspects of Andalusian identity as it was cultivated over these first cen-turies. It was, in fact, part and parcel of the Umayyad particular-ity vis-à-vis the rest of the Islamic world. In 929, what had been understood or believed by many since 756 was said aloud: from every mosque in al-Andalus there was read the declaration that Abd al-Rahman III was the true Defender of the Faith, the legit-imate caliph of the whole Islamic world, and the religious leader of all Muslims.

This full-fledged declaration of sovereignty on the part of the Andalusians—involving a great deal more than political in-dependence, since it entailed the public declaration of legitimate stewardship of all Muslims, not just those of al-Andalus—re-vealed the fatal weaknesses of the Abbasid empire in this first half of the tenth century. No civilization anywhere had been more splendid during the previous two centuries than the Abbasids'. One of the most tenable clichés surrounding the his-tory of Islamic civilization is that this was the very zenith of its accomplishment and influence, these few hundred years follow-ing the moment when the Abbasids deposed the Umayyads and settled into their new home in Baghdad. The effects of this ad-venturous and energetic culture—which, among other things, undertook the project of translating the Greek philosophical cor-pus into Arabic nearly in its entirety—did reach from Baghdad to Cordoba, as well as to other places within its wide orbit. Despite their move inland, away from the old Roman sea to an ancient spot on the Tigris near where it meets the Euphrates, the Abbasids were the beneficent force of revival in the Mediterranean during these centuries, and quite directly responsible for the return of both material prosperity and intellectual vitality throughout that inland sea.

Chaos in the Abbasid capital had led directly to the declaration of independence and superiority by the Andalusians, who until then had been reasonably content to live with the half-fiction that they were a mere province, no matter how luminous, of the caliphate centered in Baghdad. In 909, the center lost its hold and the almost unthinkable happened: a breakaway group of Shiites, who saw themselves as descendants of the murdered Ali, the Prophet's son-in-law, succeeded in taking control of the empire's western provinces. In Tunis — not so far from al-Andalus — these pretenders, led by an imam who claimed direct descent from Fatima, the Prophet's daughter and Ali's wife, proclaimed their breakaway Islamic state to be the legitimate caliphate. From the Andalusian perspective, it had been one thing for the quite reasonably independent Umayyads to pay lip service to the authority of the far-off Abbasids. There had been considerable profit all around from that comfortable arrangement, and free and easy travel back and forth between the rival cities of Cordoba and Baghdad had helped feed the Andalusians' insatiable appetites for every latest fashion from the eastern metropolis. But by the turn of the tenth century, Cordoba, which from the outset had a distinct sense of its own legitimacy, scarcely imagined itself a provincial capital at all.

Unlike Iraq, however, where the Abbasids lived, Tunis was practically around the corner, and the Fatimids, as they were called, thus represented a dangerous rival for the Andalusians. It was quite another thing, then, when the Fatimids proclaimed not just independence but rival authority, a rival claim to represent what an Islamic state was and should be. The Umayyad counterclaim, that the authentic leadership and very center of the Islamic world resided in Cordoba, was thus made very loudly and very publicly that day in 929 by the young Abd al-Rahman III, a fitting heir to his ancestor and namesake. Cordoba, and not just from the obviously prejudiced view of the Cordobans, was probably justified at that moment in believing it was the center of the known universe. But that public declaration, as satisfying as it may have been, helped trigger particularly hostile and rivalrous reactions, from both the Christian north and the Islamic south. Resentful rivalries would come to haunt the golden city on the Guadalquivir. But let us not go quite yet to the undoing of the great caliphal capital of Europe, not until we have lingered a bit in the short century of its deserved celebrity.

Cordoba, by the beginning of the tenth century, was an astonishing place, and descriptions by both contemporaries and later historians suffer from the burden of cataloguing the wonders, much like the counting off of Don Juan's conquests by the dozens and hundreds: first the astounding wealth of the caliph himself and of his capital, then the nine hundred baths and tens of thousands of shops, then the hundreds or perhaps thousands of mosques, then the running water from aqueducts, and the paved and well-lit streets . . . The cultivated nun Hroswitha of Gandersheim was involved enough in the diplomatic and social circles of the court of Otto I that she wrote a glowing account of the Muslim city based on her conversations with one of the emissaries to Otto's court sent by the caliph Abd al-Rahman in 955. "The brilliant ornament of the world shone in the west, a noble city newly known for the military prowess that its Hispanic colonizers had brought, Cordoba was its name and it was wealthy and famous and known for its pleasures and resplendent in all things, and especially for its seven streams of wisdom [the trivium and quadrivium] and as much for its constant victories."

But Cordoba was luminous not just by virtue of a necessarily invidious comparison with those lands to the north, barely progressed, materially or culturally, beyond where they had been in the eighth century. Renowned Arab chroniclers and historiographers were also responsible for Cordoba's image throughout the rest of the Islamic world — where running water and libraries were part of the familiar landscape — and they left a powerful vision and memory of that city as "the highest of the high, the farthest of the far, the place of the standard." Not just Cordoba shone, of course, but the whole of al-Andalus over which its caliph presided. In the end, it would be al-Andalus's vast intellectual wealth, inseparable from its prosperity in the material realm, that made it the "ornament of the world."

The rich web of attitudes about culture, and the intellectual opulence that it symbolized, is perhaps only suggested by the caliphal library of (by one count) some four hundred thousand volumes, and this at a time when the largest library in Christian Europe probably held no more than four hundred manuscripts. Cordoba's caliphal library was itself one of seventy libraries in a city that apparently so adored books that a report of the time indicated that there were seventy copyists in the book market who worked exclusively on copying Qurans. In one of the dozens of pages he devotes to Cordoba, the historian Edward Gibbon describes the book worship of the Islamic polity he so admired (and found incomparably superior to what he saw as the anti-book culture of medieval Christianity) using a somewhat different measure: the catalogues alone of the Cordoba library ran to forty-four volumes, and these contained the librarians' information on some six hundred thousand volumes. Islam was indeed a clerisy: its privileged elites were the religious lawyers who studied the sacred texts and the scribes and bureaucrats who

staffed the royal chanceries. But beyond that considerable segment of the population, these libraries were the monuments of a
culture that treasured the Word, built by rulers who had the resources to enshrine it. Many of the volumes they housed, it is
safe to assume, were on subjects of little concern to visitors who
were not Muslims or Arabophiles: works on religion and on language played a dominant role in the Islamic library. But there
was a great deal more, and there were books that would have astonished any Christian visitor, with his necessarily vague knowledge of the classical world. The Andalusians, thanks to their
regular intercourse with Baghdad, which had made translation of
the Greeks a prized project, also housed the libraries of crucial
traditions long lost to those in the rest of the Latin West, and unknown to them still, in the tenth century. Hroswitha's informant
about the marvels of Cordoba (including, centrally in her description, the knowledge of the trivium and quadrivium) was,
tellingly, not a Muslim but a Christian, and none other than
Racemundo, the bishop of Elvira, the metropolitan see of all of
Andalus. Hroswitha's description of Cordoba also speaks to the
sensation no doubt created by the Latin- and Arabic-speaking
Christian who came from a place where they not only knew the
long-forgotten Greeks but where the bishop was an esteemed
member of the caliph's diplomatic corps.

Cordoba's libraries were a significant benchmark of overall
social (not just scholarly) well-being, since they represented a
near-perfect crossroads of the material and the intellectual. The
sort of libraries built in Cordoba—unseen and unimagined for
hundreds of years amid the intellectual spolia of the Roman
empire—ultimately depended on a vigorous trading economy
throughout the Mediterranean. This in turn encouraged energetic technological innovation, so that at some fundamental level
what allowed those libraries to exist, and on such a previously
unimaginable scale, was a paper factory in Jativa, a town near the
prosperous coastal city of Valencia. Paper was dramatically

cheaper and thus more plentiful than old-fashioned parchment, which was still being used in less developed places. Just as essential to the social and cultural project embodied in those libraries was a series of attitudes about learning of every sort, about the duty to transmit knowledge from one generation to another, and about the interplay between the very different modes of learning that were known to exist—modes that might contradict each other, as faith and reason did, and do now. These sat happily in those libraries, side by side, unafraid of the contradictions, first-rate.

In the eyes of the Christians who lived in the territories of Galicia and Asturias in the northwest, and in the uplands north of the Ebro River valley in the northeast, it was unambiguously the Iberian Peninsula that had most successfully recovered, well before the turn of the millennium, from the economic and cultural depressions that had followed the full collapse of Rome. The glorious city of Cordoba, and the polity of al-Andalus of which it was the capital, had filled the black hole of cultural, material, and intellectual well-being in the West. Within the first century after the year 1000, all sorts of byways would open up, and notice would start to reach the outer corners of the lands on its far northern outskirts about what life could be and what a culture could achieve. Intellectual as well as material traffic between the hungry markets of the north and the prosperous merchants of the south would begin in earnest and eventually expand everyone's horizons. But in the meantime, there sat fat, complacent, and conceited al-Andalus, sure of itself and its own superiority vis-à-vis not just the northern Christians but all other Muslims. After the Abbasid hiatus of nearly two hundred years, the Cordobans, the Andalusians, were unembarrassed to reclaim the Umayyads' rightful place on the center of the world's stage.

᪥

In some ways the caliphate of Cordoba was a victim of its own prosperity and its own successes, and what came with them. Despite every cliché, this story is far from that of a simple conflict between infidels and believers. Provocative and damaging raids against Christian strongholds in the north had been undertaken during the late 900s by a notorious vizier named al-Mansur, who had become more powerful than the young and feeble caliph whose protector he was supposed to be. But at the turn of the millennium these raids and tauntings of the northern kingdoms were not the cause for the collapse of central caliphal power.

Bitter civil wars among the rival Muslim factions of al-Andalus began in earnest in 1009, and for the subsequent two decades they tore apart the "ornament of the world." Appalled contemporary observers rather poignantly called those self-destructive years the *fitna*, "the time of strife." A culture that not long before had been at the peak of its powers was being brought low not so much by barbarians at the gate as by all manner of barbarians *within*—within its own borders and within the House of Islam. On the one hand, internal arrogance and the excesses that came from extraordinary wealth began to color the caliphate in the late tenth century. At the same time, the cocksureness of Abd al-Rahman III in declaring the Andalusian caliphate had incited other pretenders to authority, and at precisely the moment when other powerful Islamic polities, hostile to the idiosyncratic Umayyads on both ideological and political grounds, were on the rise in North Africa.

The violent destruction of Madinat al-Zahra, the Versailles of Cordoba, in 1009, just after the beginning of the civil wars, is as good a marker as any of the end of the political well-being of an Islamic polity in medieval Europe. That lavish palatine city on Cordoba's outskirts was one of the most fabled architectural and urbanistic achievements of the Islamic world. Although to this day the lost city is only partially excavated, what is now visible, combined with the written accounts of what there once was, reveals breathtaking levels of architectural sophistication. Madinat al-Zahra had been built in the early tenth century by Abd al-Rahman III, and this architectural complex was part of the declaration of worthy rivalry to the Abbasids. But when this monumental Umayyad site was sacked, less than a century later, it was not by the Christians with whom the caliphate had been sparring on its frontiers. Rather, the destruction was perpetrated by other Muslims, marauding and rampaging Berbers ferociously venting all manner of resentments. These soldiers were part of the mercenary armies brought into al-Andalus by the last desperate rulers of the caliphate to help keep the peace. That devastation of 1009, not at all unlike the Goths' sack of Rome of 410 in its symbolic freight, was the sign of a civil society that had lost control of itself and whose erstwhile order had been left to foreign armies. The ruins of the palaces and gardens of Madinat al-Zahra became the touchstones in Andalusian memory for human grandeur—and its ultimate fragility.

In part, too, the destruction of Madinat al-Zahra reveals the dramatic divisions among the various communities of Muslims that were part of the struggle to carve out both political and religious legitimacy, and that had been visible a hundred years before, when the Andalusians had declared themselves the true caliphs. Particularly ferocious were the divisions between Berber Muslims from North Africa, traditionally far more conservative, even fundamentalist, and the Andalusians. Many Andalusians were, of course, descendants of Berbers who had first settled the peninsula in the eighth century, when there were already destructive ideological and political rivalries between the Arab-Syrian leadership and the Berber hoi polloi. But in the end, their Andalusian identity had been decisively shaped during those subsequent 250 years as a quasi-mythical Umayyad polity in exile; and the citizens of al-Andalus, even those descended from the original Berber settlers, were in many ways at cross-purposes

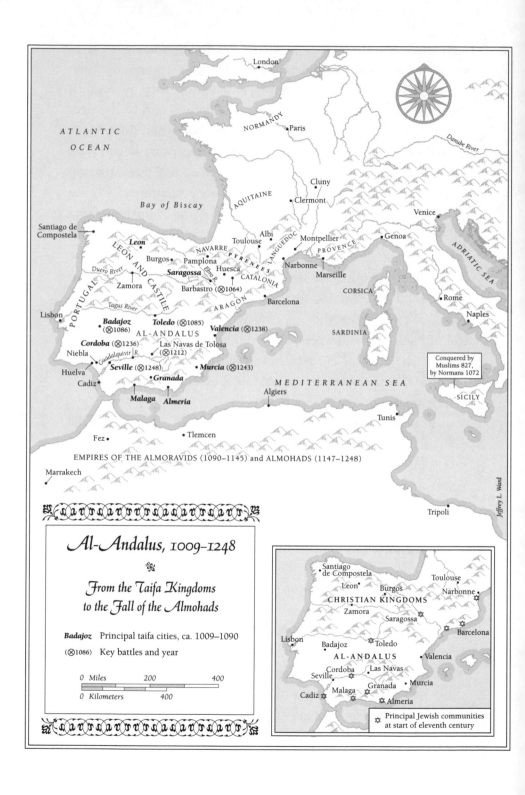

London

NORMANDY • Paris

*ATLANTIC
OCEAN*

Danube River

AQUITAINE

• Cluny
• Clermont

Bay of Biscay

Venice

Santiago de
Compostela

Leon

LEON AND CASTILE

NAVARRE
Toulouse
PYRENEES
LANGUEDOC • Montpellier
• Genoa

PROVENCE

ADRIATIC SEA

Burgos • Pamplona
Huesca
Narbonne
Marseille

Duero River
Zamora
Saragossa
Ebro R.
Barbastro (⊗1064)

CATALONIA

CORSICA

• Rome

PORTUGAL

ARAGON
Barcelona

Tagus River

• Rome
Naples

Lisbon

Badajoz
(⊗1086)
Toledo (⊗1085)

AL-ANDALUS

Valencia (⊗1238)

SARDINIA

Conquered by
Muslims 827,
by Normans 1072

Cordoba (⊗1236)
Niebla
Guadalquivir R.
Las Navas de Tolosa
(⊗1212)

Seville (⊗1248)
• **Murcia** (⊗1243)

MEDITERRANEAN SEA
Algiers

SICILY

Huelva
Cadiz •
• **Granada**

Malaga **Almeria**

Tunis

Fez •
• Tlemcen

EMPIRES OF THE ALMORAVIDS (1090–1145) and ALMOHADS (1147–1248)

Marrakech •

Tripoli

Jeffrey L. Ward

Jeffrey L. Ward

Al-Andalus, 1009–1248

❧

*From the Taifa Kingdoms
to the Fall of the Almohads*

Badajoz Principal taifa cities, ca. 1009–1090

(⊗1086) Key battles and year

0 Miles	200	400
0 Kilometers	400	

Santiago
de Compostela
Leon •
Toulouse
Burgos •
Narbonne •

CHRISTIAN KINGDOMS
Zamora
Saragossa ✡
Barcelona ✡

Lisbon •
Badajoz •
✡ Toledo
AL-ANDALUS
✡ Valencia

Cordoba
Seville ✡
Las Navas
• Murcia

Cadiz ✡
Malaga ✡
Granada
✡ Almeria

✡ Principal Jewish communities
at start of eleventh century

with the Berbers across the Strait of Gibraltar. As a viable political entity, al-Andalus ended under conditions not unlike those under which it began, as one more chapter in the bloody struggle within Islam for legitimate authority, the intense and often rancorous competition for the succession to Muhammad.

The full and official dissolution of the Cordoban caliphate came in 1031, slightly more than a century after its optimistic and triumphant proclamation. And although Madinat al-Zahra would never recover, a phoenix of sorts did rise from the ashes of the caliphate in the taifa, or party, kingdoms. In Arabic *taifa* means "party" or "faction," and in this case it means a splinter party, a breakaway from the mainstream. In the aftermath of the fragmentation of the caliphate of Cordoba, individual cities and their hinterlands became independent or quasi-independent states and began years of struggle among themselves to acquire the prestige and authority that had once belonged to the now ruined Andalusian caliphal capital. In the early years there were some sixty states of differing sizes and differing political provenances. Some of these were dominated by Umayyad loyalists, others by the old tribal groups who saw themselves as the true Arab aristocracy, others still by Berbers, or even disgruntled military adventurers. As time went by, incessant warfare among these rival cities winnowed the survivors down to a powerful few.

A vital part of this cultural landscape in full bloom at this time was the Jewish community. As was the case with many other well-off Cordobans, whole sectors of the prosperous and well-educated Jewish populace left the ruined and dangerous former capital. Emigrating to newly formed taifas, many Jews resumed the influential roles they had enjoyed in Cordoba. The taifa of Granada, to take but one conspicuous example, recruited a gifted young man whose family had fled Cordoba and settled in nearby Malaga. Samuel ibn Nagrila succeeded, as his employers had hoped, in bringing his Umayyad-Cordoban refinements to this backwater, and he quickly became vizier, or prime minister. At the same time, he became the first *nagid*, or head, of the Jewish community—and, as one of the most accomplished of the new Hebrew poets of the Golden Age, is remembered by his Jewish honorific, Samuel the Nagid.

Precisely at this point also, the northern Christian territories began to consolidate as unified and increasingly powerful kingdoms. Expanding slowly southward throughout the eleventh century, the Christian-controlled cities were in the same general melee of competition for territories and widespread leadership and cultural prowess as the Muslim cities. The Cid, an ambitious military adventurer (who would enjoy a long career in Spanish myth and legend), lived and led his various armies into all manner of battles at this time, when religious rivalry was more an ideological conceit than any kind of determining reality. Rodrigo Diaz, known by his Arabic epithet—El Cid comes directly from *al-sayyid*, meaning "the lord" in Arabic—had military successes chronicled admiringly by Muslim as well as Christian writers, just as he fought in the service of Muslim and Christian monarchs alike. Likewise, Muslim cities at times paid tribute to more powerful Christian neighbors, just as Christian kings at times found their most loyal allies among Muslim princes or emirs.

The rivalry for ascendancy among the various taifa cities of the peninsula, militarily and socially destructive as it was, is often likened to the jockeying for power, coupled with cultural exuberance, that was so distinctive among the Italian city-states during the Renaissance. Many of the most characteristic and influential Andalusian cultural forms came into their own in one or another of the many independent city-states that dotted the landscape, and many of them came as part and parcel of the rampant mixtures of people produced by the splintering of the caliphate. During the eleventh century, the fallout from the crash of a centralized and powerful state meant the constant reshifting of political borders and considerable resettlement of many who had once been subjects of the Cordoban caliph. Muslims now found themselves living in Christian cities—these were the Mudejars, as their Christian sovereigns called them—along with Arabized Jews and yet another hybrid group, the Mozarabs. The Mozarabs were those Arabized Christians who, during the three hundred years they had lived in an Islamic polity, had become a community dramatically distinct from their coreligionists in the rest of the Latin West. There was movement in the other direction as well, of course, and Romance-speaking Christians from the north were also suddenly traveling in and out of—even settling in—areas that were perhaps just beyond their own borders geographically. These new and previously unseen places may as well have been different planets culturally. But only for a short while: the pell-mell fraternizations soon enough produced familiarity with the sounds, smells, and colors of every kind of neighbor.

The commingling of languages, religions, and styles of every sort—food, clothes, songs, buildings—took place not only within the Iberian Peninsula, although certainly most vigorously there, but with increasing intensity far beyond the Pyrenees. The much more promiscuous and transformative interaction between Andalusian culture and the rest of Europe still lay ahead, in the twelfth and thirteenth centuries, although its beginnings became obvious during the last half of the eleventh century and were enhanced by the mobile culture of the vigorously competitive city-states, Muslim and Christian alike. But another crucial turning point reshaped the cultural and political landscapes of Europe in the first century after the millennium: the expansion and invasions of the Normans.

The outcome of the encounter between the Norman Christians and the Muslims of Sicily—Sicily, too, had been an Islamic polity since the eighth-century expansion that had created al-Andalus—is in its own way a parable for the complex shift of power and the cultural absorption of the times. In 1072, after thirty-four years of effort, Palermo, the capital of Islamic Sicily, fell to the invaders and became the center of the Norman kingdom of Sicily. Yet over the course of the subsequent century and a half, the Arabized Normans ended by becoming near-captives of the culture they had conquered. This case speaks volumes about the complicated and often paradoxical relationship between politics, ideology, and military history on the one hand and culture on the other. Though the Church had maintained a hostile attitude toward Islam from the beginning—the entire Eastern patrimony was swept under Muslim sovereignty in the seventh and eighth centuries—it was never in a position to call for a taking-up of arms against that ideological enemy. But in 1095 at Clermont, in France, Pope Urban II summoned Western Christendom to a Crusade to win the Holy Land back from the infidel Muslims; and from our perspective the times often seem stamped principally by this act of aggressive religious intoler-ance. Yet, these were also the times during which some of the vast holdings of Cordoba's spectacular libraries came to be read, translated, and in effect canonized as part of the Western tradi-tion, as often as not by men who were part of the hierarchy of the same Church promoting the Crusades.

Within the Iberian Peninsula, the tumultuous period of the independent Muslim cities of al-Andalus came to an end with an event characteristic of the times. Alfonso VI of Castile, a politi-cally astute and highly ambitious Christian monarch and long-time protector of the critically important Islamic taifa of Toledo, consolidated his power and took overt and official control of that ancient city in 1085. Victor over Christian and Muslim adver-saries alike in his bid for leadership over broad territories, Alfonso made Toledo his new capital. He also made it the heir apparent to some of the lost glories of Cordoba and al-Andalus. Alfonso and his line of influential successors became the patrons and proselytizers of much of Arabic culture, and of the vast range of intellectual goods that were subsequently made accessible to the Latin West. Toledo was made over as the European capital of translations and thus of intellectual, especially scientific and philosophical, excitement.

But to the south, Toledo's takeover by a powerful Christian monarch who was a real contender, not just another strongman of some minor city, provoked a historically fateful military reaction. Alfonso's defeated and dismayed rival for control over Toledo, the equally ambitious and accomplished Mutamid, based in Seville, asked for military help from the Almoravids, the fundamentalist Muslim regime that had recently taken control of Marrakech and established the polity we know as Morocco. The Almoravids were Berber tribesmen who had been building a considerable empire in North Africa. These fanatics considered the Andalusian Muslims intolerably weak, with their diplomatic relations with Christian states, not to mention their promotion of Jews in virtually every corner of their government and society. But the somewhat deluded Mutamid of Seville cared little about their politics, and imagined he could bring them in to help him out militarily and then send them packing. The Almoravids thus arrived ostensibly as allies of the weak taifas and quickly succeeded, in 1086, in defeating Alfonso VI. These would-be protectors, however, stayed on as the new tyrants of al-Andalus.

By 1090, the Almoravids had fully annexed the taifa remnants of the venerable al-Andalus into their own dour and intolerant kingdom. For the next 150 years, Andalusian Muslims would be governed by foreigners, first these same Almoravids, and later the Almohads, or "Unitarians," an even more fanatic group of North African Berber Muslims likewise strangers to al-Andalus and its ways. Thus did the Andalusians become often rambunctious colonial subjects in an always troublesome and incomprehensible province. They had irretrievably lost their political freedom, but the story of Andalusian culture was far from over: although bloodied, the Andalusians were unbowed, and their culture remained their glory—viewed with suspicion, yet often coveted by all their neighbors, both north and south.

The twelfth century in Europe opened with a series of ironic juxtapositions and then ran with them. While Latin Europe began to reap the material and intellectual rewards of contact with Andalusian progressiveness, what had once been al-Andalus was itself an increasingly repressive place. The Crusades, a term understood to mean the religiously motivated warfare between Christians and Muslims, have come to symbolize the political history of that moment. But at the same time, destructive intrareligious disputes within both the Christian and the Muslim communities were shaping broad social and cultural developments at least as much. Perhaps the most transforming of these was the great rebellion of the new vernacular languages against Latin, which marks the beginning of the road leading, through many twists and turns, to Dante and Cervantes and Shakespeare and all the others who would use the individual vernaculars of Europe instead of the older, unchanging, and universal language of the Church and of the long-vanished Roman empire.

This period is also the beginning of the end of hundreds of years of open Islamic and Jewish participation in medieval European culture. The years of colonial status, from the Almoravids' 1090 annexation on, were unhappy ones for the Spanish Muslims. The Almoravid attempts to impose a considerably different view of Islamic society on the Andalusians provoked relentless civil unrest: in 1109, not even twenty years after these newcomers had been invited in as allies, anti-Almoravid riots broke out in Cordoba following the public book-burning of a work by al-Ghazali, a legendary theologian whose humane approach to Islam, despite its orthodoxy, was too liberal for the fanatical Almoravids. Such violent disagreements about the nature of Islam were far from unique. Equally striking was the resistance against various Almoravid government attempts to control and even persecute the Sufis, mystics deemed far too heterodox by the Almoravids but much admired by the Andalusians.

The generally turbulent religious climate in al-Andalus drastically changed the composition of Muslim cities. A significant flight of the dhimmi, the Jews and Christians who had been a vital part of the vivid and productive cultural mix, now began. Regrettable as all this was, still worse was to follow: an even more repressive Muslim Berber regime overthrew the Almoravids in North Africa, and kept al-Andalus as its own colony. The Almohads' brand of antisecular and religiously intolerant Islam was at irreconcilable odds with many Andalusian traditions, and they ultimately failed in their attempts to "reform" their colonized Muslim brethren. Nor were they able to achieve anything like the sort of ideologically based political unity they demanded among Muslims, a failure with grave political consequences.

This severe and often violent internal discord within the tattered remains of al-Andalus coincided with the power and influence of Pope Innocent III, who ran roughshod over much of Europe during his years as pontiff, 1198 to 1216. Al-Andalus was only one of Innocent's many targets of crusade, both within and beyond Europe, and within and without Christianity. Christian civil wars had been going full force throughout the twelfth century and into the beginning of the thirteenth; the Crusade against the so-called Albigensians, a starkly puritanical heresy, also decimated the social and political structures of the once flourishing courts of Provence, the same courts, with intimate ties to those of northern Spain and al-Andalus, where the troubadours had wrought the first canonical secular literature of the modern Western tradition. Sung in defiance of the previously omnipotent Latin written tradition and often performed on a range of new instruments that challenged the traditional sounds of religious music, their songs of impossible love flourished throughout the twelfth century as the cultural chic of the times. So it is yet another paradox that this first full flower of modernity—arriving, as it did, at the very height of the medieval period—should come to an end by the mid-thirteenth century with the destruction, during the Crusade against the Albigensians, of the Provençal courts that had supported and encouraged these revivals of secular culture.

Once again, in a parallel to the events within al-Andalus that led to the destruction of the once vibrant Islamic society, the enemies here were as often within as without. With his grandiose visions of universal dominance over political enemies (Christian heretics and Muslim infidels alike), Innocent was a pope of unrivaled political reach who provoked wide-ranging changes in Europe's cultural and ideological landscape. Innocent's iron fist was also directed at what seemed to him a motley crew indeed, the Christians of the various and sundry kingdoms south of the Pyrenees. Here was a collection of disunited and all too heterodox Christians so lackadaisical in their faith that they permitted Jews to live indistinguishable from them in their midst, eventually even ignoring the 1215 decree of the Fourth Lateran Council, over which Innocent presided, that stipulated that Jews wear distinctive clothes or other external markers of difference. These were Christians who, most of the time, would just as soon fight each other as wage crusade against their Muslim enemies next door.

But one exceptional moment made all the difference. In 1212 the disunited Spanish Christians took full advantage of the offers of northern European military help against the Almohads, and this led to the second crucial turning point in the history of al-Andalus, much as the first, in 1086, had been the outside military help sought by the then disunited Muslim city-states. A pivotal military moment but also a rarity, the battle at Las Navas de Tolosa was about ideology as a fairly abstract thing, and one of the few real incidents of "Reconquest," fought with crosses and papal banners on one side and nothing but Muslims on the other. The resounding Christian victory was the clear beginning of the end; virtually nothing but further Muslim losses and retreats followed this disastrous Almohad defeat. Like dominoes, the grand old cities fell to the Christians one by one: Cordoba in 1236, Valencia in 1238, and finally Seville, the lovely orange-tree-filled city the Almohads had made their capital. Seville was taken in 1248 by Ferdinand III of Castile, the first of many generations of Castilian monarchs who would prefer Seville above all other cities. When Ferdinand died a few years later, his son Alfonso—who would be called "the Learned" and be the great patron of translations and thus of the transfer of the Arabo-Islamic fortune into the treasury of Christendom—built for his father a tomb to sit in the Great Mosque of Seville, which had been reconsecrated as the splendid cathedral of the new Castilian capital. Alfonso had the tomb inscribed, in the spirit of the age, in the three venerable languages of the realm—Arabic, Hebrew, and Latin—as well as in the upstart Castilian that only poets and other revolutionaries were writing in just yet.

But the world within which Ferdinand's tomb made sense, that first-rate world in which all those languages sat comfortably next to each other carved on the tomb of a Christian saint, was eventually destroyed, along with the mosque that originally housed it, and inside which not only Ferdinand but his successors prayed until well into the fifteenth century. The fitful dismantling of that universe, the hows and whys of the disappearance of this first-rate European culture is really a different history from the one that concerns this book, and it is a long and often treacherous road that winds from Ferdinand III's Seville in 1248 to Ferdinand V's Granada in 1492. Ferdinand III had, in effect, created Granada as the last Islamic polity on the Iberian

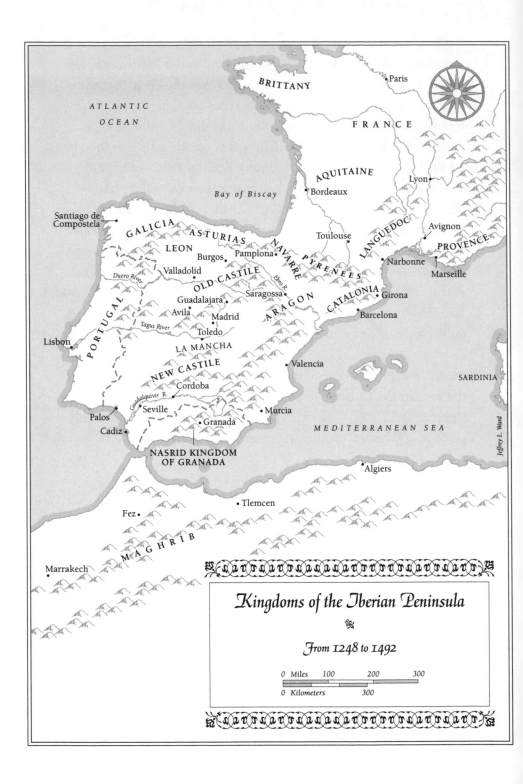

Kingdoms of the Iberian Peninsula

From 1248 to 1492

Peninsula: it had been the reward given to one Ibn Ahmar, of the Nasr family, in return for much-needed military assistance in the battle for Cordoba that the Castilian had waged against the Almohads in 1236. The Nasrids, the descendants of Ibn Ahmar, survived the *Iliad*-like 250-year siege that followed, not as Andalusians proper but rather as keepers of the memory of al-Andalus and, increasingly, as the builders of its final sepulchral monument, called the Alhambra. On a spot already inlaid with layers of memories, the Alhambra ultimately became the setting for the highly charged scenes that set the stage for the true end of the Middle Ages in 1492: Muhammad XII, the last of the Nasrids, known as Boabdil, handed the keys of his family's royal house to the descendant of Ferdinand III and Alfonso the Learned, Queen Isabella of Castile, and her husband, Ferdinand of Aragon. Some recountings of that story say that the Catholic Kings were dressed in Moorish clothes for the occasion, and perhaps they were also dressed that way just a few months later, when they signed the decree expelling the Jews.

The Palaces of Memory

The Mosque and the Palm Tree

Cordoba, 786

ABD AL-RAHMAN WAS AN OLD MAN OF FIFTY. A LIFETIME had passed since he had first arrived in the once remote hinterland of Cordoba, an ambitious young man, the sole surviving heir to a caliphate brutally stolen away in Syria. The universe had changed in those years, partly of its own accord, partly under his direction. From the outset, he had resigned himself to the permanence of exile in al-Andalus, despite the sadness that came from knowing he would never see his beloved homeland again. With that acceptance had come determination, energy, and purpose as he learned to harness what might have been crippling bitterness against the Abbasid pretenders who had destroyed his family. The Abbasids had abandoned Damascus soon after Abd al-Rahman had: by 754 their second caliph, named al-Mansur, had moved to the East, where he had a spanking-new city built to escape the very memory of the Umayyads. Baghdad was indeed a marvelous and magical place from the moment it arose, a circular city, perfectly concentric and perfectly secure on the banks of the Tigris. But Abd al-Rahman, whose enemies begrudgingly called him "the Falcon of the Quraysh" (the Quraysh was the tribe of the Prophet himself), had survived to make sure that, despite the Abbasid turn in history, the memory of the Umayyads and of Damascus would not be lost. For thirty years he had been laying the foundations for a defiantly new Umayyad polity.

In Iberia the Visigothic settlements that the Muslims had moved into were far from well tended. But part of the Umayyad tradition, developed in Syria when they had first arrived there, was to know how to take advantage of what they found lying about, especially when it came to the abundant remains of the Roman past. What could be salvaged was salvaged and reused; what had to be newly invented was. Bridges and roads were built or repaired; and water was brought to the land so new kinds of plants could be cultivated. In many cases these were themselves the fruits, both literal and metaphoric, of the eastward Islamic expansions, to places such as Persia and India, whose many riches became Umayyad staples. Many later historians, Abbasids as well as others seeking to justify the end of that glorious moment in Islamic history, would point disapprovingly to the way the Umayyads had absorbed and adapted the spolia and trappings of the civilizations they found as they spread throughout the world. To such purists, the open-hearted and eclectic syncretism of the Umayyads seemed a defect.

Like other exiles and immigrants in every generation and from every culture, Abd al-Rahman yearned for the small tokens of the old country, a favorite fruit, the look of a childhood home. But in this case, the man who craved the tastes, sights, and sounds of a native land to which he could not return was a caliph in all but name, with the wherewithal to have plants brought across the breadth of North Africa, and to have buildings built to remind him of Syria. Because he was not only a powerful ruler but the founding father of the Umayyads of al-Andalus, his memories and nearly everything he did to satisfy his cravings ultimately bore more significance than the personal nostalgia of one man forever exiled from a beloved maternal home. And these were the essential building blocks, shining with the patina of tradition and legitimacy, of this new common-wealth.

The first Muslim armies had ventured to the far northern reaches of Iberia, beyond the deep and snowy mountains they called al-Baranis, the Pyrenees, and into a place called Gaul. The farthest drives north had taken place years before Abd al-Rahman had even dreamt of al-Andalus, while the Umayyads were still run-ning things from Damascus. Armies had moved far up the Rhone valley, and well into Burgundy, and for a number of years it looked as though the extended Muslim territories in Europe would include considerable lands north of those rugged moun-tains. But a different and far worthier adversary lay in wait. When, in 732, the far-ranging Muslim armies ventured as far as a settlement called Tur—barely 150 miles from Paris—the ruler of the Franks was provoked to defend his territories. On the out-skirts of the modern city of Tours, on the plains south that lead to Poitiers, Charles Martel stood up against the Muslim forces, and the battle that ensued became legendary on both sides. The Franks routed the Muslims, killing the general at the head of their army and so many men that Muslim historians ended up calling the killing fields "the Plain of the Martyrs." For histori-ans of Europe, the Battle of Tours, sometimes called the Battle of Poitiers, would always represent the iconic end point of Muslim advances into northern Europe. This crucial turn in European history elicited Edward Gibbon's striking remark in *The Decline and Fall of the Roman Empire* that, had the battle gone differently, "perhaps the interpretation of the Koran would now be taught in the schools of Oxford, and her pulpits might demonstrate to a circumcised people the sanctity and the truth of the revelation of Mohammed."

The brutal loss forced the would-be settlers to retreat to the area that would later be called Provence, where they stayed on for about another quarter-century. But the Franks were not the Visigoths, and their determination to claim these lands for their own continued. Pepin, son of Charles Martel and father of the far more famous Charlemagne, launched a long and ultimately successful campaign to take the land north of the Pyrenees, and by 758, just a few years after Abd al-Rahman had established himself in Cordoba, the northernmost Muslim armies and settlers had been pushed back south of the Pyrenees. This did not occur readily, however, and the many battles and long sieges—of the city of Narbonne most famous of all—ended up providing much of the material, part historical and part legendary, for the vast epic tradition that would become the bread and butter of medieval French literature.

The Battle of Tours and its aftermath determined the linguistic and religious makeup of northern Europe, in effect limiting the expansion of Islam to the Iberian Peninsula instead of allowing it to reach nearby Paris and the Rhine. Yet a different and far less historically decisive battle only a generation later takes pride of place in the literary and mythological tradition of modern Europe. No epic is more central to that tradition than the *Song of Roland*, and the raw material for this *chanson de geste* ("song of deeds," as the Old French oral epics were called) comes from the years during which center stage was occupied by two great and ambitious rulers, each determined to create a vast and unified polity. The Umayyad almost-caliph Abd al-Rahman and the king of the Franks (and eventual Holy Roman Emperor) Charlemagne were neighbors whose territories rubbed against each other, at times seductively, at times abrasively, all along the Pyrenees. The Battle of Roncesvalles, which was later immortalized in the epic tradition, was triggered in part by the Franks' land lust. Their success, under Pepin, against the advancing Umayyads had whet their own expansive appetites and they had begun to dream of the lands south of the Pyrenees, much as the southerners had dreamed about settling to the north.

The opening to the lands of the south came, as these things so often did, because of civil strife and treacheries. From the beginning of his reign, in 756, Abd al-Rahman appeared determined to avoid the errors of earlier governors, and especially to eliminate the chaos that had characterized much of al-Andalus's short history. Abd al-Rahman realized that Berber and Syrian rivalries would be the enemy of a large and prosperous state, and he vigorously and uncompromisingly administered al-Andalus while refusing to play the games of tribal loyalties. In the long run his strategy succeeded brilliantly, and the result was (among other things) a thriving, powerful, and well-organized state, which he passed on to his heirs, and they to theirs, for a quarter of a millennium. But in the early years, predictably, tribal and factional leaders felt they and their age-old traditions of political patronage had been betrayed.

In 777, the twenty-second year of Abd al-Rahman's rule, a number of aggrieved local Muslim nabobs approached the king of the Franks for help. Though Charlemagne was himself heavily involved in his own ongoing struggles against the Saxons, he spent the next year campaigning with his Muslim allies throughout the lands south of the Pyrenees, struggling over cities from Barcelona, on the Mediterranean coast, to places like Pamplona, closer to the Atlantic shore. This was an unhappy venture, as it turned out. Military successes were few and far between, and by the summer of 778 the thirty-six-year-old king could no longer maintain his siege of the city of Saragossa, which sits on the Ebro River. Charlemagne may have been summoned back by yet another Saxon uprising, or perhaps he may have understood that Abd al-Rahman was not about to give in to the rebels from within his own house. In either case, Charlemagne began a long withdrawal of his Frankish army from Saragossa. But as his defeated and exhausted troops struggled back northward, they were attacked again, this time by a fighting force of highly territorial Basques, whose mountain passes they were crossing—and trespassing. The retreating army's rear guard was entirely destroyed, including its commander, the count Roland. Little more than an account of what happened survived the massacre. That report became the very stuff of early French national mythology in the twelfth century, imaginatively transformed into the most canonical of medieval epics and eventually into a story completely unrelated to its own historical moment: one of Christian versus Muslim, of religious animosity and crusader zeal.

Despite these and hundreds of other successes, military as well as civic, political as well as artistic, and despite the stability and prosperity that was his from early on in Cordoba, Abd al-Rahman waited until nearly the end of his life before he finally seemed ready to begin his most vital project, the one that would proclaim most loudly, in years to come, who he was and what he stood for. The venerable old church of San Vicente was the largest in Cordoba, and it had been built on the ruins of a Roman temple. The traditions cultivated by historians of al-Andalus record an account that would have sounded surprisingly familiar to those who knew the story of the building of the Umayyads' Great Mosque of Damascus more than a century before, in the 640s. When the Muslims first needed a substantial place to pray in that city, half the Damascus cathedral was bought and in effect became a shared house of worship, the relatively newly arrived Muslims praying in one half, the older Christian community in the other. Years later, when the caliph was ready to build a mosque worthy of his family and his heritage, he bought out the Christian half, demolished the older church structure, and on that same site began building a "Friday mosque"—as Muslims call the mosque at which the whole community prays on Fridays—for his now stable and flourishing capital.

The retelling of this story—how the newly arrived Umayyads approached building their first great cathedral mosque when they arrived in Hellenized and Christian Syria, and then how the prince in exile ended up building the first great cathedral mosque of al-Andalus—reveals the extent to which the whole project of Cordoba and al-Andalus was regarded as a conscious continuation of what had been destroyed in Syria. It is also very much about the Umayyads' care not to destroy the multiethnic and religiously pluralistic state. The aesthetics of the new Cordoban mosque, to which Muslims from far and wide throughout history would forever write odes, was typically Andalusian from the start: part adaptation of local, vernacular forms and part homage to Umayyad Syria, forever the source of hereditary legitimacy. Even the most mysterious idiosyncrasy of the great building is best understood in terms of that yearning to remake in the new land what was lost in the old: the *qibla* of this mosque—the orientation that in all mosques points the faithful toward Mecca when they pray—is not in the direction of Mecca but something more like due south, as it would be if the mosque were indeed in Damascus.

The Cordoba mosque continued to be built, and added to, for the next two hundred years, until nearly the year 1000, but the characteristic look of the place, the horseshoe arches that sit piggybacked on each other, themselves dizzyingly doubled in alternations of red and white, was established from the start. It is futile to try to describe the nearly kinetic energy of a powerful monument like this; the effort would be akin to paraphrasing a poem. Indeed, the visual poetry of the Great Mosque antici-

pates from the outset the culturally hybrid sung poetry the Andalusians invented about the time of the proclamation of
the caliphate, nearly two hundred years later, a mixture of old
and new, classical and vernacular, called "ring songs." The
mosque's look was crafted in great part out of the landscape of
this new place; the columns and capitals were all recycled, bor-
rowed from the ruins of the traditions that were being replaced,
whether Gothic churches or Roman buildings. The singular new
look is also a distinct and loud echo of the earlier forms of this
land and its characteristic styles: the horseshoe arch that has
come to seem to us prototypically Islamic was representative of
the indigenous church-building tradition of pre-Muslim Spain,
and the doubled-up arches, with their distinctive and almost hal-
lucinatory red-and-white pattern, are visible in Roman aqueducts, one prominent in Merida, no great distance from Cordoba.
Like the Christians to the north, the Muslims in Hispania used
old Roman columns and capitals and made new ones resemble
the old. They continued the Roman construction methods that
involved alternating brick and stone, a method whose most
memorable example turns out to be this magnificent mosque.

Stylistic openness, the capacity to look around, assimilate,
and reshape promiscuously, was chief among the cardinal virtues
of Islamic style, and had come west as a key part of the Umayyad
aesthetic. In casting about in this alien landscape to find the
building blocks for his monuments, and in taking from them
freely, whether they were part of the language of the Christians
or the Romans, the homesick Umayyad prince knew he was following in the tradition of his Syrian forefathers. The Great
Mosque of Cordoba, with its unmistakable gestures of respect
and longing for the most important Umayyad sites of the old
world, became as lovely an example as one might want of living
dialogue with the past, a way of bringing the past to life, or of
rewriting it so that it is intelligible in the present.

❧

> *A palm tree stands in the middle of Rusafa,*
> *Born in the West, far from the land of palms.*
> *I said to it: How like me you are, far away and in exile,*
> *In long separation from family and friends.*
> *You have sprung from soil in which you are a stranger;*
> *And I, like you, am far from home.*

In old age, aware that he would die far from his native land, Abd al-Rahman wrote a lovely, heartbreaking little poem, an ode to a palm tree. He had been a daredevil young man and a vigorous and powerful sovereign, a man who had survived the vicious rout of his family and spent three decades turning a once wild outpost, rife with internecine violence, into a prosperous and civilized world capital. He had triumphed as a warrior and a pioneer, and in his final years his greatness as a builder was every day more visible, as a mosque to rival all others, past and present, grew in Cordoba, row after row of red and white. But at the end of the day, Abd al-Rahman shared with his Arab ancestors an unembarrassed and manly love of poetry. Although he was not himself a brilliant writer, Abd al-Rahman's legacy is as crucial as the Great Mosque itself, his poetic tradition a palace that houses the memories of the oldest ancestors.

Islam had emerged from the desert with its foundational vision and the will to establish a wholly new society. But it was also armed with a body of sophisticated Arabic poetry that would continue to be recited and lovingly cultivated despite its palpable pagan, pre-Islamic, provenance and qualities. Perhaps nothing is more central to understanding the inherent complexity of medieval culture than the basic relationship between Arabic, as a language with a powerful pre-Islamic poetic tradition, and the Islamic order that springs from the same place—and whose scripture is written in the same language. This is the moment in which the distinctive taste for a complex notion of identity that allows (or, more likely, encourages) contradictions is born. Since this story colors everything around it in the same light, it is worth pausing to tell.

Much of the history of pre-Islamic poetry (the era is referred to in Arabic by the half-poetic, half-theological characterization al-Jahiliya, "the Age of Ignorance") is lost in the desert sands. Shards do survive, however, of a particularly refined oral poetic tradition. "Traces of an abandoned campsite mark the beginning of the pre-Islamic Arabian ode. They announce the loss of the beloved, the spring rains, and the flowering meadows of an idealized past. Yet they also recall what is lost—both inciting its remembrance and calling it back." So begins the presentation of some of the surviving examples of this body of poetry by their foremost translator in our times, Michael Sells. The poems themselves are usually referred to as odes—or, more revealingly, as the "suspended" or "hanging" odes, a curious expression deriving from a most telling anecdote about them.

The story told is that the many Arabian tribes would hold an annual poetry competition when they congregated in Mecca. The winning poems would be embroidered in gold on banners and then hung on display at the ancient shrine called "the House of God," which holds the impenetrable black rock at the heart of the city. The Kaaba, as it is called, would eventually become the symbolic heart of the new religion as well: Muslims pray in that direction, and a central part of the pilgrimage to Mecca is the circumambulation of the Kaaba. When Muhammad came in from the desert and stood in that town, pronouncing the Revelation he had received from God, he was a Prophet whom God had instructed to "recite." The Quran is the near-contemporary recording of Muhammad's recitations (al-Quran means "the recitation"); one of Islam's singular features is its relationship to its own founding language, Arabic, which is understood to be the language of God himself, and thus of His revelations to His prophet.

Muhammad's arrival at the heart of pagan Mecca to preach, to recite verses, many of them powerfully poetic and even hermetic, was also clearly part of the public poetic tradition that had hung banners with poems embroidered on them in the village square. Even as the Prophet's message veered away from the pagan universe of those poems and into the spiritual domain, it never had the effect of repudiating the virtues of poetry itself, not even the poetry of the pagan world of "the Ignorance." The unusual reverence that speakers of Arabic have for their own language can be explained, and usually is, by noting that it is for Muslims, as Hebrew is for the Jews, a sacred language, God's own utterance. But there is nothing intrinsic about the original reverence for the language of Muhammad's Revelation, which was explicitly meant to be spread universally and to be readily intelligible by all men—a revelation not at all meant to belong to a circumscribed ethnic community.

Love of the language itself was certainly part of the pre-Islamic Bedouin culture that first received and shaped the new religion. These desert warriors were also poets, and great lovers of poetry of extraordinary delicacy and sentimentality. As the story of "the hanging odes" illustrates, nothing was prized more highly than the language of poetry; nothing was worthier of being turned into gold and then placed at the center of Mecca. Muhammad's uncompromising monotheism stripped that pagan place of its idols but, perhaps incongruously, left what might have been the most powerful idol of all, poetry itself. Poetry not only survived the coming of Islam but flourished. Indeed, the pre-Islamic odes were collected by Islam's first generation of scholars and canonized as the only interpretative key capable of unlocking the linguistic treasures of the Quran, Islam's single inimitable book. So it is not all that surprising, a century and a half after Islam's foundation, to find Abd al-Rahman, warrior on one hand, religious head of the community on the other, writing an ode to a palm tree.

Arabic became the language of Islam, permitting no other in which to be a Muslim, which meant, historically, that Arabic spread as rapidly and as far as the Islamic empire. It became the language of religion, and quite often a second or third language for those converts from the dozens of far-flung cultures, many of them ancient and already literate themselves, from the Pyrenees to the Chinese border. The language of religion never completely quashed the older secular Arabic of the poets, the language that had never tired of reciting profoundly secular poems of love and longing, and of heroes and battles. For a long time there reigned the broad and profound appreciation that Arabic should also be at the head of an empire of profane letters. As the Islamic empire expanded, many came into the Arabic-speaking fold not as Muslims but as citizens of an Islamic polity. Christians, Jews, and Zoroastrians all developed profound attachments to the many benefits and seductions of Arabic as a secular language.

Among the memory palaces built by the exiled Umayyad prince in al-Andalus, none was more personal and poignant than a place called Rusafa. In Syria, south of the Euphrates, far out on the Syrian steppe, there had been an ancient and mysterious walled city. The Umayyads had turned it into their family retreat, and it was especially beloved by Abd al-Rahman's grandfather, the caliph Hisham, last of the Syrian Umayyads. It was there that the family was found and murdered by the Abbasids; and just outside Cordoba, Abd al-Rahman built his new Rusafa, a retreat for himself and his new family, and a botanical garden as well, a place where he could collect and cultivate the living things that had been so central to beauty and delight in Syria. With the highly advanced irrigation techniques that had been brought from Syria, all sorts of things would grow here now. Among the plants Abd al-Rahman most loved, and which he made part of the landscape he and his children and his children's children would look out on, were the palms of his native land.

As the years went by, Abd al-Rahman spent more and more

time at his garden retreat filled with palm trees. He eventually stopped living in Cordoba proper, and his descendants followed suit, even as the capital became more luminous. The new Rusafa had become the beloved family home of the Andalusian Umayyads. Abd al-Rahman died there in 788, among his beloved palm trees.

Mother Tongues

Cordoba, 855

❧

*The Christians love to read the poems and romances
of the Arabs; they study the Arab theologians and
philosophers, not to refute them but to form a correct
and elegant Arabic. Where is the layman who now
reads the Latin commentaries on the Holy Scriptures,
or who studies the Gospels, prophets or apostles?
Alas! All talented young Christians read and study
with enthusiasm the Arab books; they gather immense
libraries at great expense; they despise the Christian
literature as unworthy of attention. They have
forgotten their own language. For every one who can
write a letter in Latin to a friend, there are a thousand
who can express themselves in Arabic with elegance,
and write better poems in this language than the
Arabs themselves.*

THIS IS THE VOICE OF PAUL ALVARUS, OUTSPOKEN AND WIDELY
respected Christian luminary of Cordoba, in the mid-
ninth century. It was almost exactly a hundred years
since Abd al-Rahman had arrived in that old Visigothic city, now
so transformed visually and socially. Cordoba was all bustle, a
prosperous boomtown, new construction of every sort every-

where, its peoples, cultures, and languages reshuffling themselves along with the changing landscape. Perhaps the best contemporary witness to these changes is the decidedly partisan Alvarus, whose famous polemical book, *The Unmistakable Sign*, quoted above, gives us a snapshot of the culture wars of his time. Though he himself was a layman, Alvarus shared his horror at the spectacle of a world transformed with a small but highly visible group of conservative Christians.

The transfigurations that Alvarus's generation observed with increasing pessimism were not a simple matter. First, there was the staggering expansion of the Muslim community. Some of this increase came from new immigrants; a great deal of it came from among the numbers of the once dominant Christians, who were converting by the hundreds. Every day, the tide of converts moved from the Church toward this new religion of those who were fully and powerfully in control. Among the losses of the Christian community were the children of the countless mixed marriages. Even when the Christian brides remained Christian, or at least did not appear to have converted, and even when they brought up their children speaking their maternal tongue—the old local language of the Christians that was no longer Latin but still had no name of its own—the children were almost invariably, inevitably in the eyes of Islamic law, raised as Muslims. The example, if one was needed, was set by the caliph himself. From the time they had arrived in old Hispania, the Umayyads had mixed their bloodline with women from the old Christian families of Iberia, or from beyond the frontiers to the north. The most powerful and respected of the Muslims, the Umayyad princes descended from the caliphs of Arabia and Syria, were also visibly their mothers' sons, the often fair-haired heirs of their indigenous Iberian forebears.

There were also now many more mosques than churches, and the cathedral mosque, overflowing beyond capacity on Fridays, was being expanded once again. But Alvarus, whose allies in the resistance to the new religion were mostly the representatives of the embattled Church, knew that religion was only half the problem. The other half, directly laid out in those lines from *The Unmistakable Sign*, was that vast realm of culture intimately tied to faith and yet separate from it. The Muslims had brought to Hispania something that the half-crumbled Visigothic province could scarcely remember it had once had: a language that spoke with power and elegance about all the powerful human needs that lie outside a faith. Alvarus's own words make the case unflinchingly: the Latin the young people were abandoning in droves was the tradition of commentaries on the Scriptures. But the Arabic they were embracing was not only that of prayer, but no less the one that had allowed Abd al-Rahman to write an ode to a palm tree to express his profound loneliness in exile, and which had since then been the language of a hundred years of love poetry—songs sung in Baghdad as well as in Cordoba.

"They have forgotten their own language," Alvarus plaintively remarks, because the Christians of Cordoba, like the Jews of Cordoba, had found in Arabic—not in Islam—something that clearly satisfied needs that the language of their own religion, Latin, had failed to meet. Arabic beckoned with its vigorous love of all the things men need to say and write and read that not only lie outside faith but may even contradict it—from philosophy to erotic love poetry and a hundred other things in between. The prosperous and influential Jewish community's romance with Arabic did not provoke Alvarus-like reactions, since Jewish communities had already been in exile for a near eternity and had long spoken the language of others while keeping their own faith intact. Furthermore, a century of Umayyad rule had spectacularly improved the Jews' everyday lives and social status: a community not long before reduced to squalor and slavery was upwardly mobile now, halfway toward the day when a Jew would be the grand vizier of an Umayyad caliph.

The Christians were a different matter. They had not only their disconsolate Alvarus but a core group of radical rejectionists who detested the combination of religious and cultural conversions they perceived to be disastrous for their community and its future. The irony, however, is that most of the Christian community of Cordoba must have felt quite as the Jews did, that their adoption of Arabic was not at all a betrayal of their faith, and eventually the Christian liturgy, the Gospels, the Prophets, the Apostles, all the texts that Alvarus could imagine only in Latin, existed also in Arabic. Already assimilation—Arabization—was taking place, and at the highest levels. Alvarus's own book is full of attacks against the "traitors" within the clergy, and even the Church hierarchy, who worked with Muslim authorities and believed in accommodation and coexistence, men whose use of Arabic was a graver matter than the dalliance with mere poetry. Someone like Alvarus probably could not have conceived that one day the liturgical rites of the Arabized Christians of Cordoba would be the most resistant to any kind of reform in Western Christendom.

Even more appalling and painful for Alvarus and his cohorts would have been the foreknowledge of the name forever after used to describe Christians of the Umayyad polity: the term "Mozarab" originally meant "wanna-be Arab," and it was most likely the disparagement that Alvarus himself would have used to insult those young men so in love with Arabic elegance and poetry. It was surely a derogatory epithet first used by those Christians who believed that the language of the Muslims could and should never be countenanced by a Christian, and who believed that dramatic and violent public resistance was the only acceptable response to the Muslim dominance over their lives. But the name stuck and Mozarab was eventually used to indicate *all* Christians living in the Islamic polity, and those Arabized Christians, along with their name, became the very symbols of the endurance of Christianity alongside Islam. That militant

vision of a purely Latin Christianity was, even at the time of
Alvarus, the dream of a minority: "For every one who can write
a letter in Latin to a friend, there are a thousand who can express
themselves in Arabic with elegance."

In 855, a small number of the most radical opponents of the conversion of their Christian and Latin world openly sought martyrdom. One by one, they indulged in conspicuous public declarations of the deceits of Islam and the perfidies of the Prophet;
and although Islam was elastic in matters of doctrine, particularly when it had to do with Christians, they had zero tolerance
for disparagement of their Prophet.* The would-be martyrs thus
knew for a certainty that they were forcing the hands of the authorities of the city by expressly choosing to vilify Muhammad.
Leaders on both sides made every attempt to head off such radical behavior and its fatal consequences—in vain. The virulent
public attacks continued and the offending Christians were be-
headed in public. After about fifty of these gory executions, a
spectacle that horrified and enthralled Cordobans of all religions, it was over. The passions of the moment passed and life
went on as it had before in this city of thriving religious coexistence. The widespread civil unrest feared by both the Muslim
and Christian hierarchies as the violent events were unfolding
did not come to pass.

But the young men and women who had provided this

---

*Even the obviously partisan Christian account of a similar martyrdom as narrated by
Hroswitha makes quite clear just how widely it was understood that the practice of
Christianity was tolerated in Cordoba, but that the single intolerable offense was blasphemy of the Prophet, whom she calls "the golden idol": "[The Moslem ruler] issued a
pronouncement . . . / That whoever so desired / to serve the eternal King / And desired to
honor the custom of his sires / Might do so without fear / of any retribution. / Only a single condition / he set to be observed, / Namely that no dweller / of the aforesaid city /
Should presume to blaspheme / the golden idol's name / Whom this prince adored."

spectacle of self-immolation would not be forgotten: they were eventually transformed from a thorn in the side of a Church struggling to adapt and find its way in a complex, changing world, into the "Mozarab martyrs." These fifty-odd Christians, incongruously and ironically remembered by the name that described their opposite, eventually became the near-sainted symbols of a cause that served the purposes of Christian chroniclers and analysts of later periods as an easy enough touchstone: brave Christians resisting the forced conversion "by the sword" that conventional history tells us was the way Islam spread, and suffering death for their heroism.

This was not quite as fabulous a transformation as that which turned the slaughter of Charlemagne's rear guard by Basques into a Christian-Muslim holy war. But it was misleading nonetheless, since the evidence suggests that these voluntary and mostly adolescent martyrs were viewed as wild-eyed, out-of-control radicals by other Cordobans, both Christians and Muslims. By the middle of the ninth century, the Church had come to rather successful terms with the Islamic polity within which it lived. It is very possible, indeed, that many of those churchmen were still reading Isidore of Seville, whose *In Praise of Spain* had strained to put the best face on a Visigothic presence that was, for all its Christianity, still unintegrated on the peninsula. But the Mozarabic martyrs enjoyed very good press down the road: they had been followers of Alvarus, who wrote a whole book full of laments about the loss of Christian autonomy in an uncompromising style and from a purist perspective. They were also followers of a later sainted monk named Eulogius, himself the author of *The Saints Commemorated*, a book about the destruction of churches by the Muslims. Most important of all for the cult of these Cordobans, Eulogius eventually wrote another book that spun out their story in great (and obviously partisan) detail. His *Apologia for the Martyrs* became something of a bestseller, with its vivid descriptions of each martyr's death, which he explicitly compares to the heroic deaths of the early Christians. But were they at all like the early Christians, testifying their faith openly and thus putting their lives on the line? And was the Umayyad polity, this all-but-declared caliphate, really destroying their churches, coercing conversions, making Christianity untenable?

From its beginning, Islam explicitly recognized its special relationship with Judaism and Christianity. Muhammad had been asked to perform miracles like earlier prophets, but he refused. For him, and for the believers, the Quran, the book of God's revelations, was the ultimate and undeniable miracle. He understood that it was the existence of this book that made Muslims the scriptural equals of Jews and Christians, who had their own sacred books. In the Quran's understanding, and so a fundamental part of Islamic belief, Moses and Jesus had both been given books, which became the foundations of their communities. Thus it was that the expression "Peoples of the Book" came to be used of Jews and Christians, a phrase that is itself an explicit recognition of the genuineness of those earlier revelations. Indeed, while pagans were treated mercilessly by the Muslims and were required to convert to the new faith, Jews and Christians were dealt with under the special terms of a *dhimma*, a "pact" or "covenant" between the ruling Muslims and the other book communities living in their territories and under their sovereignty.

The *dhimmi*, as these covenanted peoples were called, were granted religious freedom, not forced to convert to Islam. They could continue to be Jews and Christians, and, as it turned out, they could share in much of Muslim social and economic life. In return for this freedom of religious conscience the Peoples of the Book (pagans had no such privilege) were required to pay a special tax — no Muslims paid taxes — and to observe a number of restrictive regulations: Christians and Jews were prohibited from attempting to proselytize Muslims, from building new places of worship, from displaying crosses or ringing bells. In sum, they were forbidden most public displays of their religious rituals.

Not surprisingly, in any given historical case these relatively abstract and general provisions of the dhimma could and did materialize as either a genuinely tolerant and even liberating arrangement or, at the other extreme, a culturally repressive policy within which religious freedom is a hollow formality. The Umayyads, whose ethics and aesthetics were the very wellsprings of Andalusian culture, had more often than not been extraordinarily liberal in their vision of the dhimma, and their social policies were largely commensurate with their aesthetic vision, whose generous and absorbing attitudes about the past and about other cultures created the Great Mosque of Damascus—and that of Cordoba. Beyond the specific policy issues vis-à-vis the Peoples of the Book, the Muslims had transformed the cultural landscape in ways that were both inclusive and, by almost any measure, vast improvements over the half-ruined place they had found. Unlike the much resented Visigoths who preceded them, the Muslims did not remain a ruling people apart. Rather, their cultural openness and ethnic egalitarianism were vital parts of a general social and political ethos within which the dhimmi could and did thrive. As time passed, the perceived need to keep visible and distinct the Umayyad articulation of Islam, with its cultural eclecticism, became more pronounced, as the Abbasids and eventually other rivals for leadership in the House of Islam established their own competing political and cultural visions.

The positive consequences of newfound religious freedom and cultural openness on the Jewish community contrast with their effects on the Christians. As the Jews' civic and political status improved dramatically within the Islamic polity, that of the Christians declined. From ruling majority the Christians had initially been demoted to being a majority governed by a minority of Muslims; from there, soon enough (and clearly by the time of Alvarus), their status had declined further, to the point where they were an ever-diminishing minority. Whereas Jewish ritual had long been, of necessity, a private and even domestic exercise, Christianity had long before expanded out of catacombs and house churches and into the public domain—and expected as a matter of course to exercise far more than mere freedom of conscience. Little wonder, given these differences, that the restriction on public displays of religion, while of small consequence to the Jews, had a seemingly catastrophic impact on the Christians.

Most difficult of all to Christian partisans was the less analyzable matter of conversions, which certainly took place within the Jewish community but were fewer than those of Christians and did not adversely affect the community's general size and well-being. By Alvarus's time, a century after the establishment of the Umayyad polity, it would have seemed that Christians were abandoning the Church right and left. The majority Muslim community was growing, mainly thanks to the high rate of conversion. Most who remained Christian were content, eager even, to be Arabized—and thus Alvarus's lamentation. Not only was his flock thinning rapidly, but the few loyal sheep that remained were so enamored of the wolf that they all wanted to dress in his clothing.

Alvarus could not quite bring himself to say aloud what he knew to be true: how thin the line might be between the seduction of a vital secular culture, of a language alive and powerful enough to speak to God and to a man's beloved, and the religion to which such a language and culture were so intimately tied. "They study the Arab theologians and philosophers," Alvarus wrote, "not to refute them but to form a correct and elegant Arabic." But he knew full well that "correct and elegant Arabic" was often a far greater temptation than the truth of any theologian. In Hispania, Arabic itself had been the first bewitchment and corruption, and many conversions of faith were inextricably tied to the cultural conversions that had preceded them. But just why had Arabic cast such an extraordinary spell? Why did even the faithful Christians love the language of their religious adversary so much that they were willing to re-create their ancient liturgy in it? What charms, in sum, did Arabic have that Latin did not?

Part of the answer we have heard already, from Alvarus himself: "They gather immense libraries at great expense; they despise the Christian literature as unworthy of attention." Christian texts were pretty much all the Latin literature that anyone had read or studied or passed on to young men as their cultural heritage for a very long time. But Arabic brought with it treasures that had little to do with religion. Though intimately tied to Islam, it was also the passageway and access to an already extraordinary canon of works that, from the poetical to the philosophical, could nourish the intellectual and aesthetic hunger that in Hispania had not been fed, or fed well, for centuries. In 850 or so, when Alvarus was observing the cultural desolation from his perspective, the "immense libraries" that were the flames to the young Christian moths were just beginning to be built. By the time the Umayyads got around to officially declaring the caliphate, less than a hundred years later, both the size and quality of Cordoba's libraries had expanded many times over. The clever young men of that generation, Muslims, Jews, and Christians alike, all knew Arabic, and the prominent Christians knew it well enough by then that the Mozarab bishop of Elvira of that generation was part of the highest levels of the diplomatic corps and served as the caliph's envoy to the German court. They could all thus read the demigods of the ancient world — Plato and Aristotle among others — authors about whom someone like Isidore of Seville could only have dreamed, and for whom, it is a fairly sure bet, that sainted churchman would eagerly have learned Arabic himself.

But it was not just about Arabic. Latin, at this same time, was losing its hold everywhere. The language of Rome was itself disin-
tegrating hundreds of years after the dismembering of its empire.
No one in Cordoba at the time of Alvarus could possibly have
known, but in 842, in the far-off city of Strasbourg, Latin suffered a blow at least as devastating as it was suffering at the
hands of Cordobans who were abandoning it for Arabic. In that
Frankish city, an official document was executed that recorded
the mother tongues of Charlemagne's various grandsons. The
Oaths of Strasbourg, as we know this small but significant
record, was the written version of a public oath of reconciliation
and allegiance among the feuding brothers who had inherited
Charlemagne's domain. This was a kingdom that did not include
any part of al-Andalus, as Charlemagne had once dreamt it
might, but it was extensive nonetheless. The circumstances of
the oaths are described in serviceable, boilerplate Latin. Then the
document proceeds to transcribe faithfully what each said and
swore out loud—this not in Latin but rather in the mother
tongues of two of the three rival brothers, one Germanic, the
other Romance.

Lovingly, we call the languages we grow up speaking
"mother tongues," since we learn them not from books or
schools but from the society of women who raise us. Sometimes
these languages are the same as the ones used in the larger institutional world of our fathers, and sometimes not. The dramatic
changes in the linguistic terrain of mid-ninth-century
Cordoba—which languages were spoken by whom, and what
conversions, cultural and religious, they led to—are not at all
isolated. They reveal the seismic cracks that existed all over the
European landscape, the ruptures that appeared when it started
to become clear that Latin had become a stranger in the house,
no longer the language of the songs women sang to their chil-

dren at night. In every corner of what had once been an empire unified linguistically by Latin, now local differences, old and new, gained strength. As long as those ever-increasing and ever more striking differences were only in the ways people spoke, while what they read and wrote was still the old and unchanging Latin, no one called it by any other name. Yet the everyday "Latin" spoken in Paris was more than halfway to being as different from the "Latin" of Florence as French is from Italian today. And these still-unnamed mother tongues that were already "Romance," the languages of the Romans' children, were every day more different, not only from each other, but from unchanging Latin, which had become more a memory than a living thing.

Alvarus himself wrote and spoke in Latin in formal and public settings. As the liturgical language of Christianity, Latin was, of course, neither unique nor even first—Jesus spoke Aramaic, and the New Testament is written in Greek—but in Cordoba in 850, Latin was synonymous with the older religion and its ways. And Latin here, as elsewhere in the former western provinces of the Roman empire, had become largely ossified. That once vigorous instrument that had served Rome's great poets, historians, and orators was now almost completely frozen in place. Those mother tongues, on the other hand, what people had been speaking for hundreds of years, had been changing inexorably, though still with little consciousness (and little need of such consciousness) of its being substantially different from what was written by everyone from the great Roman writers to the papal secretaries of the seventh century.

Even after Arabic arrived, the Cordobans—all the Cordobans, the Christians, the Muslims who were the children of Christian women, and many of the Jews—never discarded the ancestral mother tongue of their city and their community. The vernacular that was the child of Latin in that part of the world, first cousin to those spoken in Paris and Florence, was thus reared alongside Arabic from the eighth century onward. We now sometimes call it by the technical name of Andalusi Romance, which reveals its kinship with the other Romance languages as well as its ancestral home, al-Andalus. But its older and more familiar name is, ironically, Mozarabic, because it was, indeed, the other language of those Arabized Christians who lived under Islam. While Latin was disappearing even among the Christians, its Mozarabic daughter and heir thrived as the language of the nurseries, passed on generation after generation by many Cordoban mothers, Muslim as well as Christian. Mozarabic, the Romance of the Christians of al-Andalus, lived inside the House of Islam, rubbed shoulders with Arabic, exchanged words with it constantly. Arabic itself was what Latin had been long before, the language of literature that was not very far from the language of the streets, despite its ties to the immutable Quran and to all the layers of commentary accumulated around that book over several hundred years. The songs sung by mothers in Arabic, itself a language heard in nurseries and children's playgrounds, were not so far removed from the songs that were the poems of the courts, nor so foreign-sounding to the young men who were learning to write letters and read commentaries—and write love songs.

A Grand Vizier, a Grand City

Cordoba, 949

*Let it be known to you, my lord, that our land is
called Sefarad in the Holy Tongue, while the
Ishmaelite citizens call it al-Andalus, and the
kingdom is called Cordoba.*

O NE OF THE MOST PROMINENT MID-TENTH-CENTURY CORDOBANS
made this proud proclamation in a letter he was writing
to a perhaps mythical king of a far-off land. By way of introduction, he had identified himself as "Hasdai, the son of Isaac,
the son of Ezra, from the sons of the Jerusalem exile who now
live in Sefarad." But Hasdai was much more than this modest
identification of family and tribe revealed: he was the *nasi*, the
"prince," of his own religious community. At the same time, he
was a vizier, the right-hand man to the ruler of "the Ishmaelite
citizens," the caliph Abd al-Rahman III. This Abd al-Rahman,
who ruled successfully between 912 and 961, was the descendant of his namesake founder of that homeland called, as Hasdai
indicated, Sefarad in Hebrew and al-Andalus in Arabic. The extraordinary prosperity of spirit, intellect, and power these men
shared with each other glows from every page of Hasdai's

communiqué, as well it might have, since one of Hasdai's most appreciated qualities was his eloquence in Arabic.

The caliph had elevated Hasdai to higher and higher offices throughout his lifetime largely because Hasdai spoke and wrote with elegance and subtlety, and because the vizier possessed a profound knowledge of everything in Islamic and Andalusian culture and politics that a caliph needed in his public transactions. So it was that the prince of the Andalusian Jews had become the prestigious and powerful foreign secretary to the caliph. And this was no small-time, would-be caliph: during the lifetimes of Abd al-Rahman III and Hasdai, the Umayyad caliphate of Cordoba made its sweeping and plausible claim to absolute primacy within the House of Islam. Although for us it may seem astonishing that one of the most public faces of this Islamic polity, at its peak of power and achievement, should be a devout Jewish scholar, famously devoted to finding and aiding other Jewish communities in their scattered, worldwide exile, such suppleness was a natural part of the landscape of this time and place.

The compelling Cordoban panorama had been critically reconfigured one fine day in January 929, a Friday, the day of assembly observed in mosques across Islam. Hasdai ibn Shaprut was then at the beginning of his manhood, about fourteen at the time, and so he was already part of the life of intense learning and public activism of his father, Isaac, whose personal wealth supported individual scholars as well as a synagogue in that city. The Jews would have heard the momentous public announcement not long after it was read aloud from the pulpit of every mosque in the land: Abd al-Rahman III had officially taken the title of Commander of the Faithful, the caliph of the Islamic world, successor to the Prophet at the head of the entire Muslim community.

Since 756, the Umayyads, in their new home in al-Andalus, had acknowledged the caliphate of Baghdad in the Friday prayers in their mosques. And while technically and formally it was nothing more than a "province"—the emirate of al-Andalus, its rulers no more than emirs, or "governors," subservient to the caliph in Baghdad—for 173 years Cordoba had in fact been a functionally independent and distinctly Umayyad polity. Abd al-Rahman's public proclamation of 929 was first and foremost an oral declaration of what everyone had always known: that the Umayyads of Cordoba did not serve at the pleasure of the Abbasids of Baghdad, that they were not mere governors, and that the House of Islam had not been under a truly single rule since the moment Abd al-Rahman I had claimed his birthright in exile.

There were other powerful emirs in Islam—the governor of Egypt, for one—but the voice that was heard that Friday in Cordoba spoke not from power or arrogance. Abd al-Rahman I had carried his legitimacy in his blood, from Damascus to Cordoba, where it passed from generation to generation, discreetly but well tended. Now Abd al-Rahman III was shouting it from the rooftops. His pronouncement made clear that the head of the House of Islam in al-Andalus had claims far beyond that independent polity's frontiers. All sorts of questions cry out here: Why, just now, this provocative declaration of independence and superiority? Did Abd al-Rahman really believe he was on the brink of wielding the sort of political power and moral authority that would make him truly a caliph to all the world's Muslims— a leader on the far western margins of an empire that extended as far as the frontier of Sinkiang and the source of the Indus? What would a Cordoban have thought on that day when the city echoed, from one end to another, with that unexpected Sabbath-eve announcement? Could Hasdai himself, an impressively educated young man, proficient in all the languages of his native city—Latin, Mozarabic, Arabic, and Hebrew—a pious Jew and budding physician and philosopher, possibly have imagined what it might mean to him?

The Abbasids had created a brilliant civilization in Baghdad. Perhaps they did not wield direct political control over the Andalusians, but that would have mattered precious little to the political and cultural empire that knew itself to be unrivaled in wealth and accomplishments worldwide. While Charlemagne in his halting and stultified Latin was being crowned Holy Roman Emperor in 800, the Abbasid caliphs were already well into the monumental translation project that brought the Greek philosophical and scientific tradition into Arabic. Continuous traffic between Cordoba and Baghdad meant that the Andalusians were soon enough reading the same things and eagerly keeping up with the latest innovations, fashions, and products, and, eventually, capable of sending their own back in return. Despite their sometimes quirky ways—quirky by normative Abbasid standards—the Andalusians were profoundly indebted to and appreciative of the material, intellectual, and artistic emanations from the luminous eastern capital. The long first Umayyad century in al-Andalus was thus predicated on a healthy respect for the murderous, usurping Abbasids, for their political prowess and stability as well as for their cultural leadership.

In more recent years things had begun to fall apart in Baghdad. By 909, the political and military center had lost its hold to the extent that the almost unthinkable had happened. At the turn of the tenth century the Shiites, another legitimist group of Muslims, had successfully taken control in the North African provinces of what had been the Abbasid empire. The Shiites were supporters of Ali's descendants—Shiite means "of the Party of Ali," the Prophet's murdered son-in-law—as the divinely appointed and thus legitimate heir to the leadership of the House of Islam. From Tunis, the Arab Ifriqiyya, or "Africa," these pretenders, now led by an imam who claimed direct descent from Fatima (the Prophet's daughter and Ali's wife), issued loud challenges to the Abbasids' claim to true legitimacy and succession, along with the proclamation of an independent state. If the imams of this upstart Muslim polity claimed to represent what an Islamic state was and was meant to be, and to have not merely political but religious authority over all Muslims, how long would the Andalusians—who constituted far more of a threat where legitimacy was concerned—continue to publicly acknowledge the central power of the distant Abbasids?

At the time these dramatic events were taking place in North Africa, Abd al-Rahman III, the beloved grandson and heir-designate of the ruling Umayyad, Abdullah ibn Muhammad, was eighteen years old. When the latter died, three years later, in 912, the young Abd al-Rahman assumed full powers. He spent the first eighteen years of his rule reunifying a kingdom that had in recent years suffered from internal bickering and skirmishing that bordered on civil war. He also strengthened his frontiers to the north, pushing deep into the regions of Leon and Navarre, in one famous battle taking and sacking the town of Pamplona. With his own house very much in order and prospering more than ever, and with his frontiers to the north under control, Abd al-Rahman was finally ready, in 929, to make his own counter-claim to that of the Fatimids. Here was the voice of the Umayyads now issuing that house's long-delayed assertion of defiance to the Abbasids who had murdered and displaced it.

It seems unlikely that Abd al-Rahman imagined he could establish the sort of political unity across the broad Islamic universe that his Syrian ancestors had once had, and that in a limited way the Abbasids had hung on to for some time. The House of Islam was now broken down into too many separate and rivalrous polities, each in its own region and with its own character and army. But he was quite right to understand that the struggle for the symbolic leadership that the position of caliph entailed was open to contest. The Commander of the Faithful was the arbiter, in some fundamental sense, of the way Islam was to be correctly lived. And the Andalusian Abd al-Rahman surely believed that way to be as the Umayyads lived it.

"It is a fat land full of rivers, springs and stone-cut wells," wrote Hasdai in his letter to the king of the Khazars. Hasdai had heard fabulous accounts of an entirely Jewish kingdom, Khazaria, an alleged fifteen-day journey from Constantinople and to the northeast of the Black Sea. As he introduced himself to a correspondent he could only hope existed, Hasdai described his Andalusian homeland, alluding modestly to his own role there:

> It is a land of grains, wines and purest oils, rich in plants, a paradise of every sort of sweet. And with gardens and orchards where every kind of fruit tree blossoms, and those with silkworms in their leaves. . . . Our land also has its own sources of silver and gold and in her mountains we mine copper and iron, tin and lead, kohl and marble and crystal. . . . The king ruling over the land has amassed silver, gold and other treasures, along with an army the likes of which has never been amassed before. . . . When other kings hear of the power and glory of our king they bring gifts to him. . . . I receive those offerings and I, in turn, offer them recompense.

Hasdai ibn Shaprut was born in Cordoba in 915 into a world brightly lit for Jews. In the previous 150 years of Umayyad rule, the Jews of al-Andalus had become visibly prosperous—materially, to be sure, and culturally even more so. To say they were thoroughly Arabized is to acknowledge that they did a great deal more than merely learn to speak the language of the rulers, something they no doubt did in the same several first generations, alongside Berber Muslims, Slavic slaves, and Visigothic converts. Under the dhimma brought by the Muslims, the Jews,

who in Visigothic Hispania had been at the lowest end of the social and political spectrum, were automatically elevated to the
covenanted status of People of the Book (alongside the
Christians, for whom it was, instead, a demotion), which
granted them religious freedom and thus the ability to participate freely in all aspects of civic life.

This freedom meant virtually unlimited opportunities in a
booming commercial environment. Suddenly, the once economically moribund peninsula was frenetic with activity: trading
across the Mediterranean and importing products from the Far
East, it had also dramatically altered its own agricultural base,
embarked on dozens of large and ambitious building projects,
and a great deal more. The Jews' improved status also meant that
they were able to join the educated classes, which they did with
alacrity and, as the life and career of Hasdai reveal, with manifest
success. And, of course, at the heart of the Jewish community's
prosperity lay an enthusiastic attitude about Arabization, which
meant full cultural assimilation.

The Jews' often loving relationship with Arabic culture con-
trasted from the outset with the attitude of the hierarchy and
leadership of the Christian community, whose resistance to what
they regarded as unbearable cultural oppression led to the crisis
of the Mozarab martyrs. There were obvious and foundational
reasons for the critical differences in attitude: the Christians
were adjusting to the loss of ruling status, and then of wholesale
conversions that meant, just after the time of Alvarus's famous
complaint, they were a shrinking minority in al-Andalus. The
Jews' position under Muslim rule, on the other hand, was in
every respect an improvement, as they went from persecuted to
protected minority. The results of these different attitudes may
well have contributed to the paradoxical social and cultural outcomes clearly visible by the turn of the tenth century. There was
a surviving Christian community, but it was smaller and more
discrete than it had been even at the time of Alvarus, a stubborn

group of Mozarabs who believed they could use Arabic and be devout Christians, and in fact by now their scriptures and rites were all in Arabic. But the once-majority Christian community had been decimated at least in part by that Alvarus-like all-or-nothing attitude that seemed to push people to one extreme or the other: conversion to Islam, on one hand—the majority—or voluntary exile to the handful of Christian enclaves in the far northwest of the peninsula, on the other.

The Andalusian Jews universally embraced a third option: they assimilated into the Islamo-Arabic culture of the Umayyads *and* remained a devout and practicing religious community, with its religious language intact. Hasdai, growing up as the child of a prosperous (but not culturally unrepresentative) Jewish family, was thoroughly educated in two separate but complementary spheres: that of an observant Jew, learned in Hebrew and its biblical and exegetical traditions, in order that he might be at ease in the company of rabbis, or be a rabbi himself; and that of an intellectual at ease in the most cultivated Islamic society. Hasdai was a scion of a Jewish intellectual class so successfully assimilated within the sparkling Umayyad culture of al-Andalus that they had themselves become prominent contributors to it. These men were visible and significant participants in the flourishing of letters that, by the time Abd al-Rahman III was caliph and Hasdai his vizier, had made Cordoba as serious a contender as Baghdad, perhaps more so, for the title of most civilized place on earth.

The Jews understood themselves to be Andalusians and Cordobans, much as the German Jews of the late-nineteenth century—Marx and Freud most prominent among them—considered themselves Germans, or the American Jews in the second half of the twentieth century, who helped define the intellectual and literary qualities of their time, never thought twice about calling themselves Americans. But unlike many later European and American Jews, the Andalusian Jews had not had to abandon their orthodoxy to be fully a part of the body politic and culture of their place and time. The Jews of al-Andalus were able to openly observe and eventually enrich their Judaic and Hebrew heritage and at the same time fully participate in the general cultural and intellectual scene. They could be the Cardozas and the Trillins and the Salks of their times because they were citizens of a religious polity—or rather, of this particular religious polity. The Umayyads, much like the Abbasids who devoted vast resources and talent to the translation of Greek philosophical and scientific texts, had created a universe of Muslims where piety and observance were not seen as inimical to an intellectual and "secular" life and society.

So it was that the rich and varied cultural and intellectual Arabophone universe that was the House of Islam in the ninth and tenth centuries provided the backdrop for the Umayyad vision. The Andalusian scene, where a man like Hasdai could occupy center stage, was accessible to the Jewish community in far more than just a technical or linguistic way; indeed, it was a vital part of their identity and in no way at odds with their Jewishness. At the same time, the broader culture partook of their presence and contributions, and Jews added to the everyday-expanding Arabic library in areas ranging from science and philosophy to poetry and Arabic philology, this last the queen of the sciences in an Arabic tradition in love with its own language. This thoroughgoing assimilation would have all sorts of long-term effects down the road, when the Umayyad caliphate was gone and much lamented. But those are later stories.

In 949, Hasdai ibn Shaprut was at the head of the delegation representing the caliphate of Cordoba in delicate foreign negotiations. The caliph, who twenty years before had broken with Baghdad, was interested in a strategic alliance with the Byzantine emperor in Constantinople. Greek-speaking Eastern Christendom and Arabic-speaking Muslim al-Andalus had a common enemy in the Abbasids of Baghdad, who were a menace to both.* The historic and colorful encounter between the representatives of these two powers with seats at either end of the Mediterranean took place in the most lavish of Andalusian settings, the new palatine city of Madinat al-Zahra. "The City of Zahra" was a fairy-tale-like series of palaces and gardens, still in the making, that Abd al-Rahman III had begun building outside Cordoba a dozen years before, ostensibly in honor of one of his beloved concubines, and named for her. Legendary in its own time as a wonder of the world, it would eventually become one of the most powerful and enduring monuments of the caliphate, second only to the Great Mosque as an iconic memory. For these delicate and potentially momentous talks in the innermost enclaves of Cordoban power, no man was better suited than Hasdai, who was thirty-four at the time. He had risen meteorically through the capital's intellectual and political ranks, beginning as a gifted physician whose invaluable specialty was antidotes to poison, soon enough becoming a central player in the diplomatic corps attending the caliph.

Because prominent Christians also figured in these caliphal foreign policy circles, it is probable that Hasdai worked closely at this time with the Mozarab bishop of Elvira, Racemundo, who in 949 figured prominently in the caliph's diplomatic representation to the court of Constantinople. Half a dozen years later, in 955, the bishop, known in Arabic as Rabi ibn Zayd, would end up as the caliph's envoy to the court of Otto I, where he would meet the nun Hroswitha and give her the materials for both her life of the Mozarab martyr Pelagius and her enduring description of Cordoba's marvels. Among the gifts that Rabi ibn Zayd

---

*They also had common Christian enemies, a fact that would emerge vividly during the time of the Crusades, when Byzantine cities—Constantinople chief among them, in 1204—were sacked and looted by Crusaders. The four famous bronze horses that grace and even seem to define the look of Piazza San Marco in Venice were taken from the hippodrome of the capital of Eastern Christendom.

brought back from Constantinople was a green onyx fountain adorned with human figures that ended up in the newly built Madinat al-Zahra.

Another of the gifts from the Byzantines presented to the caliph by Constantine VII—whose official title, Autokrator Romaion (Autocrat of the Romans), belied his mixed political heritage—was a fundamental Greek medical work until then known only in a poor Arabic translation, itself based on a mangled Greek original. Here was a real treasure, and an opportunity for Hasdai: the Greek original, in an early version, of an invaluable resource, Dioscorides' *On Medicine*, complete and lavishly illustrated. This gift spoke to the intellectual and cultural interests and pursuits shared by the two would-be allies. But it also immediately revealed, ironically, the extent to which the Andalusians had relied on the very Abbasids against whom they were at that moment conspiring. Cordoba had benefited from the vast translation enterprise in Baghdad, where the Greek library had been translated and then passed on to the rest of the Arabophone world—and the Cordobans had been eager, even greedy, recipients, as the impressive Cordoban libraries attested. But Cordoba itself, like the rest of Europe, had no Greek readers, and thus no way to make immediate use of that extremely desirable present.

Again, it was Hasdai who seemed to be able effortlessly to shift gears from the political negotiations to the even weightier task of making this medical encyclopedia available to the distinguished libraries of Cordoba. He set to work at the head of a team of experts put together for the purpose, a group of men that included a monk sent from Constantinople, once it became clear that help was needed to even begin to translate the Greek into Arabic—although it was Hasdai himself who, reportedly, had the last hand in crafting the Arabic version (after it had been through several relays of translators), he being both a physician and an exquisite stylist. The immediate task was accomplished and thus the Andalusians had symbolically claimed one further measure of independence, small but significant, from the Abbasids. This triumph in an area so central to Andalusian concerns — the acquisition of technical and scientific preeminence in the world — made clearer than ever Hasdai's brilliance in the public arena of Cordoba, at its very highest levels.

Hasdai's success in society at large, at the heart of the just-declared caliphate, did not in the least detract from his stature within the Jewish community. He was still the nasi, its prince, and every year more powerfully and broadly so. Following in his father's footsteps, he became an important patron of religious scholarship in Hebrew. Yet he was also the founder of new initiatives for this time of unprecedented prosperity for the Andalusian Jews. Like their Muslim neighbors, they had a strong sense of their own centrality in the universe, and, like the caliph who employed him, the nasi felt the need to redefine his community's relationship to the larger world. The center of Jewish authority at that time was, like the old caliphate, in Baghdad. There, the *gaon*, the head of the community, exercised his authority by (among other things) his annual setting of the Jewish calendar. This would no longer be so, declared Hasdai, in a statement of independence that echoed that made by Abd al-Rahman not many years before. Henceforth, the nasi proclaimed, Andalusian Jewry would mark its own new moons and holy days. So it was that by the halfway mark of the last century of the first millennium of the Common Era, in their grand city of Cordoba, Muslims and Jews alike had come fully into their own.

The Gardens of Memory

Madinat al-Zahra,
South of Cordoba, 1009

ONE HAS TO WONDER WHICH AMONG THE MANY FANTASIES-come-to-life of the palatine city of Madinat al-Zahra would have most stupefied the army troops that breached its walls one day in 1009. The reception hall with the gold and silver roof to cover the giant pearl hung from its center? The quicksilver pool that sent rays of sunlight flashing in every direction? The zoo with its wild and strange animals, surrounded by a moat? The hundreds of other pools, of every kind, in every courtyard? Perhaps the fountain with the black amber and pearl lion at its center? Or the gardens filled with statuary, some preserved from earlier, barbaric times, some newly carved, with animal and human forms (sure proof of the Umayyads' lack of piety)? These sprawling palaces must have looked like the marvelous settings for tales from *The Thousand and One Nights*, but they were real enough, and symbol enough of what those soldiers had been sent to destroy.

The Umayyad caliphs lived here, removed from the citizens of the great capital, which in recent years had fallen prey to terrible chaos. To these hired Berber troops, North African foreigners in al-Andalus, its lavish splendor was an embodiment of an old order that had to be extinguished. The Berber mercenaries sent to attack the stronghold had been hired by one of the many claimants to the caliphate at that moment of ferocious infighting in 1009. But the violence that destroyed this iconic monument exceeded what mere paid soldiers would have inflicted. Its destruction was also fueled by deep resentments these foreign Muslim troops harbored against the Umayyads and everything they stood for. By the time they had done their work, the whole city of palaces and pools and wonders was in utter ruins. It was never restored or put back into use, nor has it ever been fully excavated. As a ruin it served for centuries as a romantic and complex touchstone, an image of a once glorious Umayyad past.

Abd al-Rahman III had built Madinat al-Zahra as part and parcel of his declaration of the caliphate, and in some ways it was his loudest statement. This first official Andalusian caliph understood thoroughly that beyond political and military successes, and far beyond Friday-mosque declarations, it was conspicuous cultural achievement and display that made one place, and not another, the center of the universe. During the latter part of his long and steady reign, he devoted his energies and vast wealth (nicely described by Hasdai in his exploratory letter to the Khazars) to the intellectual, material, and aesthetic show of his kingdom's accomplishments. The setting in which Hasdai and his entourage of diplomats received the delegation from Constantinople depended for its power and ability to impress everyone—from the Eastern Christians then to us now—on the Andalusians' cultural bearing.

Construction on Madinat al-Zahra had begun in 936, not long after the official proclamation of 929, and remained the caliph's personal obsession for the rest of his life. Extant accounts of the project depict Abd al-Rahman III's involvement as so all-absorbing that it even led to his public chastisement by a ranking Cordoban jurist when the caliph failed to attend prayers at the Great Mosque for several consecutive Fridays. This perhaps apocryphal story speaks to later concerns about the turning of caliphal attention away from the political capital, which was, in fact, the Achilles' heel of the whole Andalusian enterprise. But only later historians could know that a catastrophic turn in the road lay just ahead, and during these years in the mid-tenth century, awe and pleasure were the effects of this multi-tiered and many-gardened creation. Madinat al-Zahra, like the Andalusian caliphate itself, looked out proudly onto the surrounding world from its stepped levels, proclaiming its command over the then lush valley of Cordoba and beyond. Even more so, it looked inward, in toward every courtyard and cunning garden, to revel in its own self-contained beauty. In 961, the half-century reign of the man who not only proclaimed but thoroughly believed he had made Cordoba into the true heart of the House of Islam came to an end. His son and successor, al-Hakam II, inherited both the title of caliph and the achievements and ambitions that came with it. Al-Hakam took over the last stages of the extensive construction of Madinat al-Zahra, and under his direction it received its final lavish touches. Al-Hakam also carved out for himself a different but equally expansive and iconic building project, which he announced the minute he became caliph: the expansion of the Great Mosque of Cordoba.

Under his father's direction, an unusually tall minaret had been erected. Quite likely the first true minaret to grace the mosque, it no longer stands in full; only its base survives beneath the bell tower. The language of minarets in the fractured and competitive Islamic world of the tenth century was symbolic of the sectarian and political divisions of the day (much as the very different styles of Christian churches during the Reformation would be in the seventeenth century), and the new and exceptionally tall minaret of the mid-tenth century spoke clearly to the ascendance of the House of Umayya, as nearly everything that Abd al-Rahman III did.

Al-Hakam had designs beyond that lofty minaret, and beyond mere enlargement, for the congregational mosque that had become too small for the needs of Cordoba's booming population. The mosque was now the center of a distinctive Muslim community, and its transformation was central to its leadership role. Al-Hakam's legacy, his addition to the landscapes and skylines of Umayyad ascendance, was to make the Great Mosque a different order of great, not simply to enlarge it, as had been done several times before. His vision of how to take the already striking mosque to the next level, a level commensurate with the claims of primacy of the young caliphate, was creatively traditional, very much in the Umayyad style. The moving simplicity of the repetitive rows of the eighth-century mosque was strengthened: the forest of columns with their red-and-white crowns continues on and on, affirming the founding vision, bay after new bay, row after row, innumerably more horseshoe arches sitting on leftover Roman columns and capitals—or, now, on newly built imitation Roman columns and capitals.

The additional grandeur lay, however, beyond this relatively straightforward enlargement, which made the mosque roughly one-third larger than it had been. Using the visual language of the old mosque, the expanded mosque achieved an unprecedented level of luxury. Sumptuous elaborations characterized the spaces reserved for royal prayer. Dizzyingly multilobed and interlaced arches—all red-and-white, all horseshoe—were placed to create a breathtaking *maksura* (the separate royal enclosure), clearly marked off in front of the *mihrab* (the traditional prayer niche). The mihrab, repositioned in the heterodox Damascus orientation of Abd al-Rahman I's eighth-century mosque, itself became a separate room, with its own dome; dome, room, and even the front wall surrounding the entrance to this exquisite space were thickly decorated with sparkling mosaics.

At first glance it might seem that al-Hakam's turn from the relatively distant concerns of Madinat al-Zahra's splendors to the more civic project of expanding the Great Mosque was a return to an investment in the Cordoban community per se. But the additions themselves tell a somewhat different story, and in the end it is an unhappy one. The spaces carved out, with unprecedented lavishness, for the caliph's own prayers were understood, correctly, as an expression of distance from the community. This mihrab was a separate room, the room itself set apart by the maksura, clear indications of the extraordinary standing of those who worshiped beyond the fancier arches. As was the case with the now completed palatine city that lay just beyond Cordoba itself, the Cordobans' pride in the conspicuous displays of extraordinary wealth was tainted by a sense of the inappropriateness of the distances being created between the community and the caliph.

The Syrian Umayyads had in fact been criticized not only for their eclectic adoption of multiple cultural forms but also for their tendency to move toward forms of government more characteristic of "kingship." The enormous expenditures on the mosque apparently provoked open protests—and the establishment of "higher" space within a mosque strongly suggested a violation of the fundamental precept of equality before God that is enacted in the distinctively open architectural spaces of mosques. For neither the first nor the last time in history, heady success sowed some of the seeds of its own demise, and what had been a court that proudly displayed its community's wealth and superiority began to be perceived as a self-indulgent and narcissistic court unwilling or unable to tend directly to the governance of that community.

And for neither the first nor the last time in history, the lack of a viable succession or a vigorous heir had dire consequences. The era of the long reigns of the Andalusian Umayyads was at an end: al-Hakam, who was already forty-five when he inherited the caliphate from his long-reigning father in 961, died fifteen years later, leaving only an eleven-year-old son, the new caliph Hisham II, to succeed him. In a story that is archetypal and literary in nearly all its details, actual power was seized by an evil chamberlain who at first pretended to play the role of regent but whose own tyrannical control grew over the years, until the young man who was the rightful ruler ended as a powerless prisoner within his own palace walls. The caliphate was mortally wounded by this unpredictable turn of events, and by the havoc wreaked during the quarter-century of dictatorship and often bloodthirsty military rampages of that pretend regent, Ibn Abi Amir, infamously known as al-Mansur, "the Victorious."

There would be other nominal caliphs, and other pretenders to the succession of the Umayyad line, as well as al-Mansur's own successors, who bore his dynastic name (the Amirids) and made the regency hereditary. The caliphate itself would not be officially pronounced dead and beyond resuscitation until 1031, nearly twenty years after al-Mansur had died while pursuing one of his many military campaigns, and twenty-two years after the symbolically powerful sacking of Madinat al-Zahra by the Berber troops al-Mansur had brought into al-Andalus. But from the start of al-Mansur's usurping reign, which straddled the turn of the century, from 976 until 1002, the independent and unified Umayyad polity called al-Andalus, begun by Abd al-Rahman in 756, was in effect finished.

Those last years, however, especially those of al-Mansur's

colorful life and politically momentous reign, overflowed with fateful and future-shaping events. The armies of mercenaries al-Mansur brought into al-Andalus from North Africa became, as the years went by, more and more like foreign policemen, with little understanding and less love for the Andalusians. Themselves strangers in a strange land, these Berbers were increasingly resented by the Cordobans. But for al-Mansur they were a necessary part of his relentless and exhausting military campaigns against the Christian territories to the north, campaigns that under his leadership acquired a fanatical and ideological pitch scarcely seen before. Al-Mansur even acceded to the request of some that al-Hakam II's library be purged, and he was said to carry with him while on campaign a Quran he had copied with his own hand.

In 997, al-Mansur led an unprecedentedly destructive raid into Santiago de Compostela, the site of a local cult to the apostle James, whose bones had purportedly been found there in the ninth century. The vicious burning of the city, and the carting away of all the church bells back to Cordoba to be used as mosque lamps, helped catapult Santiago from local to near mythological importance in the subsequent century. The city became the very symbol of Christianity on the peninsula and a legendary pilgrimage site of international proportions, both of which remain largely true today. James himself was eventually transformed from mere apostle of Jesus to the patron saint of what would eventually be called the "Reconquest," and his name enhanced by the epithet *Matamoros*, or "the Moor-slayer." The bells for which so high a price was thus paid—and this gratuitous taking of purely religious trophies was rightly perceived as a very different matter from territorial expansion or defense— were carried back to a Great Mosque that al-Mansur had himself expanded just a few years after al-Hakam's expansion. These latest and proportionally overwhelming enlargements were done at least in part to accommodate the considerable new population of

Berbers that al-Mansur had been importing to Cordoba. But they were carried out no less, of course, so that this first non-caliph to rule might leave his own mark, a mark that disrupts the carefully crafted symmetries and continuations of the Umayyad caliphs whose political continuity he was also severely (and permanently) disrupting. And of the lost palaces of the time, perhaps none played a more dramatic role than the palatine "City of Flowers," built by al-Mansur to rival Madinat al-Zahra itself. Built on the opposite side of the city, away from the Umayyad palaces, al-Mansur's own Madinat al-Zahira (in English transliteration a nearly identical name, and even in Arabic an echo despite the difference) has never been found.

Al-Mansur was a vigorous old man still out campaigning when he died. His career and life ended in 1002, in a small city named Medinaceli, which lies about halfway between the far larger and more distinguished cities of Toledo and Saragossa. Medinaceli, too, is part of the literary quality of al-Mansur's life: it eventually became famous and is remembered today as the hometown of the half-legendary warrior called the Cid, born perhaps some forty years after al-Mansur's death. Unlike the last of the legitimate caliphs, al-Mansur did not die without ambitious and well-prepared heirs. Two of his sons believed they could and should succeed their father in the anomalous role he had carved out for himself—nominally, the caliph's chamberlain but functionally the heavy-handed ruler of the land. Al-Mansur had, in fact, married two different Christian princesses, both of them daughters of Christian monarchs who turned their daughters over to him as part of their treaties. One, Teresa, was from the kingdom of Leon; the other, whose name as a convert to Islam was Abda, was the daughter of Sancho, the prince of Navarre, whose seat was in Pamplona, and she bore al-Mansur the child who would be his final successor, a son named Sanchuelo, "Little Sancho," in honor of his maternal grandfather.

Sanchuelo triggered the final chaos that sent the Berber

armies down the road to Madinat al-Zahra in 1009. His older brother had been al-Mansur's first successor, and for a half-dozen years he had shown every sign of being a true heir, always at the head of a powerful and victorious army, until he died suddenly, apparently of natural causes, in 1008. Sanchuelo, whose given Arabic name was (of all things) Abd al-Rahman, succeeded his brother but then committed the fatal, if inevitable, error of trying to make symbolism match a certain reality: he forced the figurehead caliph, blood heir of the Umayyad line that went straight back to Damascus, to designate him—a usurper's son—the true heir to the Umayyad caliphate. It was an extraordinary provocation and very much the straw that broke the proverbial camel's back. The Cordobans, it turned out, were still deeply tied to their Umayyad heritage and its many honors, and at that moment of crisis they would prove far more willing to defend the honor of the Umayyad line than would the morally and politically impoverished heir who had signed away all appearance of patrimony.

Without honorable leadership to fill the many vacuums created in more than a quarter-century of illegitimacies, and in a city and countryside also rife with acute and long-simmering civil antagonisms created by the influxes of Berbers hostile to the old Umayyad order, there was no real chance for the restoration of Umayyad legitimacy that so many yearned for. Instead, in 1009, long pent-up chaos was loosed on that world. While one army went off to hunt down and slaughter Sanchuelo, who in the tradition of father and brother had ridden off to the north to wage war, others went off to find the cowardly caliph-in-name-only Hisham II, who had already relinquished his birthright. He was hiding in the palaces of Madinat al-Zahra in what must have been a state of abject terror. Unable to find him, the moblike troops turned on the palace structures instead, as stand-ins for the Umayyads they wanted to obliterate. Hisham abdicated to the first of a series of rival cousins and other pretenders, and he disappears from history, although his death was not announced until a few years later, during the chaos that had continued unabated since 1009.

The Umayyad dynasty and polity ends, for all intents and purposes, the night the troops tore the beauties of Madinat al-Zahra limb from limb. For the next several decades there were claimants and counterclaimants, always someone imagining he would be the next caliph, for as long as that shadow of the old caliphate was a technical reality. Perhaps there even endured vain hopes, in the hearts of the most sentimental and optimistic, that the old order might be restored, that another prince would ride out of the desert to snatch an implausible victory. It was not to be. This was truly, now, the end of the Islamic dynasty that had first left the Arabian desert for the wider world. The Umayyads had escaped destruction in Damascus once, quite implausibly and against all odds, and they had created an enviable second life in this place, their homeland for nine generations. But now the old Andalusian order, with its political unity and cultural grandeur, exploded like a star, and it suffered years of terrible civil wars, sometimes called the Berber Wars and sometimes, more simply and movingly, the *fitna*, the "time of troubles." Cordoba itself was sacked by the Berbers in 1013 and left shattered. Of Madinat al-Zahra, only the haunting ruins survived, a forever powerful evocation of the transience of glory, and an icon of the life and death of that unique moment in the history of Islam, when its caliphate was in the Far West.

Victorious in Exile

The Battlefield at Argona,
Between Cordoba and Granada, 1041

❧

*T*HE COMMANDING OFFICER OF THE ARMY, WHO WAS ALSO THE grand vizier to Badis, king of Granada, thanked God for yet another victory. After only four years at the head of the army of his taifa, his city-state, he was already a prodigious success. Just two years before, in 1039, God had blessed him with a marvelous victory over Seville, the most enduring of Granada's rivals, even though the enemy army had surprised the Granadans on the battlefield with a force far larger than expected. A year before that, at Alfuente, when he was the freshly appointed vizier, the new leader of the military forces had fought his first battle against the king of Almeria—Almeria, that conceited taifa down on the coast, with its lavish old fortresses-by-the-sea built a century before by Abd al-Rahman III himself. And Almeria was still a wealthy port trying to lord it over the newly settled Granadans, but God had smiled on him that day: the king

Zuhair himself had been killed in the battle, and Zuhair's powerful vizier Ibn Abbas had been taken prisoner. Under the commanding officer's leadership, Granada grew every day more powerful. And that day in 1041, he had won the third and most crucial battle of all, quelling the treasonous rebellion of Yadir, the king's own cousin.

So once again, as he had after his earlier victories, the vizier turned to poetry, to his psalms, to thank his God and recount the greatness of the victory. He had always written beautifully—that was why he was the vizier, after all—but these poems were different. They were an adventure to write, in a new kind of language. The third poem, to praise the third victory, had flowed most easily of all, and he could now more effortlessly flex those new muscles that sang of arms and men and God. At the end of this song, after describing the perils and ins and outs of the battle and the chase of Yadir, whom he had "pursued until he was brought like a gift, or tribute, that summer to my king," the vizier-general knew he had now truly found his voice as poet:

> My friend, for me in my straits
> > the Rock rose up,
> therefore I offer these praises,
> > my poem to the Lord:
> He recognized fear of Yadir in my heart
> > and erased it.
> So my song is sung to the healer:
> > He ravaged my enemies with pain, easing my own.
> Someone objected:
> > Who are *you* to pay homage?
>
> I am, I answered, the David of my age!

The end of the caliphate was a political disaster and a personal tragedy for many. But like its beginnings in the personal and po-

litical tragedy of the House of Umayya, that end also became a
hymn to the virtues of exile. The David of his age, as he audaciously called himself, was only one of the key players, although
one of the first, in an audacious age. The extraordinarily innova-
tive cultural life of which he was a part, and which was the hallmark of the years directly following the breaking apart of the
caliphate, was attributable in large measure to the many kinds of
exiles created by the fitna, that time of troubles. Central government was replaced by radically different civic structures: the
taifas, as the city-states that replaced the Cordoban caliphate
were called. Despite the unending political upheavals and the
continuous infighting among the dozens of independent polities,
the "party kingdoms," that grew up as fragmented centers of
power in the fallout from the explosion, cultural life not only remained vigorous but took new and unexpected turns, as if freed
and emboldened by being let loose in a world less safe and less
predictable—and infinitely more varied and surprising—than
the old one. Of the rebellions against the old order, none was
more transforming in the long run than the insurgence of the
vernaculars of which the David of his age was a part.

But who was he? And what was this poet doing out on a
battlefield, riding one of the smart and fast Arabians that had
been brought to Europe, to al-Andalus, by the ancestors of the
soldiers he led? His name was Samuel—Ishmael in Arabic, his
native tongue; Shmuel in Hebrew, the language in which he
spoke to God. The Hebrew patronymic was Halevi, but in
Arabic, the language of his family for hundreds of years, he was
known as Ibn Nagrila. Samuel was born in 993, during the last
years of the caliphate; and in 1013, just a few years after Madinat
al-Zahra had been turned into a memory palace, Ibn Nagrila's
family, like many others, was part of the general exodus from the
increasingly violent and dangerous precincts of Cordoba.

Ibn Nagrila's family was prosperous and typically well educated, part of that Jewish community integral to the highest

classes of government and scholarship in Cordoba. For them, just as for countless others (not only Jews, but especially Muslims and even the Mozarabs, the Christians), the dislocations at hand were terrifying, the apparent end of the good life and the beginning of some unknown and unpredictable existence in unknown places, all undoubtedly less civilized by far than the beloved Cordoba, with its beautiful streets and immense libraries. For many, there was no choice but to move away, and Ibn Nagrila's family was one of these. Because their wealth most likely came from the spice trade, they settled in the port city of Malaga, where vigorous trading continued and a commercial life could be reestablished. The young Samuel himself, the prodigy, did not stay for long in that seaside city but instead moved inland to a nearly brand-new city just being built along the Darro River. It was a site graced with clear views of the always snowcapped, perfectly named Sierra Nevada, the Snowy Mountains. A wonderful hagiographic account exists of this critical transformation, the tale of how Samuel ibn Nagrila was transformed from prosperous Malaga merchant to powerful vizier of the taifa of Granada. The superbly educated and eloquent young man had been working as an anonymous scribe for the vizier of the new taifa of Granada, writing elegant, learned letters that the vizier, as befitted his station, passed off as his own—or did until the king himself discovered the ruse and brought the gifted young writer to his court. There Ibn Nagrila proved a star, this cultured and cosmopolitan Cordoban, with the full range of Arabic poetic and philosophical learning at the tip of his tongue and the end of his pen, come to grace what was still a fresh, provincial outpost.

Ibn Nagrila's success in his new home was mercurial. As had been the case with Hasdai ibn Shaprut during the glory days of the caliphate, his success in an Islamic government and court, and in Arabic letters, was rewarded not only with ever higher positions in the court itself but also with positions of leadership within his own religious community. By the time he was thirty-four, Samuel was appointed nagid, the head of the venerable Jewish community of Granada, a city at times referred to in Arabic as Gharnatat al-Yahud, "Granada of the Jews." The Jews had for some time been settled mostly on the hill dominating the river valley, a breathtaking place where one side rises up cliff-like, a frightening natural fortress on top of which still stood an old castle. That stronghold was marked by the distinctive red clay from which it was built, and it was already known as the Hisn al-Hamra, "the Red Fort," or al-Qala al-Hamra, "the Red Castle." It was the tag of *hamra*, "red," that would stick, and the place would be known eventually, and then forever, as the Alhambra.

The Nagid (as he is most often called after his appointment) almost immediately began rebuilding the castle and city on that hill of bright-red clay, his buildings part fortification and part cultural show of force. Out in this backwater, Samuel's aesthetic visions, his notions of what a city and its buildings should look like, were anything but provincial. As sophisticated as his writing, which had put the locals to shame, the Cordoban's very urban tastes had obviously been shaped during his youth in the old capital of the caliphate. Samuel's son, Joseph, was his heir as nagid, and he was also the editor of his father's poetry; he gathered the poems together, copied them lovingly, and provided them with introductions. But Joseph was a maker of more than those *diwans*, or anthologies, of poetry: it is believed that it was he who first laid out the elaborate gardens that began the long tradition of the-gardens-next-to-the-palaces on that hilltop. The first gardens built on the red hill by those exiles from Cordoba were, like Abd al-Rahman's palm tree, the echoes and reconstructed memories of a mourned homeland. The exilic memory of the ancient and noble gardens of Cordoba, transplanted to Granada when it was young and Cordoba was lost, haunts the crown of that hill to this day.

❧

The memory gardens and other palaces built by the Jewish vizier of Granada are now deeply buried and mostly invisible under the many layers of other buildings and other gardens that were piled atop them. But the foundational poetry that the David of his age wrote became and remains to this day the most visible cornerstone of a crucial chapter of Hebrew poetry known to most as the Golden Age. This Cordoban in permanent exile was the first poet and founding father of the new Hebrew poetry. His distinctively Andalusian voice not only rewrote the history of Hebrew poetry in a groundbreaking way but was also part of a landscape filled with all manner of poetic experimentation. As Samuel the Nagid rode home from his victories, composing versions of his new poems in his head, he was firmly a part of Europe's burgeoning avant-garde. All sorts of disparate yet kindred movements were beginning to redraw the map of our own poetic languages, carving out spaces for mother tongues of all sorts.

At the end of the road, this revolution in poetry would affect all of Europe, but it had its conspicuous start in the Iberian Peninsula and was well under way by the mid-eleventh century. The new Hebrew poetry was only one of a variety of new poetries that crystallized in the exiles that followed the collapse of Cordoba. Along with the loss of many of the orderly and constraining traditions of the old Umayyad order came a complete reshuffling of populations, and thus of languages, religions, and styles on the peninsula. In the melee of peoples and city-states constantly at war with who-knew-which other city-state, unexpected neighbors appeared on every block, in nearly every city. The heady admixtures of their styles became more and more the vivacious trademark, the soon-to-be internationally famous style, of this place. Sparks seemed to fly off the new encounters and the unexpected comings-together. The old Christians of Cordoba moved into exile in the north, to find that their coreligionists were far stranger than their old Muslim neighbors, and much-coveted Islamic craftsmen were hired to build fine buildings, including churches, in newly Christian cities, and now Hebrew songs could be heard in distinctly Arabic accents. The constant rivalry among the taifas also sparked poetry, and every other art form—a rivalry, implicitly at least, for the succession to Cordoba. Who knows how many of the taifa kings ever really imagined they would have the political and military power necessary to reunify the peninsula? But almost all dreamed that they might succeed Cordoba as the cultural center of that world, and so they filled their courts, their walled cities, with philosophers, architects, musicians, but most of all with poets, who could make them shine more brightly than the other Andalusian stars. And if one of these poets was also a brilliant military strategist and field marshal, so much the better.

Samuel the Nagid was not the first of the Arabized Jews of Islamic Spain to write poetry in Hebrew that, like the Arabic poetry that was their heritage as well, spoke of lovers and battles and other worldly things, as well as of God and the spiritual world. A century earlier, when Hasdai ibn Shaprut had also played a prominent role at court—the caliphal court of Cordoba—an immigrant to Cordoba from the East named Dunash ben Labrat had laid the groundwork for the radical changes ahead. Dunash had come from Baghdad, the capital of the rival Eastern caliphate of the Abbasids. He almost certainly carried with him many of the conceits of superiority that Jews from the East, like Muslims from the East, brought with them to al-Andalus, only to have their eyes opened at what they saw in this western capital. During his years in Cordoba, Dunash first suggested that Hebrew poetry might be written as Arabic poetry was, using the sort of formal techniques the Jews already knew intimately. Hebrew, the Jews' liturgical language, had not been a truly living poetic language for a very long time; for as long as anyone could remember, it was only the language of prayer, the

language of a religion and of a liturgy. What struck Dunash, perhaps more vividly than those living there because he was a
stranger and was seeing the vitality of the Jewish intellectual
class of Cordoba from outside, was the contrast between the narrow precincts of Hebrew and the wide universe of Arabic. For
Dunash, the way to begin to make Hebrew a language that could
speak outside the synagogue was to dress it in Arabic prosody,
and he created a minor revolution by doing just that.

The Cordoban Jews had been too content with what they
could do with Arabic—in public life as well as in their intellectual and literary pursuits—to be enthusiastic revolutionaries of
Hebrew. Despite Dunash's newfangled verses, which were received with some interest, the community of socially and intellectually prosperous Jews remained satisfied with their success
within the capacious House of Arabic as long as the caliphate
lasted. Only in exile, in the taifas, in that less stable and more adventurous world, was Arabic's challenge to Hebrew finally taken
up in earnest.

The answer to this challenge, however, was not merely a
question of making Hebrew verses sound to Arabophone Jews as
elegant and sophisticated in their rhythmic structures as the
countless poems they already knew by heart in Arabic. At the
core of the matter were all the fundamental questions of what
poetry was *for*, and the revolution in Hebrew was based precisely
on the Andalusian Jews' profound appreciation of the tolerance
and openness of the universe of Arabic poetry. At some profound
level a pious Jew could unashamedly recite a pre-Islamic ode or
a homoerotic poem because a pious Muslim could; piety and poetry, in other words, in the universe in which those Jews had
been educated, were not to be confused with each other. Out of
that understanding, gleaned from the use of Arabic as a religious
and a secular poetic language—out of the recognition of the
fundamental need that a true poetic language has to shelter and
nourish contradictory values—a new Hebrew poetry was born
in the eleventh century. It took men like Samuel the Nagid, and

perhaps only at that moment of internal Andalusian exile, no longer as complacent in their full Arabization as they had been in Cordoba, to fully and unflinchingly embrace that principle of contradictory values for their own religious language. In that loving and revolutionary embrace by a powerful and supremely self-assured man, Hebrew was redefined, and cultivated as a language that could transcend the devotional and theological uses to which it had lately been limited.

For the first time in a thousand years, Hebrew was brought out of the confines of the synagogue and made as versatile as the Arabic that was the native language of the Andalusian Jewish community. Almost miraculously, Hebrew was once again used as the language of a vibrant, living poetry, what we call secular, because the immensely successful Jews who had been satisfied with being a part of the Arabic universe of the caliphate found themselves in an altogether different world. On the other side of the divide that is the exile from the Cordoban caliphate, they rediscovered the long-masked aspects of their own heritage, and they came to believe that the language of their God, like the language of the Muslims, which they had long shared and continued to share, should be great enough to transcend mere prayer. Ironically, perhaps, because devout Jews had learned to love the heterodox Arabic love poetry that pious Muslims loved to recite, it became possible, in the eleventh century, to once again read a biblical text like the Song of Songs with its full complement of erotic charges, and even to appreciate that what had once made Hebrew great was that it could be used to write poetry that not only lay outside the synagogue but might well contradict its teachings. When Samuel the Nagid proclaimed himself the David of a new age, he understood fully what he was saying, and what he was doing: he rode at the head of an army (a Muslim army, at that), he was the hero of his taifa, and he could go home and write poems about it all. He also wrote about other things, including erotic love, in the language of the David of old.

"And though some [of his verses] speak of desire, he wrote in full faith," observed Joseph, Samuel's son and first editor, speaking of the poems in his father's collection. No doubt he referred to poems such as this one:

> I'd give everything I own for that fawn
>   who betrayed me—
> my love for him locked in my heart.
>   He said to the rising moon:
> "You see how I shine
>   and dare to be seen?"
> And the circle was set in the sky
> like a pearl in a dark girl's palm.

It is impossible to know to whom the protective son Joseph is speaking in his preface to the collection he edited, called *Ben Tihillim* ("After Psalms," or perhaps more suggestively translated as "Psalms, a Sequel"). When he insists on the allegorical meanings of the erotic poems in the collection, is he speaking to the Jews of Granada, less cultured than those of his family and class? Or is he speaking to posterity, to future generations of readers who, like the Jews of the thousand years before him, might once again forget that Hebrew could be a living poetic language—and might forget, once again, all about David's many loves, his many different kinds of poems? Is he speaking to other Jews of his own time, whom he knows live far from al-Andalus, far outside the poetic universe of Arabic? They would be hearing these kinds of love songs for the first time in Hebrew. In Samuel's poetry, as in the poetry he made possible for those who followed him to write, love is ubiquitous, multifaceted, and at times troublingly ambiguous in its obsessions, in the source of its devotion.

The Nagid was a charismatic leader of armies, and then of poets. But the poetic revolution in Hebrew instigated by this vizier of the taifa of Granada was far from isolated, and the Nagid was far from a lone soul in the taifa world of the eleventh century. Indeed, the David of his age was part of the age of the avant-garde of then-modern poetry, poetry written in recognizable versions of the spoken languages, what we call vernaculars. His was a world in multiple kinds of upheavals, witnessing insurrections of every kind. Battles like those Samuel recounted in his poems followed one on the heels of the other, and everywhere throughout the peninsula, among the dozens of competing cities. As if in tandem with those constant skirmishes among the rival taifas, and among and against the Christian cities to the north, the vernaculars (or what was once poetically called "the common speech") began to rebel against the stranglehold that the written traditions had exerted on literature—on poetry—for so long.

Hebrew was made nearly vernacular by being sung and recited in the native accents of the Andalusians, who were native speakers of Arabic. Their Hebrew lyrics sounded like Arabic, they were sung to the rhythms and enunciated in the accents of Arabic. At the same time, classical Arabic found itself no longer alone in the poetic arena. By its side there was heard another Arabic, as tainted and reshaped by that spoken version of Latin we call Romance as Hebrew was by Arabic. Mozarabic, the mother tongue of the old Christians of Cordoba and of so many of the other citizens of the caliphate, Muslims and Jews alike, began to be heard alongside Arabic in songs. And far to the north, where Samuel the Nagid's counterparts had to battle not against other Muslim cities but against Christian ones, other maternal forms of what had once been Latin were heard on the streets—and were themselves on the verge of joining the ranks of this small army of new poetic languages all proclaiming, each in its own way, that their age had arrived.

Love and Its Songs

Niebla, Just West of Seville, on the Road to Huelva, August 1064

Love, may God honor you, is a serious illness, one
whose treatment must be in proportion to the
affliction. It's a delicious disease, a welcome malady.
Those who are free of it want not to be immune, and
those who are stricken want not to be cured.

I've a sickness doctors can't cure,
Inexorably pulling me to the well of my destruction.
Consented to be a sacrifice, killed for her love,
Eager, like the drunk gulping wine mixed with poison.
Shameless were those my nights,
Yet my soul loved them beyond all passion.

—Ibn Hazm, from *The Neck-Ring of the Dove*

NIEBLA WAS A TERRIBLE PLACE TO DIE. FROM AFAR IT IS picture-book pretty, a pink-walled and towered little medieval city on the Guadalquivir, halfway between Seville and the sea. But for a man who in his mind's eye could still see the gardens of Madinat al-Zahra at the height of their splendor, a man whose hometown was the metropolis of

Cordoba, capital of the caliphate and center of the civilized world at the time of his childhood, the city whose vast libraries he knew well—for such a man, Niebla was the ends of the earth. It was there, in that isolated backwater in the summer of 1064, that Ibn Hazm, the preeminent old man of Andalusian letters, died in lonely and embittered exile. He was of the same generation as Granada's vizier Samuel the Nagid, and indeed the two men, born within months of each other, knew one another, and had even once, as young men, debated publicly, during one of their final years in Cordoba. Forced as grown men to leave their beloved homeland, they made new lives in exile that could not have been more different.

A decade before Ibn Hazm died in Niebla, after a lifetime spent defending the hopeless Umayyad cause, his counterpart, the Nagid, had died, the wealthy and much-honored vizier of his taifa and the beloved leader of the Jewish community. The man Ibn Hazm had known as Ishmael ibn Nagrila had left Cordoba to move into the brave new world of the eleventh-century taifas, still sufficiently optimistic about the future to be a principal innovator of audacious new poetries. Ibn Hazm, very much Samuel's opposite, savored his bitterness at disappointments and was never able to put the past behind him. But the emotional energy and relentlessness of purpose that came from Ibn Hazm's determination not to let the glories of the Umayyad world simply die, or be utterly vulgarized by the barbarians at the gate, also made him one of the keenest minds the caliphate had ever produced. His prodigious writings on nearly every imaginable topic mark him as an outstanding intellect in Andalusian history, although much of his later writing was marred by vitriolic ad hominem attacks on his enemies, real and imagined, including Samuel the Nagid. The viciousness of many of his polemics, against all sorts of people and causes, led later Muslims to approach him gingerly, or not at all—yet the twentieth-century Spanish historians and writers who studied Ibn Hazm seem more struck by his sad-countenanced side and remember him as a Quixote-like figure. He was, in any case, an astounding intellectual, his life a fitting tribute to and a noble and melancholy end point for the caliphate he never ceased to long for and lament, as if it had been a lost lover. The caliphate could not be said to be truly gone, with no one left to recall her in all her once-vivid beauty, until Ibn Hazm passed on, fifty-five years after the sack of Madinat al-Zahra.

Ibn Hazm came by his tenaciousness of spirit honestly. His own father had worked loyally for the Amirids—al-Mansur and his sons—the chamberlains who had presided over the downfall of the caliphate. When the impressionable young man was only fifteen, Sanchuelo, the last of the Amirids, was overthrown and murdered, events that led to the sacking of Madinat al-Zahra in 1009. And Ibn Hazm's father died imprisoned for political reasons. But Ibn Hazm, who had been raised in a harem (and as one might imagine, he eventually wrote a great deal about this experience), was perhaps even more misguidedly idealistic, more quixotic, than his father: he took up the Umayyad cause after 1009, after his father's death in prison, and stuck with it even after the devastating sack of Cordoba itself in 1013. He then spent the better part of his early manhood in a series of dangerous struggles to restore some sort of viable Umayyad caliphate. These were years of political intrigue, exile, and wandering, as well as of battles in which he himself fought. Ibn Hazm shared with Samuel the Nagid the physical courage to risk his life for his political beliefs on the battlefield. These were also years of imprisonments, which Ibn Hazm suffered when the political tide turned against him, and when the horse he was betting on failed, as happened time and again. And these were years of personal disaster: the love of Ibn Hazm's life died just as Cordoba was being despoiled. In his description, many years later, of his inability ever to come to terms with the death of this young woman, a slave girl, one can discern also an echo of his grief for the death of Cordoba: "I have not found consolation for her loss to this day. . . . I have never forgotten her memory."

For a very brief moment Ibn Hazm, too, had been a vizier, though far less happily than his counterpart in Granada, since he served the last nominal Umayyad caliph, Abd al-Rahman V. After the overthrow and murder, in 1023, of this completely incompetent young man, who had been the pseudo-caliph for some seven weeks, Ibn Hazm landed in prison once again. Only after this disaster did he acknowledge the futility of the situation and abandon his active involvement in politics. He rode off alone sometime around 1024, not exactly into the sunset but as something of a crusty and irritable wanderer and peripatetic scholar. Ibn Hazm never found a real home again. The jewel-like heart of Islam, as he had known it as a young man, had disappeared, and in its place arose a hundred small towns, some no larger than Niebla, each taifa existing only for itself, for its own cause and its own party. As Ibn Hazm wrote of his other lost love, "My love for her blotted out all that went before, and made anathema to me all that came after."

Nevertheless, during the time so intolerably different from that of the grand world of his childhood, and in the midst of the new culture that was, in his eyes, intolerably inferior to the culture that produced him, the prolific polymath wrote against the wind. As if single-handedly to keep the libraries well-stocked, he produced some four hundred books, of which only a few remain. Ibn Hazm wrote on a vast range of subjects, from law to philosophy, from volumes on comparative religion to a hermeneutical meditation titled "On the Division of the Sciences"; yet the work that has most captured the imagination of posterity and made him the best-known of Andalusian writers was on that most basic and compelling subject, love.

It is ironic that *The Neck-Ring of the Dove*, as his little book is generally known, became as celebrated as it did in the aftermath of the vernacular revolutions of the era that Ibn Hazm so despised, and thanks in great measure to the love poetry that was the very banner of those revolutions. The fundamental changes in the cultural order that were beginning to be seen and heard were anathema to this uncompromising champion of the old values. But the triumph of the vernacular poetries broadcast the contours of love, as they had been cultivated, imagined, and written about endlessly in the classical Arabic tradition. Ibn Hazm's little treatise on love became the explanation par excellence of the whole phenomenon, a handbook of sorts, providing easy access to his culture's elaborate codes of love, its complex conceits about the tortures and ecstasies it brings. It would no doubt have mortified Ibn Hazm to know that, above all his other works — the dozens of neo-Platonic treatises and the argumentative texts on jurisprudence — it was this youthful romantic confection, *The Neck-Ring,* that would make his fame and fortune in posterity.

This meditation on love itself, its nature and problems, its traps and rewards, is made up of thirty small chapters, each of which addresses some problem or theme: "On Those Who Fall in Love at First Sight," "On the Signs Given by the Eyes," "On Betrayal." Each subject is first discussed in prose and then exemplified with a poetic example. In almost encyclopedic fashion, Ibn Hazm lays out the contours of passionate love as they were understood in the refined courtly society from which he had come and elaborated on within its vast corpus of love poetry: the different ways in which it is kindled, its obstacles, the different ways it comes to an end, and, perhaps most of all, the ways in which it can be an all-consuming illness that wastes the lover away, robs him of sleep, appetite, and tranquility — the sum of which creates an incomparable ecstasy and is also the very source of great poetry. This résumé of complex conceits, and some of the poetry that exemplified them, was a work of powerful nostalgia and recollection, both personal and communal. Written in those first tumultuous years after the destruction of Madinat al-Zahra and his father's death—and then the sacking of Cordoba itself, which coincided with the terrible death of his childhood love—*The Neck-Ring* was a tribute to a world of courtliness that Ibn Hazm had just seen obliterated, and that seemed every day more likely to vanish completely.

But *The Neck-Ring's* lasting popularity came precisely from the ways in which the vulgarizations of the world of the taifas— a world Ibn Hazm saw as the sure sign of the end of civilization as he knew and loved it—made highly refined romantic notions of love widely accessible, brought them out from within the walls that had once hidden places like Madinat al-Zahra from common, public view. In fact, none of this was lost in the destruction of the caliphate but instead was scattered to the many winds, and in poems sung in the veritable army of vernaculars claiming that they, too, could sing of love. Part of the endurance of Ibn Hazm's book lies in the sometimes uncanny and nearly always clear way his writing and thinking anticipate those notions about love that soon enough came to dominate the European sensibility.

Niebla, where Ibn Hazm died, is in the province of Seville, not far from the port of Palos, from which Columbus would one day set sail. He died an angry old man, alienated from almost everyone around him, having written terribly vitriolic attacks on dozens of his contemporaries. He also died believing that the culture he had loved and defended was dead as well, a ruin like the abandoned Madinat al-Zahra. But the culture was not dead; it was just beginning a second life, one that in its metamorphosed shapes and forms, in languages just breaking out of their cocoons, would endure and multiply. Far to the north of Niebla, in another small town, a vibrant market center with stark views of the towering Pyrenees, songs of love that are recognizably a part of Ibn Hazm's universe—but also recognizably of our own—were already being sung. They were about to be carried away farther still.

Barbastro, in the Foothills of the Pyrenees, on the Road to Saragossa, August 1064

The same summer that Ibn Hazm died in the southernmost part of the peninsula, an army of Normans—adventurers from the Breton coastline—along with what amounted to a light escort of neighboring Aquitainians (Aquitaine was that long-independent duchy just north of the Pyrenees, stretching east as far as the Rhone) appeared well to the north. They had wandered, purposefully, just slightly south of the Pyrenees into the region called Aragon. Along with most of the rest of the peninsula, the territories that led to these mountain passes and beyond were now a mosaic of ever shifting, ever competitive taifa kingdoms. In the north—unlike in the south, where the Muslim taifas had only each other to face in battle—there were also taifalike Christian cities to contend with. There were also foreigners who appeared, from time to time, from beyond the rough passes that had, since time immemorial, slowed but never stopped traffic there, where the peninsula begins.

The troops that appeared in the summer of 1064 laid siege to Barbastro, a prosperous and thriving trade center on a busy crossroads that led to Saragossa, the large and powerful taifa that dominated that area. The Franks among the troops were far from unknown, coming from nearby regions—from the Catalan areas to the northeast, for instance, where kingdoms often straddled the Pyrenees. Others came from cities on the far side of the mountains and were themselves no strangers to the well-traveled merchant communities in Iberia. But along with all of these, and apparently at their head, were other soldiers, not Franks—or at least not the sort of Franks known to the Barbastrans.

Soon enough, the citizens of Barbastro got an intimate look at just who these new players on the complicated political and military stage were and how they liked to live. The northerners' siege of Barbastro dragged on through the summer, but then in August, after some forty days, the city capitulated and opened wide its doors to the troops of soldiers flying their Christian flags. Numerous chroniclers, writing from various political points of view, eventually described this siege and the occupation that followed it; the events captured the imaginations of an unusual number of those who wrote the histories of the time. Nearly all report that the strangers among the troops, the contingent from the northernmost reaches of the Frankish lands, the Normans, walked into this first Andalusian city they had ever seen and immediately went native. With alacrity and ease they adopted the ways and unexpected pleasures of this previously unknown land. They fell in love with the fine clothes, clean streets, flavorful food, and just about everything else in this near and yet marvelously different place, including a fair number of the women. The citizens of Barbastro quickly learned what citizens of lands as far from each other as England and Sicily would learn about the Normans: how quick they were to settle where they went, and with what ease they seemed to do it.

The Christian Normans, like the Muslim Arabs before them, regarded the original minuscule corner of the world allotted to them as but a starting place. In 1064, when that victorious force of Normans moved into Barbastro, they were at the same time embarking on the rapid-fire spread that would take them to nearly every other corner of Europe. In their expansiveness they made over a great deal of what they found in their own image, and in our Anglophone culture we understand the general effects of what we call "the" Norman Conquest. In 1066, just two years after their forces made themselves at home in little Barbastro, much larger Norman forces crossed the English Channel and made themselves rather decisively at home there, on the island that lay twenty-two miles from their own shores. We understand, at least in some general ways, how that overlay of Norman culture affected the island kingdom they made theirs for so long, and we especially understand that the language of the conquerors reshaped the English of that time so fundamentally that our own English still wears a distinct veneer of that tattered-Latin-becoming-French the Normans spoke.

But in other cases, and most strikingly where the Normans went head to head with the Islamic centers in Europe and wrested control from them, the effects of acculturation were, conversely, that of the conquered upon the conquerors. As was the case in this small corner of old al-Andalus, when the Normans took political control of places with a seductive local culture, they mostly made themselves over, and with alacrity. One of the most striking stories told by historians who wrote about Barbastro was that of a Jewish merchant, the close friend of a Muslim citizen of Barbastro who had been forced to flee the city at the time of its capitulation. The Muslim asked his friend to enter the Norman-controlled town — the Normans had stayed on, while the Aquitainians had left with their booty — to ransom his daughter, a captive of the Christians. The no doubt dramatized story had the would-be rescuer of the young Muslim woman standing open-mouthed at the scene he found in his friend's old house in Barbastro. The Christian who had appropriated the property had taken over everything that came with it and was sitting on the floor in full mufti, enjoying a meal of local foods, chatting in pidgin Arabic with the members of the household who had stayed behind, including his friend's daughter, whom he appeared to have taken as his wife. After dinner, they all listened to the favored entertainment of the locals, the songs performed by the singing girls called *qiyan*.

Even if we suspect this anecdote of being a little too well wrought, the broader historical picture confirms its basic points. The spongelike and extremely mobile Normans played a crucial, if somewhat inadvertent, role at the end of the eleventh century in familiarizing Latin Christendom with Islamic Europe. They went, they saw, they conquered—and in the process, they learned, adopted, and spread wherever else they went. There is no case more telling than that of Sicily. In 1072, after thirty-four years of effort led by two brothers, Robert and Roger Guiscard, Palermo, the capital of Islamic Sicily, fell and became the center of the Norman kingdom of Sicily. Sicily had always been a crossroads of peoples, a place where both Latin and Greek survived and coexisted. Beginning in the eighth century, the island had been colonized by North African Muslims, as part of the wave of expansions that led them to Iberia.

But Islamic Sicily's political and cultural status had always been subordinate to Cordoba's, until that extraordinary center fell. Shortly thereafter, in 1038, a mere seven years after the official end of the caliphate, the Normans began to muscle in, although Muslim Sicily would be a far tougher nut to crack for the Normans than little Barbastro, even tougher than that other island they had so coveted, Saxon England. By the time the Guiscards had seized complete political control of their island in the Mediterranean in 1072, their kinsmen had been ruling England for half a dozen years. In something of a replay of the Barbastro anecdote, writ very large, the Norman rulers of Sicily for the subsequent century and a half became so thoroughly Arabized, and so outstanding in their role as the premier patrons of Arabic culture, that Sicily had its golden years as a center of an Andalusian-like culture *after* political control there passed from the Sicilian Muslims to the Norman Christians. The "turbaned kings" is what the Muslims eventually called the Norman rulers of their island, the descendants of the Guiscard brothers. And to them were dedicated important books in Arabic, including the foremost work of geography of the Middle Ages.

This love of things Arabic was no passing fancy or momentary cultural fad. Nearly two hundred years after the Norman conquest of Sicily, its half-German ruler, descended on his mother's side from the Normans, wrote letters in Arabic to Muslim philosophers in North Africa with whom he carried on a correspondence on a whole range of intellectual problems. Frederick II, the last of the line of Arabized Norman Sicilians that began when the Normans first spread wide their wings in the mid-eleventh century, was an exceptional man and recognized as such even in his own lifetime, when he was already known as the *Stupor Mundi,* or "Wonder of the World." But he was also the product of complex Norman attitudes about the difference between politics (which often as not meant religion as well) and culture—a difference that the Jewish merchant saw strikingly illustrated that day in 1064 when he walked into his friend's house and saw the Norman entranced, moved, listening to the love songs sung by the young women of Barbastro.

Not all the Christians involved in the taking of Barbastro stayed. The Aquitainians, who comprised a significant part of the conquering forces, decamped almost immediately, perhaps because they were closer neighbors and not so surprised by what they saw there, or perhaps because they were better satisfied with the immediate material results of the raid than with the long-term responsibilities of moving in. But whatever the reasons, Christian and Muslim historians alike recorded that, with William VIII of Aquitaine at their head, they returned to their home courts weighed down with booty of every sort, having taken nearly everything they could carry. What the Normans were happy to enjoy and adapt inside their own new homes, the

Aquitainians preferred to carry away with them. The great prize that was hauled back across the Pyrenees was a large number of qiyan: women like the ones singing for the Norman-gone-native in the earlier anecdote, women who sang for a living, young and attractive entertainers much prized in the Andalusian courts. Sources vary wildly on the numbers of women who were taken as prizes of the battle for Barbastro—500, 1,500, 5,000—but they all agree that a great many went back with the Aquitainians. In that expedition, and no doubt in others, Andalusian singers were the greatest treasure among the spoils taken back to the newly ambitious Christian courts that lay just the other side of the Pyrenees, from the Mediterranean coast in the east to the Bay of Biscay in the west.

The aristocratic courts that lay to the north and northeast of those still-Islamic territories, the land we vaguely (and often inaccurately) refer to as Provence, were just then beginning to develop a considerable appetite for many tokens of the good life: silks, exquisitely crafted musical instruments, ivory jewelry boxes. These things came from their neighbors to the south, not exactly new neighbors but in some ways newfound neighbors. The number and type of cultural, material, and linguistic affinities and dependencies among cities on either side of the diaphanous and always shifting divides of religious ideology and political loyalty increased dramatically over the next several centuries. Crucially, there was nothing like the sort of linguistic separation we observe today. The way Latin was spoken throughout those territories—a vernacular in a dozen different street guises, none of them possessed quite yet of independent identities and names—was still more similar than different in places like Barcelona and Montpellier and Toulouse. The languages ran into each other in a crescentlike swath of land along the Mediterranean, where the mountains gently slope down toward the sea. This stretch of land ignored the modern national divisions and treated the mountain range as a middle instead of a division, and it was happily dubbed Languedoc—the name of the land taken from its language, *langue d'oc,* that is, "the language that says *oc* for 'yes'" (as opposed to the *si* of the Italian peninsula and the *oïl* of the northern French areas).

The cultural exchange at Barbastro rather dramatically marks the beginning of the end of the long period during which neighbors, al-Andalus on this side and Latin Christendom beyond the Pyrenees, glimpsed each other only rarely, and to very little effect. The new neighborliness sometimes came from relatively friendly impulses, but far more often it arose from ideological hostility or military aggression. It mattered little. As was the case in the siege and conquest of Barbastro, or in the far more extended and flamboyant example of Sicily, it may well turn out that a moving love song captivates the men who have come to capture a city. Barbastro is the memorable marker of the expansive new era that began in the mid-eleventh century, when the walls between the neighbors began to be dismantled and all of a sudden one could see into the other's courtyard, and beyond. The doors were opened wide by every conceivable kind of contact, from the numerous royal and aristocratic marriages that linked courts to each other, to the increasing traffic along pilgrimage routes to and from Santiago de Compostela, and the spread of the monastic center Cluny's dominance over dozens of linked religious houses on both sides of the mountains. As both the Aquitainians and the Normans involved in the taking of Barbastro learned, sometimes what could be heard coming from the neighbors' courtyard was exceptionally beautiful. The art of singing, and especially the art of singing songs of love, was the great vogue among the Andalusians. And after Barbastro, they were being sung by qiyan on both sides of the Pyrenees—qiyan whose mother tongue was most likely Mozarabic and for whom the language of *oc* was a kissing cousin to their own form of Romance.

Curiously, the man whose poetry was saved and canonized as "the first" in a modern European language was the son of the same William VIII who led the Aquitainians at Barbastro, the man who had returned to Provence with the human treasure that was a veritable small army of singers. William IX, the young troubadour-to-be, was raised in Aquitainian courts where the singing of those women was part of the aristocracy's cultural and material well-being. The young William, along with many others of the first generation of troubadours, grew up in cities and courts that did not imagine themselves distant in space, language, or culture from many of the courts and cities on the southern side of the Pyrenees, courts and cities that, like Barbastro, were part of the Arabic cultural orbit, regardless of whether they were controlled politically by Muslims or Christians. Armies of merchants and singers as well as soldiers crossed the mountains every day, in both directions, well-provisioned with forms of Romance as well as forms of Arabic. As both a child and an adult, William, several of whose wives were from cities south of the Pyrenees, was one of that privileged class of Christians in the Latin world who could hear their neighbors singing. He also belonged to the avant-garde generation that rebelled vigorously against the strictures of a Latin that was no longer the mother tongue and began to write love songs, and other kinds of songs, in the new vernaculars of the time. These were not those modern national languages we know—French, Spanish, Portuguese, Italian—but others: Mozarabic, Provençal, Sicilian, Galician, which were the first generation of the Romance family. And among these, none would ever be a better icon of the revolution, of the invention of the modern European sensibility, than William's song-language of Oc.*

---

*The modern cult of the troubadours and their linguistic and poetic revolution has been developed by a series of influential philosophers and poets, among them Nietzsche (who described the troubadours as having invented "ourselves" and whose *Gay Science* is a play on the Provençal name for poetic manuals), as well as by Ezra Pound, a prodigious translator of their poetry.

Pass us the cup around! In it the heartache's forgotten.
Open the festivities! The ties of love are broken.

Make love your religion, your law,
Friend! As long as you're alive.
Turn your ear from
The blamer's persuasion.
Your duty is ordained, the wine
Awaits you, hasten!

Our drinking companion's repented. Sing, chant,
Show him a cup of wine! Perhaps he'll apostatize!

The singing of songs was an art cultivated widely and ferociously by the Andalusians, who, with customary and due respect for their ancestors, believed they had taken the much revered pre-Islamic cult of poetry one important step further. They had invented something called "ring songs," lyrics quite unlike the hanging odes of the beloved pre-Islamic tradition, or the classical poems brought to near perfection in the East over the past several hundred years. In the old days, the ones that Ibn Hazm's book of love poems perfectly captured, the refined court poets recited their own lyrics rather formally, even when they were accompanied by music. But these newfangled ring songs that had become so much the vogue since the fall of the caliphate, in the fifty years or so before Barbastro, were meant wholly to be enjoyed, and sung along with, even danced to, rather than just listened to and admired with detached connoisseurship. At the very heart of their popularity was their most revolutionary gesture: they brought the mother tongues of the Andalusians up to share the stage with classical Arabic poetry, a language and a poetry that had never had to share the stage before.

These songs reflected explicitly the complex and hybrid identity that had been the self-conscious hallmark of the

Andalusians from the time of Abd al-Rahman I. The ring song (in Arabic it is called *muwashshaha,* from the word for "sash," "circle," or "girdle") broke all the rules of the classical Arabic poem that had come out of the desert and been cultivated lovingly and carefully in Baghdad and everywhere else among the Arabic-speaking peoples. Where the poetry of the old world had a single rhyme linking all the verses, whether five or five hundred, the ring song did quite otherwise. As its name suggested, this kind of song made rhyme an encircling device, repeating rhyme patterns of sometimes dizzying complexity, with internal rhymes as well as those linking one stanza to another.

The stanzas themselves were a new thing, also a part of the insurrection of the vernaculars of the time. The courtly performance of the traditional Arabic lyric had no need for stanzas, for breaks between one thought in the song and the next. On the contrary, its specific aesthetic called for seamlessness, a single continuous strand of lyrical expression whose outward form is in part marked by the single rhyme sound and in part by the absence of distinct regular breaks. This new song form was different: this was dance music that had come in off the streets. The song was broken into stanzas that were then "ringed" with the most astonishing part of all, a simple little refrain to be repeated after each of the stanzas, much as in any modern song of ours. These simple few lines turned the whole tradition upside down because they were so impudently unclassical. The main stanzas of the song were still in classical Arabic, although now sung to the beats and rhymes of the little refrain. But the voice in the refrain was that of a woman, and she was singing in the vernacular. Beyond that, in terms of content, the refrain almost always upset the expectations and intentions of the rest of the song: whereas the classical voice sings of love with the usual high-flown metaphors and allusions, the vernacular voice replies with a curt "shut up and kiss me." In these new songs, the mother tongues thus literally run rings around the classical poets and their fine language: in their kitchen Arabic or in that tattered

Latin spoken by the Mozarabs that was consanguinous to langue d'oc, these final lines were the key to the Andalusian proclamation of cultural ascendance and uniqueness, no less than the horseshoe arches in the Great Mosque.

Much like the brilliant synthesis visible in the Great Mosque, and much like those rhyming alternations of brick and stone, of the old and new parts, of Roman spolia and new constructions, the ring songs are the loud Umayyad voice in the stanzas half arguing with and half making love to the women who sing out their handful of lines in Mozarabic, iconically the mother-tongue of the Christian women of Cordoba. Later ring songs would have refrains in other vernaculars, in the vernaculars of the times and places they were sung, including vernacular Arabic; the distinctive feature was vernacularness as such, and its abiding contrast with the formal language of the rest of the song. This was the artful and inspired combination of Ibn Hazm's world—the refined universe of the courts, with its ultra-refined poetic tradition—with the world just outside those courts—that of the popular women singers who performed to the stirring beats of a whole repertoire of instruments that would soon become standards in the European musical picture: guitars, drums, and tambourines. As if it, too, were a new instrument, the vernacular, the antidote and rival to the classical languages, was brought into the courts.

The popular song tradition in al-Andalus, as everywhere, went back further than history can track with any certainty. There is ample evidence that songs in vernacularized and even part-Romanized Arabic had been sung, alongside Arabized Romance, for a long time in the streets of Cordoba and in other parts of the old caliphate, at least as far back as the time of the Mozarab martyrs in the mid-ninth century, when the language wars were already at a fever pitch. But as in the case of Hebrew's makeover into a language that could sing songs of love, it was not until after the collapse of the cultural certainties of the

Umayyad caliphate, and the invigorating cultural mixtures characteristic of the taifas, that this new song form flaunting Andalusian hybridness became widespread, and just fashionable enough to entice the court poets themselves to sing in its accents—or to write so that the qiyan could sing.

The cultural commentaries and histories of the Arabs all record the impact of this vogue, this very Andalusian way of doing songs, especially love songs. The new generation of Hebrew poets, those who followed in the footsteps of Samuel the Nagid, also fell in love with this form and it became a distinctive part of the repertoire of forms in the new Hebrew poetry. It was so powerful that memory traces of it survived, along with the notion that there is an Andalusian aesthetic of love songs, a notion that lives to this day throughout the Arabic-speaking world, in places and among people who have little idea of what al-Andalus was.

This Andalusian legacy in the lyrical song tradition was powerful in its ability to speak lucidly and movingly, in the only partly symbolic guise of a simple love song, to the problem of marrying the different strands that had made up Islamic culture since Umayyad times. The very shape and languages of this kind of song bring the key players in the drama out to sing at the same time: the revered ancestral poets who can remember the way poems were once recited at the center of Mecca, in front of the Kaaba; and the women they courted and married from among the great variety of peoples they encountered as they left the Arabian peninsula and spread throughout the world. As a structure that would far outlast the Andalusians themselves, the ring song was an ode to the sort of union so electrifyingly visible in the Great Mosque: the back and forth of two contradictory strands, in love with each other, tied to each other indissolubly, and yet their languages autonomous, each with its own place within the capacious House of Islam and the even more capacious House of Arabic.

The Church at the Top of the Hill

Toledo, 1085

I T SITS VERY QUIETLY, AT THE TOP OF THE HIGHEST HILL OF A craggy mountain stronghold. The little-visited site is now the Museum of Visigothic Culture, but it was built as the Church of San Roman, in the aftermath of what is called the Christian Reconquest of Toledo of 1085. Toledo had been the ancient Visigothic capital, and the original site almost certainly had seen a Visigothic church on it. In their more than 250 years in the city, the Muslims had never used this highest point for a mosque, but when the Castilians took control of the Muslim taifa of Toledo, toward the end of the tumultuous eleventh century, they recognized its obvious symbolic importance. Sometime in the century after they seized the venerable old city and made it the new capital of the kingdom of Castile, the Christian conquerors decided to build a brand-new, commemorative church on the spot where their already mythologized

Visigothic predecessors had worshiped, and from which they had surveyed their old dominions, the whole of the peninsula, before losing them to the Umayyads in the eighth century.

The first thing pious worshipers saw when they entered their new church was a vivid visual memory of the Umayyads. The wall that dominates the entry is a series of horseshoe arches with alternating red-and-white voussoirs, unmistakable echoes of those of the Great Mosque; these arches are themselves framed by Latin inscriptions all around, while inside the curvaceous horseshoes are painted Byzantine-looking figures, presumably saints. Finally, and most strikingly, above the arches sit a series of lovely and delicate interior windows, also decorated with writing—except this is Arabic writing, and the sight of it locates the Latin inscription within an artistic context. The complex uses of writing, a superbly allusive form of visual ornamentation, were (like the red-and-white voussoirs atop the horseshoe arches) the unmistakable decorative signatures of a religion that, quite unlike medieval Christianity, eschewed icons.*

But what in the world are these Muslim echoes doing here, in this church that was a clear marker of the triumph of Christian over Islamic rule? The small concession made to the audacious suggestion that the God of the Christians of twelfth-century Toledo was also the God of the Muslims—an impression one might easily walk away with after a first glance at this sanctuary   was that the Arabic writing itself was made impossible to decipher. It is, on closer inspection, not just a difficult-to-read Arabic script, but an ersatz Arabic, a symbolic evocation of the language of the other God. Yet why, inside this church that (unlike others) was never a mosque, do we find unmistakable

---

*The aniconic ("without icons") principle in Islam is far less rigidly observed than most people assume: the vast and luxurious tradition of Persian manuscript illustration is a conspicuous but not unique example of an Islamic art form that violates it, and as in other instances it is likely a case of early Islam's accommodation of indigenous traditions.

emulations of the characteristic features of mosques, especially of the Great Mosque that was the spiritual center of the Umayyad caliphate? Why do the conquerors intertwine their own heritage and culture with the most distinctive aspects of the heritage and culture of the conquered? The squared-off arches do not sit in a different chapel or in a different part of the church; they surround the horseshoe arches, the Latin writing alternating with the "Arabic," the two visually dependent on each other.

In this sacred place, Christians of the twelfth century—who were supposedly engaged in unrelenting religious warfare against the Muslims—paid an unambiguous tribute to the culture of the enemy, and created a space in which to pray that surrounded them with visions of their remarkable intimacies. This was the church built for and by the rough-and-tumble Castilians, who so nakedly aspired to replace the Umayyads, or rather, to triumph over the squabbling children of the Umayyads, the dozens of bickering taifas of the eleventh century. Why did they want their place of Christian worship to speak the languages of worship of that other God so eloquently? What kind of city was this Toledo they had now made the capital, first of the kingdom, then of the aspiring Christian empire?

Toledo was a natural capital city from the outset. In the post-Roman period, this craggy citadel, naturally fortified by the encircling Tagus River, and already noteworthy as an urban center, became the heart of the first independent Visigothic kingdom. After the formal union of the Visigoths with the Catholic Church in 589—the Visigoths had entered Iberia in the beginning of the sixth century as Arians, a condemned version of Christianity that did not accept the full divinity of Christ and saw the Son, Jesus, as subordinate to the Father—Toledo itself was transformed from a secular to a religious center, the seat of what were called the "councils" of Toledo. The councils of Iberian bishops were increasingly powerful during the chaotic last years of the kingdom of the Visigoths, but after 711, and especially after 756, what the Church said and where it sat ceased to matter as much. In the new order of the Umayyad world, Toledo was eclipsed as a political capital, but it was far from forgotten. Some of the old luster and sense of its centrality were never lost, and Toledo lived on as one of the prominent cities of al-Andalus in its prime. When the caliphate disintegrated, just after the turn of the eleventh century, and the peninsula fell into that period of cultural and political rivalry among the taifas, Toledo soon enough emerged as one of the most luminous and powerful of those independent city-states.

From the beginning the taifa of Toledo was ambitious and proud, and its government and leaders were notorious for their luxurious court life and far-flung military aspirations. In 1043, while Granada's armies were still being led to their battles against other taifas by the Jewish vizier Samuel the Nagid, the leadership of rival Toledo fell to a charismatic and cultured man named al-Mamun. His long reign, during which he filled the city with the intellectual and artistic luminaries of the moment, further polished Toledo's already bright cultural life and reputation, and al-Mamun seemed to be moving Toledo toward some sort of succession to the peninsula's Islamic leadership. Toledo's most powerful rival in this was the huge taifa of Seville, ruled by a series of no less cultivated strongmen called the Abbadids, after the first of that line, Muhammad ibn Abbad. As in the Toledo of al-Mamun, the Abbadids' military and cultural ambitions were purposefully intertwined, and their Seville became the new haven for poetry in al-Andalus. The Abbadid-sponsored academy of poets played all sorts of important roles in poetic history, attracting poets from inside and outside the peninsula (including the most memorable of the Sicilians, named Ibn Hamdis) and leaving us an important *diwan,* or anthology, of the poetry of the period. The last of the line of the Abbadid military rulers was al-Mutamid, a poet ranked among the very best in the whole of the Andalusian canon.

The relentless warfare among all the Muslim-held cities, and the especially ferocious competition between al-Mamun's Toledo and Abbadid Seville, defined political life for decades. Other taifas, as well as the increasingly important Christian-held cities and small kingdoms to the north, were involved in the ever shifting and often unpredictable alliances that dominated the long aftermath of the collapse of central Cordoban authority. It seemed that everyone wanted some version of what Cordoba had once had, and adventurers and the ambitious were everywhere involved in the often chesslike complex of rivalries and battles among cities of every stripe. Alliances and rivalries crossed religious lines every day: Christian cities whose Muslim allies helped them defeat Christian rivals became as commonplace as the Muslim taifas whose Christian allies helped them take other Muslim cities.

The brilliant al-Mamun led Toledo to a series of significant military victories. He took over Valencia, a city of crucial strategic importance, and for a short but delicious period he held the most coveted prize of all, Cordoba. The old capital was far more than a half-ghostly place on the banks of the Guadalquivir, although much of it was still in ruins from the brutal rampages that had ravaged it at the time of the Berber wars. Toledo and Seville, the two taifas most intent on making themselves the new capital of whatever phoenix might be coaxed from the ashes of al-Andalus, understood that Cordoba was the repository of the powerful memories of the ancient and legitimate capital. Al-Mamun's symbolic and thus especially sweet triumph when he took Cordoba was, however, as short-lived as most of the other military triumphs and alliances of this period. Cordoba soon enough returned to the orbit of al-Mamun's bitter rivals, the Abbadids of Seville.

By the eleventh century it must have seemed as if the

fratricidal Muslim conflicts would never end. Perhaps, though, this appeared not to matter much, since the material and cultural wealth of the courts inside nearly every city became more conspicuous while political and military chaos reigned. But in fact these small centers could not hold forever, and the great cultural triumphs of the taifas could not, at the end of the day, forestall the heavy price to be paid for the lack of political stability and continuity. At the top of the highest hill in Toledo, in the triumphant Christian church inscribed with its love for the Islamic arts, we can see both the aesthetic victories of the Andalusian taifas and the political price paid for them, the loss of power.

Where does the road to that church in Toledo begin? From among various moments, one might choose the two-year interval of 1065–66 as a snapshot crowded with the sorts of events that would lead to San Roman. In April 1065, Barbastro, which had fallen to the Normans the year before, was retaken by the taifa king of Saragossa, almost certainly with the military help of Ferdinand I, the powerful sovereign of the combined kingdoms of Castile and Leon. That Christian monarch considered a number of the northern taifas his Muslim vassals and allies, whereas he viewed the Christians from Normandy and Aquitaine as enemy intruders.

In 1066, ferocious anti-Jewish riots broke out in Granada. Among the many victims was Joseph, the son of the city's much loved vizier; Joseph, the editor of his father's earthshaking poems in the new Hebrew of the age; Joseph, who had laid out the gardens at the top of the fortified hill, next to the old Red Fortress. There are, as always, conflicting accounts and interpretations of the causes of this relatively isolated Muslim uprising against what had been a warmly favored Jewish community. The taifas were notorious for precisely the sort of intimacy with Christians and Jews that both Joseph and Ferdinand represented, the first as the powerful and prestigious heir to his father, the latter as a close and reliable ally whose help allowed the retaking of Barbastro from the Normans. All of this seemed normal to the Andalusians, who were heirs to the Umayyad interpretation of the dhimma and who now lived in cultural circumstances where Muslims were even more rarely isolated from Christian and Jewish communities than they had been during the caliphate. But the ages-long Andalusian forging of political and cultural accommodations with Jews and Christians was interpreted as a lax or even heterodox view of Islamic law by the more purist Berber Muslims of North Africa, who had already wreaked havoc in the last days of the caliphate and who were seemingly always aware of what was going on just across the Strait of Gibraltar. Not too many years down the road—the same road that takes us to that church in Toledo—these nearly irreconcilable differences would loom very large.

But before that, back between 1065 and 1066, the political scene throughout the peninsula was most shaken by the death of Ferdinand I, who had managed to unite two of the most fractious northwestern Christian kingdoms. Ferdinand died in December 1065, and by the turn of the new year his kingdom was once again divided, by the terms of his will and by the resulting fratricidal struggles among his three sons. Ferdinand left his kingdom split so that Sancho, his oldest son, inherited Castile itself; Alfonso, apparently his father's favorite, got the kingdom of Leon, a considerably richer prize; and the youngest, Garcia, was allotted the farthest and poorest corner, Galicia. There was yet another key player in this nearly Shakespearean chain of quarrels among the brothers that began in 1066 and continued all the way into Toledo in 1085: a man named Rodrigo Diaz, one of the most prominent warriors and courtiers in the service of Sancho, the oldest of the brothers. Rodrigo Diaz would be remembered far and wide and across history as the Cid, while Ferdinand's sons, rivals for the kingship of Castile, remain obscure historical figures to all but specialists in this period.

The brothers themselves were much like the neighboring Muslim taifas: they were sometimes allies and sometimes enemies, with and against other Muslims, with and against other Christian cities; they were sometimes at each other's throats, and sometimes allied two against the third. Not long after their father's death, Sancho the eldest and Alfonso the favorite were allied, momentarily, to depose their younger brother, Garcia, from his Galician share. But once that was accomplished, Sancho turned against Alfonso and, in 1071, beat him decisively in battle and took him prisoner. The defeated Alfonso was soon enough released, under mysterious circumstances, and went into exile, as had Garcia before him. Garcia had taken refuge not in any of the neighboring Christian courts but in the poetry-mad Abbadid taifa of Seville. Alfonso, however, headed for the rival taifa, al-Mamun's dazzling Toledo, where he was warmly welcomed as the son of Ferdinand, who had often protected the city. In lively and prosperous Toledo, the young Alfonso licked his wounds and, no doubt, plotted his next move against his brothers. Suddenly, the following year, there was a drastic turn of events: Sancho was murdered while putting down an insurrection in a city called Zamora, which lies along the Duero River, due north of Salamanca.

It was of course presumed that Alfonso himself had engineered the uprising and the murder, from his comfortable exile in al-Mamun's court. Alfonso's supposed ally in the uprising at Zamora—the trap that led to the murder—was the princess Urraca, the sister in the divided family. The other famous participant in the battle of Zamora was Rodrigo Diaz, who, as the doomed Sancho's principal military leader, acquitted himself with great valor. Rodrigo then returned to Castile for the royal burial of the king who was his longtime patron and who had made possible an already distinguished career. But at some point shortly thereafter, he went into the service of the newly minted king of Castile, the principal beneficiary of his brother's untimely death, Alfonso VI. The relationship between the new king and the old king's loyal vassal was highly fraught from the outset; from these tensions, and from the dozens of other whirlwind political events of the ensuing years, were found the raw materials for Spain's great epic poem, named for Rodrigo, whose followers called him "the Cid." In the Arabic and Arabized lingo of his troops, this honorific, *al-sayyid,* meant something like "the chief," "the lord."

Sancho of Leon, Ferdinand I's oldest son, was not the only principal player to die of foul play in these closely intertwined tales. Just a few years after the drama at Toledo and Zamora, in 1075, while Alfonso was just managing to consolidate his territories of Castile and Leon, the great al-Mamun of Toledo, who had not so long before protected Alfonso from his own brother, also fell victim to treachery and political assassination. Al-Mamun had ruled Toledo for thirty-three years and made it the cultural showplace of the peninsula. At the time of his murder he had recently succeeded in the military mission that would also have made Toledo politically preeminent among the taifas and perhaps unified them, which was certainly al-Mamun's ambition: after a lifetime's effort, al-Mamun had taken the coveted city of Cordoba from his archrivals in Seville. But beneath the superficial similarity of the kings' murders—the Christian king of Leon and the Muslim king of Toledo—the two situations could not have produced more different outcomes. Whereas Sancho's death led the various kingdoms over which he and his brothers had feuded out of fratricidal violence and civil wars and into Alfonso's long, prosperous, and unifying reign, the death of al-Mamun, who had powerfully and profitably guided Toledo to a position of stability and expansiveness, resulted in a series of catastrophically weak and rivalrous successors and a period of bloody civil unrest in Toledo. The possibility that a single taifa might emerge as a unifying leader of al-Andalus was lost.

Among the weak and embattled protagonists angling to replace al-Mamun was a grandson named al-Qadir. When his moment of need arrived, al-Qadir took the perhaps inevitable next step in the back-and-forth cycle of Toledo-Castile protection and turned for help to Alfonso, who by then was king of the reunited kingdoms of Castile and Leon. Ferdinand I, Alfonso's father, had for years taken tribute from Toledo in return for protection against the city's Muslim rivals, and later that relationship was reversed. During al-Mamun's great success and independence, and especially during the years shortly after Ferdinand's death in the late 1060s, when Alfonso had to seek refuge from his brother, Sancho, he had found it in Toledo. By 1075, the wheel had turned once again, and it was Alfonso who was in a position to provide al-Qadir the help asked for, at a steep price. An embattled Toledo, coveted by other taifas—but especially by arch-rival Seville—thus came under Alfonso's protection at al-Qadir's request, and there it remained for the next ten years.

This was an eventful decade, during which Alfonso continued to expand his territories and consolidate his holdings. These were also years during which Rodrigo Diaz established his reputation as a warrior and earned his honorific "Cid." The politics of the taifas remained as convoluted and chimeric as ever, marked by all manner of alliance and enmity. The Cid himself was involved in major skirmishes on behalf of the king of Seville against the king of Granada, both powerful Muslim monarchs, each with strong Christian contingents in his army. By the time that this Christian warrior with the Arabic name was leading troops into battles between one Muslim and another, few citizens of the peninsula lived in any sort of innocence of the various languages and faiths that surrounded them. Nor did they have any reason necessarily to assume that the enemy was someone of a different faith, or spoke a different language, since that had not been the case in recent memory—certainly not in the ten years the Christian king Alfonso served as the protector of Muslim Toledo.

Most fatefully of all for Toledo itself, these were ten years during which the various factions within Toledo continued to feud, with dozens of treacherous alliances formed with rivals from other taifas, but without clear resolution. Al-Qadir, who had sought Alfonso's expensive help, was every year a weaker puppet of his increasingly strong protector. In 1084, the puppet evidently decided that he could not hold his own inside Toledo, where the factions against him had become extremely violent, and he offered direct control over Toledo to Alfonso in return for help in getting him out of the city and into exile in Valencia. This was an offer Alfonso had no reason to refuse and which in any case presented few difficulties and very limited military expenditure.

Toledo had to be besieged for a time, as al-Qadir's enemies in Toledo had nothing to gain from this transfer of power. But the siege did not last long, and in the spring of 1085, with not a drop of blood shed in battle, Alfonso VI of Castile and Leon entered venerable Toledo, a city he already knew and loved, a city that al-Mamun had spent more than thirty years grooming to be the successor to Cordoba itself. In all sorts of ways, that was exactly what it became, but with the remarkable twist that Alfonso and his successors were Christians, not Muslims. Yet they were the Christians whose descendants, as late as a century or more later, would build the Church of San Roman, with the horseshoe arches that pay loving homage to Cordoba itself, and who would keep other aspects of Cordoba's legacy alive and well.

The Toledo that Alfonso VI walked into and soon made into the new capital of his kingdom was already a vivacious place with a strong sense of its own cultural superiority. Very little of either the spirit or the particulars of the conviction that Toledo was the center of the civilized world was lost in the transfer of power that made Alfonso a worthy successor to al-Mamun. But precisely because Alfonso's formidable leadership was evident to all, and because of the obvious danger that Toledo, as a Christian capital, would rapidly succeed in reuniting the peninsula after nearly a hundred years of political chaos, near panic set in among the remaining Muslim taifas.

Alfonso began his expansions almost immediately, and in less than a year he had established poor al-Qadir, who had handed him Toledo, as his puppet in Valencia; he had laid siege to Saragossa, where his former vassal Rodrigo Diaz was probably in charge of the opposing Muslim army; and he did what even the ambitious al-Mamun had not quite dared to do—demand that his only true rival, Seville, submit to him. It must have seemed quite possible that Alfonso could have accomplished this ambitious reunification for which he had obviously developed quite a taste. But he encountered a glitch of extraordinary proportions when a force that he had not reckoned on appeared on the scene. That not only stopped Alfonso in his tracks but also fundamentally changed the character of the peninsula's old Islamic traditions.

In October 1086, Alfonso's armies abandoned their siege of Saragossa in order to move south to meet invading armies from North Africa. The Almoravids, a powerful Berber dynasty with a particularly fundamentalist interpretation of Islam, had arrived on the peninsula, to aid their Muslim brethren. It had been one thing to accept the taifalike Christian kingdoms as players on the chaotic scene of a disunited al-Andalus, but quite another for the remaining major Muslim taifas to see the threatened, perhaps imminent, unification of the old Muslim realms by the formidable Alfonso. With considerable trepidation the Andalusians had asked their North African coreligionists to send them military aid. And so it was that on a battlefield not far from Badajoz, a city about 115 miles north of the Mediterranean coast and just on the modern border with Portugal, the Almoravid army soundly defeated Alfonso and overnight brought his territorial and political ambitions to a skidding halt.

The Andalusian Muslims, the old taifas, were momentarily relieved and returned to their squabbling ways, but not for very long. The Almoravids, once they had gotten a close look at the Andalusians, were filled with contempt for their obvious military ineptness and chaotic politics. At the same time, they appeared seduced, and full of the sort of greedy desire for the still-palpable delights of al-Andalus that had so affected Alfonso. Within a few years of defeating Alfonso and returning to their lands across the strait, the Almoravids came back with the clear intention of staying and making al-Andalus a province, the jewel in the crown of an empire that began on the banks of the Senegal River in Africa. By that time the Andalusians had gotten as much of a taste as they wanted of the rough Berbers from beyond the Atlas Mountains, barbarians by Andalusian standards. Most of the taifa kings had concluded that Alfonso himself would be a more congenial overlord than those stiff-necked, morally self-righteous, and culturally backward Muslims, and al-Mutamid, the poet-king of Seville, and others ended up appealing to Alfonso for help in opposing the very Muslims they had originally brought in to protect themselves against him. But it was too late. Within a few years, the Almoravids made the shredded remnants of al-Andalus, the remaining taifas, their unhappy colony, while also attempting a radical reform of the Muslim ways of the peninsula.

Toledo, however, which had remained in Alfonso's hands and became his capital and his home—and that of his successors for generations to come—flourished as never before. This was at least partially the paradoxical result of the reining in of Alfonso's vast ambitions and of the Almoravids' harshness and intolerance. Alfonso, who had first lived in Toledo while it was a taifa, and who had only ever lived in the world of the taifas, with their promiscuous intermingling of the three religions and their mixed languages and cultures, kept Toledo as the sort of open city he knew and loved, even as many of the old taifas became closed or hostile to Jews and to Christians. After the momentous turn of events of 1085–86, Toledo became the most important city for many of those Arabized Jews and Christians. The Arabized and, more recently, re-Hebraized Jews were culturally the heirs of Hasdai ibn Shaprut of Cordoba and of Samuel the Nagid of Granada, and the Christians, who arrived with their old-fashioned Catholic liturgy in Arabic, were the descendants of the Mozarabs of Cordoba.

The narrow and winding streets of Toledo, already lined with the elegant buildings and other markers of the rich Islamic cultural legacy of al-Mamun's taifa, now began to fill up with ever larger communities of the sort that had made Umayyad Cordoba so culturally complex. In 1088, just as the Muslim taifas were being annexed to the Almoravid empire, Alfonso supervised Toledo's ascendance in the larger Christian sphere, ensuring that his new capital was declared the principal see of the Church on the Iberian Peninsula. Toledo, virtually overnight, went from being a Muslim taifa that few Christians from beyond its borders would have reason to visit, to an archepiscopal center that, conversely, few among the Church hierarchy could afford not to visit. As the Church itself became more mobile, in more intimate contact with the rest of the Latin Christian world, Toledo was the open door to the treasures of the Old World. And so, the old Mozarab community that once produced the martyrs of Cordoba now found itself, perhaps to its own surprise, at considerable odds with the Latin Christian community with whom it now shared the old Visigothic capital. The Mozarabs, some of them natives of Toledo and others immigrants from other Andalusian cities, saw themselves as the Christian old guard. And for them, the new Christians who now began to move into the city, especially those who represented faraway and foreign Cluny, were a menace to their own traditions, which went back to the times of the Visigoths. The new Christians, who from the outset occupied the most powerful ecclesiastical positions, were a community whose reformed liturgy was, in the eyes of the Mozarabs, corrupted by newfangled notions, while their own rite, kept pristine in its Arabic wrapping and thus unchanged since the eighth century, was by far the more traditional.

But Toledo was not doomed (at least not for a very long time) to be nothing more than a museum of the Islamic culture that had shaped the city for the preceding three hundred years. The rich Arabo-Islamic heritage that the Latin Christian visitors discovered in Toledo was carried on—preserved as a living thing, not merely fossilized—not only by the Muslims who had stayed (as many had, and Alfonso left the city's mosque open for worship) but also by the Jews and Christians who immigrated there. The generous and often promiscuous Umayyad vision left a living legacy among those non-Muslims, and it is likely that Alfonso himself wrote only in Arabic. The various artistic styles that were used and developed by these communities in exile from their Islamic surroundings are now called Mudejar, and are loosely defined as an Islamic style as understood, reinterpreted, and celebrated by others, by Christians and Jews. This became the signature style of Toledo in every respect for generations, and for nearly every purpose, including synagogues and churches. The church at the top of its highest hill, built at least a hundred—maybe even two hundred—years after Alfonso first made Toledo into a Christian city, was part of that living tradition that declares itself allied with the aesthetics and traditions of the Great Mosque of Cordoba. And this style, and these traditions, were now visible to Latin Christendom.

The great love of Alfonso's life was reputedly a Muslim concubine, Zaida, who was the widowed daughter-in-law of his old rival, al-Mutamid of Seville. She bore him his only son, who was killed in battle as a young man, and a daughter, named Teresa, who eventually became queen of Portugal. But Alfonso also had a string of politically advantageous marriages, and he added to the rapid internationalization of the city through his many other alliances with princesses who were all from north of the Pyrenees. The first of these, Agnes, was the daughter of William VIII of Aquitaine, the duke who had taken part in the Norman capture of Barbastro, and thus the sister of William IX, first of the Provençal troubadours. Alfonso's second wife was a Burgundian named Constance who was the niece of the abbot of Cluny. Cluny at this time was rapidly becoming the most powerful of the expanding Christian monastic houses, and with Alfonso's various blessings it added Toledo and its environs to its sphere of influence. This was just the beginning. The doors of Toledo opened wider and wider as Toledo gained in stature in the Latin Christian world and welcomed more and more northerners, many of whom, among them Church fathers, were as dumbfounded and appreciative as the Normans and Aquitainians had been when they had arrived in Barbastro.

In the long aftermath of 1085, and under the line of Alfonsos and other descendants of Alfonso VI, Toledo became the radiant intellectual capital of Europe, a Christian city where Arabic remained a language of culture and learning. This was a city with vast libraries of Arabic books, libraries begun long before, during the glorious Umayyad years, and then added to during the years of the ambitious al-Mamun, who sought to remake Cordoba in Toledo. These collections were added to by the Castilian Christian monarchs and all sorts of prelates. Among these, one Raymond, archbishop of Toledo from 1125 to 1151, gave the institutions that had arisen around these libraries the semiofficial title School of Translators, and it stuck. It was by way of Toledo that the rest of Europe—Latin Christendom—finally had full access to the vast body of philosophical and scientific materials translated from Greek into Arabic in the Abbasid capital of Baghdad during the previous several hundred years. That a Christian city rather than a Muslim one should have played this role may seem unexpected and perhaps even ironic to us. But how surprising can it have been to Christians who prayed at that church at the highest point in the city, under horseshoe arches that echo those of Cordoba's mosque, and where Latin and Arabic writing together adorn the walls?

An Andalusian in London

Huesca, 1106

I was baptized in the episcopal see of Huesca, in the
name of the Father, the Son and the Holy Spirit. . . .
My godfather was Alfonso, glorious Emperor of Spain,
who took me from the baptismal font.

—Petrus Alfonsi, *Dialogue Against the Jews*

ONE DAY IN 1106, IN THE CITY OF HUESCA, NO MORE THAN thirty miles to the west of Barbastro, in the kingdom of Aragon, a forty-something Jew was baptized. He took his new Latin Christian name from Saint Peter, whose feast day it was, and from his local patron, Alfonso I of Aragon. Alfonso, whose nickname was *el Batallador*, "the Warrior," had great imperial ambitions and eventually a hugely successful career consolidating his kingdom by the Pyrenees, although Petrus Alfonsi was exaggerating considerably when many years later he called him the "glorious emperor of Spain." Alfonso never quite managed to succeed to the throne he coveted, that of Alfonso I of Castile and Leon, the conqueror of Toledo, who died in 1109 without a male heir. The Aragonese Alfonso married but later divorced Urraca, the Castilian Alfonso's daughter and heiress. After failing to attain Castile by marriage, Alfonso of Aragon subsequently took to the battlefields and spent most of the rest of his long reign in perpetual wars with Castile and Leon, whose armies were led, with some enthusiasm one imagines, by his ex-wife.

All of these efforts still lay ahead of Alfonso when, in 1106, he took a central and public part in the baptism of a converted Jew in the bustling town of Huesca, which lies in the foothills of the Pyrenees. Like many other cities in Aragon, Huesca had been in Muslim hands until just ten years before. Alfonso's brother Pedro, who had ruled before him, had taken Huesca in 1096, when the taifas of the Upper Frontier were embattled on all sides, Almoravids to the south and Christian kingdoms at every compass point. Although it was elevated to the status of capital of Aragon—and was such at the time of Petrus's baptismal ceremony—Huesca had this kind of importance only temporarily, until 1118, when Alfonso crowned his expansion to the south by taking the great city of Saragossa, a taifa of unusual cultural and political importance.*

Petrus Alfonsi knew little or nothing of these momentous events when they took place, a decade and more after his baptism. Just as he left his ancestral religion behind in the public baptism in the heart of Huesca, along with his birth name of Moses (Petrus is thus sometimes referred to as Moses Sefardi, or "Moses the Spaniard"), he departed his newly Christian home-

---

*Saragossa (from the Roman name for the already important center, Caesar-augusta) had an often grand role in these histories. The first was as the city coveted by Charlemagne himself in the years after Abd al-Rahman had arrived in Cordoba and was consolidating the peninsula as part of his new Umayyad kingdom. It was in the retreat through the Pyrenees from the unsuccessful siege of Saragossa that Charlemagne's army was ambushed by Basques, events much later transformed into the *Song of Roland*. During the taifa period, Saragossa's monarchs built an extraordinary and influential palace (the Aljaferia), which still stands, an emblem of the cultural flourishing during those times of ceaseless military conflicts. During the years just after the building of those palaces, one of their constant visitors was the Cid, who spent years in Saragossa as the hired chief of its Muslim armies.

land shortly after his conversion. Although very little is known about the reasons for his emigration or his whereabouts during his years abroad—most of what we know we glean from his own writings—it is believed he ended up making his fame, and perhaps fortune, as something of a wise man in the land he first chose for his exile, England. He was probably among the retinue of physicians attending Henry I, the son of William the Conqueror, who ascended the English throne in 1100. This was an altogether likely role for a man like Petrus, since an educated "physician" at that time was expected to be well versed in natural philosophy, a field of learning that was relatively commonplace for a Jew of even middling education in late eleventh-century Spain. Although the details of his early years are uncertain, he had been born and reared somewhere in Islamic Spain, perhaps in the south, before he emigrated to the still-Muslim, still-independent northern cities, as did many others in the chaos of the last years of the taifas. Whatever his exact peregrinations before settling in Huesca, he had managed to receive, beyond his religious training in Hebrew, the conventional Arabic education in the sciences, philosophy, and rhetoric.

Regardless of why he left his homeland, Petrus discovered on the far northern side of the Pyrenees, in Norman England and later back on the continent, possibly in Normandy, that he was a celebrity sage. This new-fashioned Christian with the freshly minted Latin name had a level of learning that, customary as it might have been in the Jewish-Muslim circles of educated Andalusians, was astonishing in the far northern climes of Europe in the early years of the twelfth century. It represented knowledge of a forgotten past, of wisdoms that were deeply buried there, while at the same time it suggested a hard-to-believe future. Petrus became a widely read author on high-tech subjects that were just beginning to be apprehended and coveted outside the Arabic-reading world: astronomical tables, astrology, calendrical calculations, astrolabes. His mind was far from first-class in these matters, however, and his scientific work would eventually be supplanted by the next generation of scientists and philosophers—other émigrés from the peninsula, but especially northerners who would go to places like Toledo to study.

When he first arrived in England, Petrus was still something of a rara avis: he could speak on subjects that revealed a different and intriguingly more advanced universe, and so he became the earliest expert in England in several scientific areas. Later translations and dozens of citations of his scientific writings, whose level would have been that of a rudimentary schoolmaster back in Huesca (let alone in Toledo or Saragossa), made Petrus a revered authority, particularly in astronomy. Astronomy was a master science in the Middle Ages, and Petrus's most conspicuous contribution was on the critical matter of the calculation of calendars, where expertise was dependent on the long tradition of Arabic translation of and improvements on Ptolemy's cosmography. In the references and dedications of the first generation of English translator-scholars, and even as late as Chaucer himself, some two hundred years later, Petrus Alfonsi (or "Piers Alphonse," as Chaucer called him) stands out as a scientific pioneer and benefactor: he had brought news of a new intellectual universe from the Arabophone Mediterranean and, having whet the appetite, he had shown the way to satisfy it. He had become, in effect, England's first professor of Arabic, which meant a teacher not of the technical aspects of the language itself. Rather, Petrus was one of the first native teachers of the aesthetic and intellectual culture he had known in the places he had left behind, a land of libraries full of books, libraries scarcely imaginable in his new home.

It was not as a scientist-philosopher, as a scholar in those respectable disciplines, that Petrus derived his claim to fame in the years that followed, when he became one of the most widely read and translated writers in Latin Christian Europe. Rather, it was as a popular writer, with a little book called *The Priestly Tales,** that Petrus's name became widely known. In this bestseller, the Arabized Jewish convert to Christianity introduced and popularized a form of writing that became one of the mainstays of imaginative fiction for generations. Petrus was eventually known to a whole gallery of brilliant later writers who took the framed tale he had introduced in rudimentary form and ran with it. Among these, principally, were Chaucer, whose *Canterbury Tales* belongs to the same genre, and Boccaccio, whose *Decameron* not only works within the genre but also transforms a number of Petrus's tales into its own Italian masterpieces.

The little Latin book that Petrus wrote during the last part of his life spent as an émigré in England and France was a version, a cultural translation, of what was a pervasively popular form of literature throughout the far-flung Arabic-speaking world. What Petrus brought out of the House of Arabic and into the House of Latin, and thence into all the vernaculars that became the literary languages of modern Europe, was not merely individual stories but the taste for a particular way of telling tales. The pseudo-scholarly book audaciously titled *The Priestly Tales* came out of the least rarefied bags among Petrus's Andalusian baggage: it was a vigorously popular and until then mostly oral tradition that Petrus transformed into the beginnings of a written tradition. This way of reaching and teaching the unwashed—these tales that were supposed to make listeners think carefully about what we like to call "the moral of the story"—were very much the everyday clothes that Petrus had brought with him, a far cry from such finery as the complex calculations of calendars. Petrus had left his homeland carrying this

---

*The Latin name for this book is *Disciplina clericalis,* which would translate fairly literally as "A Clerical Education" but which I call *The Priestly Tales* to better represent its content, a collection of aphorisms and tales.

unwritten and highly vernacular form, which was not part of his formal learning, as the scientific materials were, but rather an incidental part of his intellectual makeup, part of the very languages he spoke. At some point during his years as a sage in the northern courts, he must have decided that part of his complex conversion—and part of the mission that had been thrust on him in these remote places, where he was regarded as a wise man—entailed rendering that particular brand of storytelling, and those kinds of stories, into something that would also be Latin and Christian, like himself.

The book is scarcely more than a suggestion, perhaps meant as a prompter for storytellers and sermonizers, a series of basic story lines that a first-rate raconteur or preacher could then fill in and round out. We can see the difference clearly by the time an author like Boccaccio makes use of them, the original plotlines turned out as full-fledged stories that we can read on our own. *The Priestly Tales* is a slim handbook that turns out to be more like a pod full of seeds, and many of the stories that are quite embryonic in Petrus (some of which are themselves skeletal versions of stories we know in other forms, including biblical stories, especially parables) can be traced over the next several hundred years, in story collections throughout Europe. But more important than all those basic plotlines is the self-conscious model *The Priestly Tales* provides for the modern narrative. The storyteller telling his stories to a captive audience is a model that allows for an infinite variety of possible pretexts for the narrator to launch into an infinite variety of stories. These may be of all types: tales, exempla, fables, even aphorisms.

Petrus's version of the framed tale was not the first in literary history, far from it. But he happened to be in the right storytelling place at the right time, and he wrote one of the bestsellers of the age in this form. At the beginning of the twelfth century, when the new European languages were inventing themselves and their new traditions, Petrus hit a true note, no doubt largely by accident. The storyteller telling stories, in this case the sage telling tales to his young acolyte, caught on as a malleable and pervasive conceit for imaginative prose—and for good reasons, all of which are on display in *The Priestly Tales*. In them, anyone can tell a story at any time, under any circumstances, even inside someone else's story; and they are richly literary in the way they inevitably become an explicit reflection on the art, circumstances, and purposes of making and telling stories. The conceit is always concerned about the most difficult and yet necessary part of the whole process, the art of interpretation, which is of course very much at the heart of the arts of teaching and learning. Despite the fact that Petrus actually wrote out only some thirty-four relatively brief tales, these are (like his translations of a handful of astronomical texts) the tip of a very large iceberg. What he revealed was the existence of a virtually limitless sea of stories—and the map for how to get to the far shore.

In Petrus's *Priestly Tales,* the elite Latin-reading world got its first real taste of a feast that in al-Andalus was available to nearly everyone on an everyday basis, and that tied al-Andalus to the rest of the Islamic empire. Even the humblest Andalusian Christian, because he could understand spoken Arabic, or because his neighbor could and retold stories in his Aragonese vernacular, was able to hear tales that had once been told in Greek or Persian and now were being retold in Arabic, and a thousand and one permutations, from one end of the empire to the other, by the master storyteller herself, Scheherazade. What Petrus's book accomplished was a translation from an oral to a written form, as much as from one language to another: from the vernacular, and indeed by some standards vulgar, Arabic tradition, to a written Latin form with the veneer of learning. Within these complex traditions, stories running the gamut from retellings of biblical parables to tales of extreme raunchiness are told by storytellers who were very much in charge and on center stage. Roles that seem as disparate to us as a woman telling stories to save her life on the one hand, and a philosopher talking to his students on the other, are intimately related and even inter-changeable. Petrus's book is filled with teachers trying to en-lighten those who know less: the philosopher Enoch (called Idris in Arabic) relays a series of little aphorisms to his son; Socrates speaks to his followers; dozens of unnamed philoso-phers and as many anonymous teachers, named simply "an Arab," present their various charges (sometimes a son, some-times a "pupil") with little philosophical riddles—and a great many tales.

Here, there is no sharp distinction between a storyteller like Scheherazade and a scholar or teacher, between "entertainment" (as suggested by the title of one of the English versions of the Scheherazade collection, *The Thousand and One Nights' Entertainment*) and "education" or "morality." Because of the complex admixture of the moral and the amoral, of the aesthetic and the philosophical, there are only a handful of unambiguous morals to these tales: that there are no easy answers or unam-biguous truths in these stories any more than there are in life it-self, which they mirror, and that although God is all-powerful, he sometimes works in inscrutable ways. Some might be tempted to observe that the most mysterious thing about *The Priestly Tales*—surely the most ironic—lay not inside the best-seller but in its very authorship: that a recent Jewish convert to Christianity should play the role of moral teacher, and that his vehicle should be the popularized philosophical and narrative tradition of Islamo-Arabic civilization. His pupils were enthusi-astic and numerous for hundreds of years to come.

The Priestly Tales was not Petrus's only bestseller, nor for that matter his first. His *Dialogue Against the Jews*, written earlier, was almost certainly related to Petrus's otherwise unexpected emi-gration from his homeland. One plausible theory is that he encountered community disapproval and perhaps worse for what had been a very public baptism inside a newly Christian community where both Jews and Muslims still lived and expected to be able to live with their religions protected. Whatever the case, the *Dialogue,* much like the framed-tale collection, was not only popular but instrumental in popularizing the dialogue form as a way of writing about certain subjects. Petrus, with his traditional if unexceptional education, invented nothing and in fact worked centrally within traditions he knew well, in this case the religious debate, which in the Islamic tradition went back at least as far as the Abbasid caliph Harun al-Rashid. But he was, once again, in the right place at the right time. Within his lifetime as an exotic and famous professor and writer in England and France, and within years of the widespread reading of his *Dialogue Against the Jews,* the dialogue form became the nearly standard form for laying out the cases of the competing religions of medieval Europe. Two of the most famous of these dialogues were written within a few years of Petrus's, almost certainly without knowledge of his *Dialogue:* Peter Abelard's *Dialogue of a Philosopher with a Christian and a Jew,* and Judah Halevi's *The Book of the Khazars.* The need for such a form was increasing exponentially, in great measure because as the doors to the Andalusian universe flew open, they revealed those religions in complex relationships. Philosophy was one of the competing religions in many of these dialogues. The more philosophical texts from the Aristotelian tradition found their way into more and more hands—and this began to happen with great speed in the latter part of the twelfth century, just after Petrus's books began to make the rounds—the more it was understood that philosophy presented at least as great a challenge to belief in the True Faith as any other of the faiths.

Whereas *The Priestly Tales* remains a delight to read, among other things because it directly and indirectly teaches the difficulty of absolute truths, the *Dialogue Against the Jews* is an uncompromising and often vituperative theological polemic, offensive toward both the communities Petrus was leaving behind. The book is not merely an attack on Judaism, staged as a dialogue between Moses (representing the old religion) and Peter (representing the new), it is a wholesale, embittered abandonment of that entire community of civilized people who could read and write Arabic and its astronomical charts, Muslims as well as Jews. As an extended and often vitriolic diatribe, it became a crucial source of later anti-Jewish and anti-Muslim rhetoric. But at the same time, paradoxically, it contained a detailed and largely accurate exposition of both Judaism and Islam, written by a man who knew both religions and their texts quite well. As an insider, fluent in Hebrew as well as Arabic, Petrus brought the use of rabbinic literature and methods into the fray.

Petrus's story—or rather, the tales told by his books, since we know a good deal about them and very little about his actual life—provides a miniature version of the paradoxical perceptions of each other held by the cultures of al-Andalus on the one hand and those of Latin Europe on the other as they began to come into closer contact at the turn of the twelfth century. Petrus was an Andalusian, but as a convert to Christianity and the author of a widely read anti-Jewish and anti-Muslim polemic, he embodied the essence of the conflict. At the surface level, there is the expected veneer of Christian disdain for these sister religions. But not far beneath that surface rhetoric, there is a powerful perception of the superiority of the material and intellectual cultures of these other peoples who are not of the True Faith. Petrus himself embodied that paradox and many of the other complexities that shaped the age. Negative reactions to his ostentatious conversion in Huesca in 1106—being taken to the baptismal font by none other than Alfonso I of Aragon—seem to have provoked his passionate and vindictive self-defense in the *Dialogue Against the Jews*, and perhaps his departure from his homeland. But then, once in the far Christian and Latin north,

Petrus found himself with something like the shoe on the other foot: his past as an Andalusian and a Jew educated in Arabic sciences and letters made him, in this locale, a veritable font of learning and wisdom. From this perspective, *The Priestly Tales* is also a book of proselytizing, although of a very different sort, an introduction, as it were, for neophytes—possessors of the True Faith who in other ways are not very enlightened—to a world of philosophical and literary subtleties.

Petrus thus set the standard for a Christian Latin polemic against both Judaism and Islam, and at the same time successfully introduced Christian Europe to a whole range of cultural and intellectual advantages that until then had been enjoyed only by Andalusians. Above and beyond his astronomical works, his little Latin book of tales gave people a taste of the popular wisdom of an extensive framed-tale tradition that was one of the glories of Islamic civilization at its peak of breadth of spirit and assimilation. Christianity, for Petrus and his new audience, may have owned the Truth, but Jews and Arabs possessed Wisdom: education, philosophy, culture—and the framed tales. Even the *Dialogue* opened doors to a world where Jews and Muslims played natural and vital roles inside Christian polities and communities. Peter the Venerable, the legendary abbot of Cluny and an intellectual engaged throughout his lifetime in refuting the militaristic mentality of his great rival, Bernard of Clairvaux, read the *Dialogue* and took from it the Talmudic quotations he used in his own writings. Who knows what role it played in his grand decision to make a trip to Toledo himself.

Sailing Away, Riding Away

Alexandria, 1140

> *Anxious or secure, my soul is Yours,*
> *submissively and gratefully.*
> *I roam, I wander, filled with joy in You*
> *and thanking You in all my wanderings.*
>
> *And when this ship unfurls its falcon-wings*
> *and carries me away;*
> *and when beneath, the Deep shrieks,*
> *howls, storms like my bowels,*
> *pot-boils the abyss and turns the sea to stew;*
> *when Christian ships slip into the Berber sea,*
> *and pirates descend to set up their trap,*
> *when ocean monsters pound against the ship,*
> *and dragons are looking forward to a meal,*
> *when you scream for fright like a woman in labor,*
> *in labor with her first, when it first breaks through,*
> *when she screams until she has no strength to scream . . .*

—Judah Halevi, from his "Sea Poems"

JUDAH HALEVI, THE REVERED PILLAR OF THE ANDALUSIAN JEWISH community and the most celebrated poet of his age, an age of poetry and many great poets, arrived in Egypt's ancient port city of Alexandria in 1140. He had sailed away from Sefarad, having chosen to exile himself from the land of his ancestors. For years he had been saying he would, but who could believe he would really pack his bags and leave that beloved place? But he finally did it. He was already sixty-four years old and had spent years preparing himself for this voluntary exile, bracing for the long and arduous sea voyage by writing poems about what the trip from the far West to the East might be like, as if by imagining the worst, the ocean monsters pounding against the ship and the dragons looking for their meal, it would be easier when it really came. To go was a painful choice, and the voyage, for an old man, was bound to be arduous, so it was easy to understand why he delayed it, as he did for years and years, and perhaps forever.

But no, not forever, as his appearance in Alexandria testified. He had left Spain—al-Andalus, ha-Sefarad—the same year that his great rival, the poet and philosopher Moses ibn Ezra, had died and the same year that Judah's own great book, his anti-philosophical masterpiece *The Book of the Khazars,* was finished and began to be read. Halevi had set off, bound for his beloved Jerusalem, to whom he had been writing poems for years, a city that not so long before, in 1099, had fallen into the hands of the crusading Christians. Jerusalem at that moment was an exceptionally inhospitable place for a Jew, and for this reason, among others, his friends and neighbors were both mystified and upset with Halevi's decision. They were right, of course, from their perspective, yet he almost made it. The ship that carried him across the Mediterranean was not eaten by dragons, nor swallowed by the deep; in fact it got him all the way to Alexandria.

In Alexandria, and in nearby Cairo, Halevi was received like royalty. His fame as the greatest of the great Andalusian poets had preceded him in this prosperous Jewish community. So he decided to stay for a bit, resting from the arduous voyage before going on. It was hard to set out again, though, and the Egyptian community that welcomed him did not seem to understand or accept that the celebrity in their midst had renounced the hypnotic poetry that had made him famous, that this trip was about retiring from a life of singing his wildly popular songs about everyday loves. The Egyptians begged him to sing for them, to be an Andalusian in their company, so Judah Halevi stayed awhile, and once again sang his beautiful songs, in those incomparable Andalusian cadences and accents.

Did he stay too long? What happened no one really knows. Most accounts say that he did finally tear himself away from his newly comfortable life among those who loved his songs and headed off for the place that was guaranteed to be inhospitable, if not impossible to enter. Some stories say he never actually reached land at all in Palestine, that he died at sea even before disembarking. Others say he did reach the far eastern shores of the Mediterranean, at the opposite extreme from his ancestral home, but that he never managed to make it very far inland. The most dramatic versions of the story have him making it all the way to Jerusalem, among the chaos of roaming bands of foreign Christian soldiers, only to be trampled to death at the city gates. There are no versions in which poor Halevi actually reaches Jerusalem, so in the end he died in exile from his homeland, without ever reaching the Zion he, above all other poets, had made into so luminous an object of desire.

> My heart is in the East, and I in the West,
>   as far in the west as west can be!
>   How can I enjoy my food?
>   What flavor can it have for me?
>   How can I fulfill my vows
>   or do the things I've sworn to do,
>   while Zion is in Christian hands
>   and I am trapped in Arab lands?

> *Easily, I could leave behind*
> *this Spain and all her luxuries!—*
> *As easy to leave as dear the sight*
> *of the Temple's rubble would be to me.*

Halevi was the last in the line of great Andalusian poets of the Golden Age, as it was dubbed by the nineteenth-century German Jews who became their historians and editors, men who saw in those urbane, philosophically mature, and socially successful Jews of the eleventh and twelfth centuries a winning reflection of what they wished the European Jews of the nineteenth to be. The golden Andalusian line that ended far from al-Andalus — symbolically trampled underfoot at the gates of Jerusalem — had begun with the self-styled David of his age, Samuel the Nagid; it was the line that had made writing in Hebrew a living thing once again, so that Halevi's love songs to Jerusalem were not part of the fossilized liturgical Hebrew that was all Jews could chant before these Andalusians had come along.

The brilliance of the Golden Age came from Hebrew's redemption from its profound exile, locked inside temples, never speaking about life itself. Maimonides, born in Cordoba just five years before Halevi left al-Andalus, described this post-exilic, pre-Andalusian state of things in his *Laws on Prayer:* "When any one of them prayed in Hebrew, he was unable adequately to express his needs or recount the praises of God, without mixing Hebrew with other languages." It was not that Jews should speak other languages but that the Hebrew they spoke was no longer the language of true love, of complex emotion, of seemingly contrary ideas and feelings: maternal, erotic, spiritual, material, transcendent. Maimonides, Andalusian that he was, believed that God needed and wanted to be spoken to in a language alive with that whole range of possible emotions. It was an attitude that later allowed English to find its voice in the love sonnets of

Shakespeare as well as in the prayers of the King James Bible. The prayers prove more satisfying, perhaps even more true, for being in the language of the love songs.

Hebrew's redemption had come at the hands of writers who were masters of Arabic rhetoric, the Andalusian Jews, men as thoroughly and successfully a part of the cult of Arabic grammar, rhetoric, and style as any of their Muslim neighbors and associates. A century before Halevi took his final leave to find Jerusalem, Samuel the Nagid had first made Hebrew perform all the magic tricks that his native tongue, Arabic, could and did. He had been made vizier because his skill in writing letters and court documents in Arabic surpassed that of all others. He then went on to write poems in the new Hebrew style, among them verses recounting his glories leading his taifa's armies to victory. In one fell swoop, Samuel's Hebrew poetry, with its Arabic accents and prosody—the features essential to making it alive for the Arabic-speaking Andalusian Jews—vindicated and completely exceeded all the small steps that others had taken in the centuries before him to revive the ancestral language, to reinvent it as a living tongue. Everyone, from Halevi to the nineteenth-century Germans who made the Andalusians into the noble heroes of Jewish history, knew that Hebrew had been redeemed from its exile thanks to the Andalusian Jews' extraordinary secular successes, first during the several Umayyad centuries and then in the taifas. Because they had absorbed, mastered, and loved the principles that made Arabic easily able to sing to God and Beloved in the same language, they had been able to revive Hebrew so it could, once again, sing like the Hebrew of David's songs, and Solomon's songs. It was a great triumph, and Judah Halevi was arguably its greatest champion.

Yet he chose to leave it all, to abandon the culture that had made this poetry possible. He repented not merely for himself; he also denounced a culture, his culture, which he saw as decadent, and he wrote treatises against the very poetry that he had

SAILING AWAY, RIDING AWAY 🏵 163

once brilliantly composed and performed. Halevi's defection caused disquiet and discomfort among the vast majority of Jewish intellectuals and literati of the twelfth century, most of whom took for granted that civilized people—like themselves, and unlike so many of their unwashed Christian and Jewish neighbors to the north—could as a matter of course do things like read philosophy in Arabic and recite reams of poetry in Arabic and, more recently, in Hebrew, too, if they were Jews. The mostly hagiographic accounts say it was around the time he was fifty, about 1125, that Judah Halevi, scion of this great culture, declared that it was all folly and inimical to Jewishness and had to be forsaken, in spirit certainly and—if possible, as he intended to do—physically. People were astonished, and some of them offended.

Almoravid rule was making life for many Jews more difficult, and many even had to emigrate to the north, once considered a land of savages; but at the same time, some Christian cities, among them the Castilian capital, Toledo, were becoming thriving centers of Jewish life. There was in any case a vast difference between the vicissitudes of modern life, with the tyranny of the detested foreign Muslims, and the old and fruitful traditions that had made the Andalusian Jews the very center of the Jewish universe in the post-exilic period. Yet what Halevi was attacking was not the difficult political moment but the very bases of the Jews' culture, the love of Arabized Hebrew poetry that Halevi himself had developed with such moving beauty, along with the study of philosophy, which Halevi began to call, contemptuously, "the Greek religion." Halevi was saying that all men of True Faith should, as he was going to do, exile themselves from everything Andalusian, from al-Andalus itself. That, for most of his contemporaries, was the threat of a truly terrible exile.

⚜

*[The reason for the delay in my writing is] the long
and difficult exile in which fate has tossed me, in a
faraway land in the end of my days. I am trapped in
prison, or rather, buried in a grave. The intellectual
requires his native land as much as his bread. In the
Quran of the Arabs it is written: "And if we had
commanded you: kill yourselves or leave your homes,
only a few would have obeyed." Thus the Quran
equates he who kills himself with him who leaves his
home.*

—Moses ibn Ezra, on his exile from Granada
to the Christian north, sometime after 1090

Halevi was an exile of sorts from the start. He was a native of the desolate northern places held in contempt by those who defined being civilized as being part of the Islamic orbit. Halevi was born in 1075 in the mountainous area of Navarre, in the Pyrenees, in the city of Tudela. Tudela was still under Muslim control in 1075, but frontierlike and heavily influenced by the important Christian kingdoms of the time, especially Castile and Leon, which had been reunified by Alfonso VI after his brother's untimely death a few years before. Indeed, Halevi's lifetime, and the Granadan Ibn Ezra's as well, coincided almost precisely with the last decades of the taifas, when the peninsula's political landscape was reconfigured by the complex and overlapping rivalries at hand.

When Halevi was perhaps about fifteen years old, he left Tudela and emigrated southward to Toledo, which had recently changed hands and become the Christian capital of Alfonso VI's kingdom of Castile. With Toledo serving more or less as his home base, Halevi spent much of the rest of his life traveling from one city to another, from north to south, from Christian to

Muslim. He led a surprisingly peripatetic life during a period of political turmoil, and yet his life was also emblematic of the continuing prosperity of the Jewish communities in a broad range of cities—cities that might be Muslim taifas one day, Almoravid-held the next, and besieged and taken by a Christian free agent like Rodrigo Diaz yet another, only to fall eventually to the kingdom of Castile. From the time of Halevi's birth, and especially from the time of his emigration from Tudela at the beginning of his adulthood, around 1090, the Almoravids were trying to consolidate their hold on the taifas, but they were meeting vigorous resistance from the old Andalusian Muslim regimes. In these years, too, Rodrigo Diaz, the Cid, was campaigning against both Alfonso and the Almoravids throughout the eastern part of the peninsula.

With this tumultuous political scene as a backdrop, inside the far-from-isolated Jewish community of al-Andalus— Sefarad—the great intellectual and artistic drama of a generation was played out. Indeed, it was the great drama of the whole Golden Age of which Halevi and Ibn Ezra's generation was in many ways the culmination. At the very outset of Judah Halevi's career, when he was a promising young man but as yet without reputation or important connections, he had been welcomed into the Andalusian Jewish upper crust, which was spread out over many different cities, since many of the old and "good" families had emigrated out of Cordoba and settled throughout the taifas. It was the grand old man of Granada, Moses ibn Ezra, who had made this happen when Halevi first appeared, seemingly out of nowhere, a stranger from the land that Ibn Ezra described contemptuously as being that of provincials and boors—and by this he meant both the Christians and the Jews, un-Arabized and uncivilized, who lived in their midst.

Unlike Ibn Ezra, Judah Halevi did not come from one of those prominent and quasi-noble Andalusian families who claimed direct descent from the best families of Jerusalem. But

the aristocratic Ibn Ezra also believed strongly in merit and recognized genius when he saw it, no matter how unlikely the quarter from which it emerged. At that time Ibn Ezra was the living
master of Hebrew poetry and the most eminent philosopher of
the community, and he invited the ambitious and talented young
Halevi to leave Toledo, where he had arrived from Tudela, and
join him in Granada. In spite of the anti-Jewish riots of 1066
(which had killed Samuel's son, Joseph the Nagid, a close relative of Ibn Ezra's), Granada was still home to a thriving community of Jewish intellectuals, poets and philosophers alike, as well
as public figures, and would remain so on and off for many years,
nearly oblivious to the political upheavals of the time. The most
disruptive of these came in 1090, just about the time the young
Halevi appeared on the cultural scene, when the victories and
advances of the Almoravids brought them to Granada's doorstep
and then, in their wake, the armies of Alfonso of Castile and his
momentary ally, Rodrigo Diaz.

The Almoravids won the day, and they deposed the last of
Granada's line of taifa kings (the first of whom had made Samuel
his vizier). Indeed, the ideological position of the self-righteous
Almoravids, who were subjugating their fellow Muslims very
much against their will, was often rooted in what they considered the Andalusians' inappropriate relations with the Jews and
Christians. These relationships were clearly illustrated by the
city's eminent, thriving, and fully integrated Jewish community,
and by the fact that the Christian Alfonso's armies were there in
part at the behest, or at least with the connivance, of the handful of remaining Muslim taifas. Like many of the Andalusian
Muslims, who had reluctantly come to the conclusion that the
Andalusian Christians might be a lesser evil than the puritanical
Almoravids, a large number of Granada's Jews, including Ibn
Ezra, left their beloved native city, at least for a time.

A supremely civilized man like Ibn Ezra, who until then
had only heard about the north but, unlike Halevi, had never ac-

tually been there, was appalled at the cultural conditions he found in the Christian regions during what he always called his own terrible and certainly unlooked-for exile. For years he wrote scathingly about the cultural wasteland to which he felt banished: "Among them I am like a lone human among so many wild animals, a lion among monkeys and parrots. . . . I live among desert wolves." It is easy enough to understand how such a man might have little patience for Judah Halevi's preaching a gospel of voluntary renunciation of that civilized culture.

Halevi wrote his most famous and best-read prose work during those years after 1125, and it is the principal manifesto of his renunciation of Andalusian culture. Other writings of his provide detailed documentation of a fifteen-year period of turning away from his native culture, but most are fairly technical studies on poetic meter. And in some of the new poetry he wrote, rejecting the Arabized Andalusian accentual and metrical patterns, as well as in a great deal of literary-theoretical writing, Halevi insisted that the language involved in the new Hebrew poetry, Arabized as it was, was a corruption of Hebrew. But it was in the dialogue form that he wrote his signature book on the subject; composed in Arabic, it had two titles, one *The Book of the Khazars,* the other, *The Book of Refutation and Proof: On the Abased Faith.** The Khazars were a perhaps legendary people assumed to have lived in areas bordering the Black Sea; Halevi takes off from the story of Hasdai ibn Shaprut's reputed exchange of letters with their king in the mid-tenth century while Hasdai was the foreign minister to the caliph Abd al-Rahman III. Halevi's book is in that old and flourishing tradition that allowed religions to confront each other directly, much like Petrus Alfonsi's roughly contemporary attack on Judaism, *Dialogue Against the Jews.* Halevi's defense of the "abased" faith emerges from an

---

*Many translations use the term "despised," but I follow the translation of Ross Brann, who uses "abased." *The Book of the Khazars* is also referred to by many as *The Kuzari.*

imaginary dialogue suggested by the exchange between Hasdai and the Khazar king, who had supposedly chosen conversion to Judaism for himself and his nation.

In *The Book of the Khazars,* Halevi makes his starting point the old story of the Hasdai letters, the story of how the king of the Khazars had summoned before him representatives of the different faiths, each to argue his case, so that he (the king) might choose the true one among them for his people. Hasdai's mid-tenth-century version of the story reflected a worldview within which the Jewish community defined and compared itself with Islam and Christianity, and the whole of that early dialogue involved a Christian and a Muslim competing with the Jew for the king's heart, soul, and respect. But that was at the very onset of the transformations and triumphs that reshaped culture (and created the Golden Age) between Hasdai's time and the moment, nearly two hundred years later, when Halevi wrote his own very different version of the king's conversation. In Halevi's story, the Jew's competitors for the king's attention were no longer either Islam or Christianity—the representatives of those religions are trotted out at the beginning but disappear after perfunctory appearances. The rabbi's real adversary, rather, is a philosopher who argues his case before the Khazar king, who is, from the outset, on the rabbi's side, often enthusiastically amplifying his arguments. The philosopher, some subtle readers have argued, is perhaps an unflattering caricature of Ibn Ezra himself, Halevi's old patron, who in real life remained a staunch defender of Andalusian culture and of the Jewish enthusiasm for both philosophy and Arabized poetry.

Just as Petrus Alfonsi's *Dialogue* was an argument between two versions of the author's own self, pre- and post-conversion, Halevi's *Book of the Khazars* is about the different ways of living as a Jew, which he takes the rabbi and the philosopher to represent. Its central question—whether faith and reason can be held simultaneously or are inherently contradictory, to put it reductively—would soon emerge as one of the great debates of the age and would occupy many great thinkers of all three of these monotheistic traditions. Indeed, in nearby Cordoba, the two most brilliant and subtle writers on this thorny question in the twelfth century were at present being educated much as Halevi had been. In 1140, Ibn Rushd, who would later be known mostly by the Latin name Averroes and as the author of the great commentaries on Aristotle, was already fifteen, and Musa ibn Maymun, who as Maimonides would be revered as the "second Moses," was five years old. Neither would give much credence to Halevi's conventionally pietistic rejection of the strong philosophical tradition the Jews had participated in along with the Muslims—what Halevi dismissed as "the flaunted Greek wisdom whose end is folly, seems to enlighten but leaves desolation."

Halevi's turn was by no means simplistic or one-dimensional like Petrus Alfonsi's; it was not, for example, a turning away from philosophy to religion, or from rationalism to faith, from unbeliever to believer. Instead, Halevi was rejecting— and this was precisely what his own community found so inexplicable—the very premise of the commensurability of the two, philosophy and religion. The bedrock of Andalusian Jewish culture for hundreds of years, what had allowed it to flourish in the ways it had, was the premise that genuine Jewish culture and devout faith in Judaism were not at destructive odds with the whole complex of secular activities they had been cultivating, neatly represented by both Greco-Islamic philosophy and the unabashedly Arabized new Hebrew poetry. This community did not imagine it had bought its secular and cultural success by renouncing, hiding, or in any way diminishing its Jewishness. On the contrary, against Halevi were those who argued that the Andalusian Jews' radical degree of cultural assimilation had allowed them to become more fully Hebraized than any Jewish community had been for a thousand years, and thus far more profoundly in touch with their heritage as Jews. Although of course no one in *The Book of the Khazars* makes this argument directly, the case is made most brilliantly by Halevi's own extraordinary corpus of some eight hundred poems, among which are his gorgeous love songs to Jerusalem and Zion, songs that come directly out of the same poetic traditions and complex Arabized culture he now rejected.

> *His eyes, grievously weeping,*
> *he turned his head and looked back upon them.*
> *He saw doors standing open, and gates without fastenings,*
> *the porches empty without cloaks or coverings*
> *and without falcons and without molted hawks.*

So opens the *Song of the Cid,* a work that, much like Halevi's *Book of the Khazars,* is today read and employed as the rousing beginning of a national tradition, as an emblem or rallying cry for a certain kind of cultural purity. In this moving opening scene — from the single mutilated manuscript, which begins only some way into the story — Rodrigo Diaz is about to ride into dolorous exile from the court of Alfonso VI, the monarch for whom this gifted warrior and leader had worked since the murder of Alfonso's brother. The two strong-willed and ambitious men had a stormy relationship during the tumultuous political era at whose epicenter was the taking of Toledo in 1085 and the invasion of the Almoravids that followed. The Cid was continually accused of treachery of some sort and was almost as continually being exiled from court — only to be forgiven and summoned back by Alfonso when the king returned to his senses and once again recognized his need for the obviously brilliant military leader.

The historical incident represented in this opening scene of the poem is almost certainly Rodrigo Diaz's exile from Alfonso's court sometime around 1091. Alfonso and the Cid, momentarily reconciled, had been thinking to mount an assault on the Almoravids, who took Granada in 1090, but for reasons that are unclear they turned back and, on their return to Toledo, had another of their fallings-out. Rodrigo was once again accused of working against the king's interests, and off he rode, once more, into exile from the Castilian court, as Alfonso returned to Toledo. The poem depicts this as the singularly undeserved exile of the loyal hero Rodrigo, and one of the poem's loveliest and best-known lines follows soon after this scene—when the good citizens of Burgos, the city to which the Cid first travels in his exile, cry out, *"Dios, que buen vasallo, si oviesse buen señore"* ("God, how fine a vassal, if his lord were but worthy").

These were turbulent times, when loyalties were anything but unmixed, and history records a very different story than that of the "faithful vassal." Rodrigo's relationship with Alfonso and the kingdom of Castile was stormy and largely antagonistic, and, not unlike Alfonso himself, it was rarely driven by pure ideological or religious motives. Neither Rodrigo nor his king ever shied away from alliances with Muslims against other Muslims—nor against fellow Christians, for that matter. Even the most schematic narrative of the Cid's history is revealing. From 1081 to 1086, during the years Alfonso was consolidating his murdered brother's part of the kingdom and taking Toledo, the Cid was the military commandant of the Muslim taifa of Saragossa. A desperate Alfonso persuaded him to rejoin his own forces after the Castilians' terrible defeat at the hands of the Almoravids in 1086, but the alliance was no better than sporadic over the next few years, and by 1091, after the abortive campaign against Granada, the breach became permanent. During the following several years, Rodrigo was back in Saragossa with his Muslim beneficiary and led direct attacks on Castilian territories. By 1094, the Cid had acquired enough wealth and military strength, through campaigns like those against Alfonso's lands, to mount a successful assault on Valencia—an event depicted in the poem in somewhat different terms, with the loyal Cid taking the city for his king Alfonso. As the self-declared king of that lovely city by the sea, Rodrigo had to defend himself from attacks from all sides, but especially from the ever encroaching Almoravids, who were almost done removing the Muslim taifa kings from power and were certainly not going to suffer a renegade Christian holding a major port on the peninsula's eastern coast. Yet the great warrior was never defeated by them, although Valencia was, in 1102. Rodrigo had died, apparently in his bed and of natural causes, in 1099, the same year that the first Latin Crusaders took Jerusalem, exemplars of a new ideological age, a narrow political culture far removed from anything the Arabic-speaking Cid would have understood.

The anonymous Castilian poem that celebrates the Cid's exploits, and which survives in written form in but a single mutilated manuscript, was part of a vigorous oral tradition, an epic poem performed over an extended period, and in any number of venues, before being committed to the manuscript version that has come down to our own times. Its period of popularity is not very far from that of the *Song of Roland,* the anonymous old French epic, and both poems, in the forms we have them, are the cultural products of the ideology of crusade that was first announced by Pope Urban II at Clermont, France, in 1095 and was followed directly by the bloody capture of Jerusalem in 1099. Both poems were involved in shaping public attitudes on turbulent contemporary issues, the Crusades in one case and the ascendance of Castile in the other, and they seem to have been in popular circulation, in some form, by the middle of the next century, by about 1140, when Judah Halevi set out for Jerusalem (the *Roland* a bit before and the *Cid* a bit later). The stark difference between the two is that whereas the Roland poem uses historical events more than three centuries removed as the basis for its story—Charlemagne's abortive attempt in the eighth century to take Saragossa from Abd al-Rahman, recently arrived on the peninsula from Damascus—the historical events we find in the Cid poem seem virtually contemporary by comparison. The Roland poem's depiction of warfare with the Muslim enemy is treated in a mythological and even fantastic fashion, partly as a result of historical distance; but the Cid poem's transformation of its historical materials is far less obvious. And whereas few nineteenth- and twentieth-century Frenchmen are likely to have taken the images of the Moor's three-headed gods as anything like historical truth, the other poem's depiction of the Cid as the loyal vassal of the Castilian king Alfonso, and as the dedicated leader in the wars against the Moors, is routinely accepted as pretty much just that.

But as with the story of Halevi's life and the culture he is said to represent, these proto-nationalist stories are to be taken not only with the customary grain of salt but with considerable irony. The Cid was infinitely more complex—for better and worse—than the loyal vassal to a not-quite worthy sovereign, and the dizzyingly complex political circumstances of his moment were such that simple loyalties—for better and worse— were rarely to be found. It is not only the Cid but the Castilian monarch himself who is at times the enemy and at times the indispensable ally of the Andalusian Muslims of any given taifa. And the Halevi story (which is never told in the same breath, and rarely in the same language as the Castilian epic) is intertwined with that of the Cid in many ways, perhaps even literally so, since Judah Halevi and Rodrigo Diaz, both men great wanderers, traveled so many of the same roads and at the same time. Where could their paths have crossed? Perhaps in Toledo around 1089, at that moment when the young Jew from Tudela was just arriving there and Rodrigo, too, was in the city, at least for a bit, during one of his rare moments of favor with Alfonso. Or perhaps it was a few years later, out on the dusty roads they both spent a lifetime on, perhaps on those roads leading to Granada, Judah headed in, at Ibn Ezra's invitation, ahead of him still his stardom as the greatest singer of the new Hebrew style, and the Cid headed out, at Alfonso's side for the last time, his moment of glory ahead of him, too, in the exile and the wars that lay just up the road.

The Abbot and the Quran

Cluny, 1142

*Fulfil then, my brother or rather, my lord, what you
promised to your sister, or I should say, to your
servant. May it please you too to send me also under
seal an open document containing the absolution of
our master, to be hung on his tomb. Remember also,
for the love of God, our Astrolabe, so that you may
obtain for him some prebend either from the bishop of
Paris or in some other diocese.*

—Heloise to Peter the Venerable, abbot of Cluny

ONE COULD BE FORGIVEN FOR IMAGINING CLUNY AS THE EPI-
center of the Latin Christian world in 1142. Here was the
newly completed largest church of Christendom, seat of
a vast empire of hundreds of religious houses and monasteries.
At its head was the formidable Peter the Venerable, the abbot
and, indeed, the venerated prince of Cluny for the previous
twenty years. Peter was himself heir to a position of extraordinary prestige, since Cluny was founded about 910 by the first
William of Aquitaine, the pious ancestor of William IX, that less-
than-pious troubadour. In those two centuries Cluny had acquired a wealth and prestige second to none, and it had entrenched itself as the undisputed heart and soul of the monastic

The Carolingian Astrolabe, tenth or eleventh century, the earliest astrolabe inscribed in Latin. (Photo IMA/Ph. MAILLARD)

The Great Mosque of Cordoba, eighth to tenth century. (Abigail Krasner)

The Church of San Roman, built by the Castilians of Toledo, twelfth century. (H. D. Miller)

The Tomb of
Ferdinand III
(Saint Ferdinand),
Seville, 1252,
with inscriptions
in Arabic, Latin,
Hebrew, and
Castilian. (Abigail
Krasner)

Miniatures from the Toledan school of Alfonso X, last half of the thirteenth century. Top: Muslim and Christian knights embracing in greeting. Bottom: Musicians.

The Alhambra, built by the Nasrids of Granada, from circa 1250 to circa 1360. (Abigail Krasner)

The Palace (Alcazar) of Peter the Cruel, Seville, circa 1364. (Abigail Krasner)

The Synagogue of Samuel Halevi Abulafia (later known as the Church of the Transito), circa 1360. (Abigail Krasner)

Depiction of the parting of the Red Sea, illumination from the mid-fourteenth century Haggadah, produced in Christian Spain, now known as the Sarajevo Haggadah.

reform movement of the age. Over the years, Cluny's original mission of ecclesiastical reform was more than accomplished, and its clergy had long before ceased to be involved in the sort of manual labor that had made the Benedictine brothers little more than glorified peasants. Instead, the houses of Cluny had increasingly gone down many roads of learning and scholarship, and sometimes they led to difficult places.

In 1140, Peter the Venerable successfully outmaneuvered both his archrival Bernard of Clairvaux, head of the younger, up-start, right-wing militant Cistercians, and the pope himself. Peter had taken under his wing the enfant terrible of the day, Peter Abelard.* Abelard was the most famous man of his age by his own reckoning, and certainly something of a controversial celebrity by anyone's reckoning. And he had been the most renowned teacher at the schools of Paris just a few decades be-fore, during the years of infancy of that supremely important in-tellectual center of northern Europe, not quite officially yet but soon to be the University of Paris. Abelard's charismatic teach-ing, in both its content and its methods, was crucial in the shap-ing of the university, but as a member of the clergy (and all the teachers at all the schools and universities of Latin Christendom for many generations to come were clerics), Abelard was often in some sort of trouble, provoked by his combative style as well as by his increasingly passionate attachment to aspects of philoso-phy, and to a philosophical style, that were difficult for many or-thodox churchmen to swallow.

His Parisian teaching years now far behind him, Abelard, a broken man of sixty-one, was still being hounded, and aggres-sively so, by the righteous Bernard, the head of the more austere

---

*Because of the potentially confusing overabundance of characters named Peter in this cluster of stories, I have systematically used "Peter" alone to refer only to Peter the Venerable, the abbot of Cluny, and "Abelard" to refer to Peter Abelard. Petrus Alfonsi, an occasional presence here, is still "Petrus."

Cistercians. Abelard was eventually put on trial in Rome on charges of heresy, and in 1140 he was condemned by the pope himself. Bernard was then given license to take Abelard prisoner, but when Abelard appeared at Cluny's doorstep and asked for asylum, the abbot himself granted it, and then some: Peter made Abelard a Benedictine monk of Cluny, wrote the pope the cleverest of letters justifying this peremptory maneuver, and kept Abelard, who was ill, well protected in one of his nearby houses for the next two years. The most famous man of his age and, in his wife, Heloise's, recounting of it, the most famous lover of his age, died under Peter's generous protection in 1142. Peter wrote to Heloise to tell her of the death of her beloved and to report that he had absolved Abelard of his sins. Peter thus made it possible for Abelard to be properly buried, as Heloise had asked, and he was prepared personally to take the body to the convent where Heloise was abbess, a religious house called the Paraclete, established long before by Abelard for Heloise, as her own nunnery.

But the long trip north from Cluny, in Burgundy, to the outskirts of Paris was postponed for several years in favor of a different trip. This would be a long one, too, since it involved Peter's going south of the Pyrenees. Peter the Venerable's trip to Galicia and Castile, undertaken immediately after Abelard's death, was an intellectual adventure. Although there is no record of the meeting in 1144 between Heloise and the recently returned Peter, when he finally fulfilled his promise and delivered Abelard's remains to her, it is easy to imagine that he would have discussed his travels with the woman who had named her own child Astrolabe, after the scientific innovation that so well characterized the complex allure of Islamic Spain. The astrolabe was a mechanical instrument capable of accurate astronomical measurements, which enabled astronomers to calibrate the positions of the stars and, thus, relative time. This allowed for reasonably accurate navigation at sea, which opened up not only the most rudimentary avenues for the transportation of material goods and peoples but all the mental avenues, the visions of the universe, that went with such travel. At the time of Heloise and Abelard's famous affair—which lasted roughly two years, beginning in 1117, when Heloise was seventeen and Abelard her thirty-eight-year-old teacher—the astrolabe was the epitome of something like radical chic, despite the fact that it had been introduced to northern Europe more than a century before. It had not yet lost the allure of a slightly mysterious device from very foreign places, and often with mysterious writing on it.

The first news of the marvel had been brought to the Latin world by Gerbert of Aurillac, an adventurous scholar who eventually became Pope Sylvester II at the time of the first Christian millennium. In the last half of the tenth century he had spent years studying in various cities of what was then the Umayyad caliphate of Cordoba, still very much in its prime. Gerbert returned to Liege with detailed knowledge of that technological advance and perhaps even with one of the instruments, a precious astrolabe. The book that Gerbert wrote about it, *The Book of the Astrolabe,* was not only the first on the subject but also a trendsetter: for many years afterward, intellectuals with any pretensions to a grounding in modern science were virtually compelled to write something about astrolabes. Beyond the direct material effects of these mathematical and mechanical wonders, one senses some rather broad cultural fallout, which in some measure explains the oddity of the name of Abelard and Heloise's son, born in 1118, a century after Gerbert's book had first brought it to the lands north of the Pyrenees. Even more astonishing, as late as 1391, by then some four hundred years after Gerbert had returned from his Andalusian sojourn with this extraordinary little instrument, it retained its cultural cachet: *A Treatise of the Astrolabe* is among the incomplete works Chaucer left behind.

❧

The abbot of Cluny traveled without difficulty to the Pyrenees and beyond, staying at the dozens of Cluniac monasteries on the way. Many of these dotted the pilgrimage route to Santiago de Compostela, but above and beyond those, the abbot's own domains spread far, with some twenty-six monasteries south of the mountain passes. The influence of Cluny in Iberian Christian territories had been growing rapidly, especially so after Alfonso VI had taken Toledo and made it the archepiscopal see of the Church—with a Frenchman, a Cluniac monk, as its first archbishop. Alfonso's father, Ferdinand, had first established ties with Cluny, providing the monastic houses with large sums of money that came from the vast tribute he was collecting from his Muslim taifa vassals. But with Alfonso, the Cluniac connections went even deeper, since his second wife, Constance, the mother of Urraca, his heiress, was the niece of the then-abbot Hugh of Cluny, and it was during Alfonso's reign that the controversial reform of the liturgy, the substitution of the Roman prayer book and mass for those that had been used uninterruptedly in Spain since Visigothic times, was imposed.

In Toledo especially, where the large and influential Mozarabic community felt it had been the privileged guardian of the oldest preserved rite in Christendom, there was resistance to these newfangled changes, and to the foreign domination that had imposed it. From the ninth through the eleventh centuries, the Mozarabs had preserved their own way of celebrating the Eucharist, not in Latin, the liturgical language of Western Christendom, but in Arabic. In this cultural and linguistic isolation from other changes in Latin Christendom, the rite thus survived in its most conservative form—but after 1085, its survival was threatened by the Cluniac reform of the liturgy, which sought to universalize the practices of Western Christendom. The tensions between the two groups of Christians there, Mozarabs and "Romans," would last for hundreds of years and may be broadly understood as symbolic of the conflict between a special indigenous tradition and the foreign-born impositions that were required if Spanish Christians were to be fully integrated with the rest of the Catholic community.

Even if the ostensible purpose of Peter's visit to this new center of the Church was in part diplomatic—to continue the process of convincing the stubborn Arabized Christians that the French (that is to say, the Roman) way of praying was what they needed to adopt—his real mission, and its difficulties, emerged soon enough. The abbot announced that he was looking for translators to work on the sacred book of the Muslims, only to find that there were no volunteers for the job, an unusual one indeed. The abbot of Cluny was undertaking nothing less than the first systematic Christian project to study Islam, and the first translation of the Quran itself, into Latin. Before Peter's remarkable trip of 1142, in fact, the goal of most of the research trips made to the lands where there was access to Muslim learning was far from religious. The prize, for almost all the adventurers in this realm, the heirs of Gerbert of Aurillac, was acquisition of the sort of abstract scientific knowledge that, as with the astrolabe itself, often enough yielded up valuable technological benefits. By the turn of the twelfth century, there was a fast-growing body of professionals responsible for the dissemination of most of the pure-research, or high-tech, Arabic materials. Although we normally speak about their work as translation, these men, especially those of the first generation or two, were not translators at all, in our sense of the word. Like Gerbert, they were intellectually ambitious men driven to discover the treasures of their lifetimes, closer to explorers than anything else. They learned Arabic—or at least enough Arabic to allow them to work alongside their multilingual Mozarab and Jewish collaborators—Arabic being the language of the map that led to El Dorado itself.

Eventually, Peter was able to hire one of these explorers, one Robert of Ketton, an Englishman living and working in and around the libraries of Toledo. It is difficult to pinpoint the exact location of the peripatetic Ketton when Peter found and hired him, and some of the sources suggest it was not in Toledo proper but rather somewhere "in the vicinity of the Ebro [River]," perhaps toward Pamplona, where Ketton eventually settled as an archdeacon. But the collection of texts commissioned by the abbot of Cluny was ultimately dubbed the "Toledan Collection," and the epicenter and source for this sort of work was clearly Toledo. In any event, wherever Ketton was when Peter tracked him down, the man had no interest whatever in working for the abbot, at least not on the job Peter was proposing. It was only when the abbot of Cluny made it worth his while financially that Robert agreed, grudgingly, to put aside his chosen work, his driving passion for the astronomical sciences and mathematics, to become the first "authorized" European translator of the Quran.

For Robert, this project was a small and mostly distracting chapter in a fertile career that included introducing an entirely new branch of mathematics to Latin Europe through his translation of the *Algebra* (from *al-jabara,* the term for reduction of an equation through the "Restoration [*al-jabr*] and Compensation" of its parts), the work of al-Khawarizmi, a ninth-century scholar who had worked in the caliphal Center for Advanced Study in Baghdad. Al-Khawarizmi's own name became the word "algorithm," from the form in which it appears in the very first line of Robert's Latin version of that work: *"Dixit Algoritmi . . ."* ("Al-Khawarizmi says . . ."). The so-called Arabic numeral system also came to Latin Europe in this era, and through many of the same works that were being translated in Toledo by Ketton and others. Itself a Baghdadi adaptation of Indian systems—the Arabs themselves call them, more accurately, "Hindi numerals" —it made many advanced mathematical calculations possible with features absent in the Latin system, among them, crucially, the zero (from the Arabic *sifr*), as well as the use of positional notation, in which the position of the digit represents the magnitude of ten, a system that makes calculations substantially easier than with Roman numerals.* These were heady days for those who had the gumption and wherewithal to mine the magic bookcabinets of cities like Toledo; and many years later, Robert of Ketton eventually wrote his own, inevitable, treatise on the astrolabe.

The makeup and profile of the European intellectual was transformed by the work that Robert of Ketton and many others like him accomplished, even during those several decades immediately after Abelard's death, when what they did amounted to opening the doors just enough to let out the first trickle of the flood of intellectual treasures that would follow soon enough. Abelard himself missed the revolution almost altogether. He was the French Aristotle, as Peter the Venerable called him, in some measure because there was no other, and Peter was in fact still reading "Aristotle" through the fifth-century Latin version by Boethius—thus only the bits of Aristotle that had been known within the early Latin tradition. That meant, until then, very little other than the philosopher's reputation as a logician, author of the *Categories* and *De interpretatione*. Even though he was a nearly exact contemporary of Judah Halevi, Abelard was familiar with virtually none of the body of philosophy that Halevi was already attempting to reject, a whole philosophical culture known to the educated throughout the Islamic world for generations.

Abelard had discovered the power of logic as a young man, and clung tenaciously to it throughout his life, even when it was

---

*The use of this Arabic system did not, however, become commonplace until it was popularized by the *Liber abaci,* or *Book of the Abacus,* written in the early thirteenth century by the famous mathematician Leonardo Fibonacci, a thoroughly Arabized merchant from Pisa who had studied accounting methods in North Africa (present-day Algeria), where his father had been a Pisan diplomat.

abundantly clear that he was in dire straits thanks to his notion that Christian faith itself could and should be subject to logical scrutiny. He created something he dubbed *"theologia"* to serve as the logical and scientific language of Christianity, and he had developed a dialectical method of dealing with philosophical, existential, and religious problems, famously called the *sic et non,* an open-ended and relentlessly inquisitive "on the other hand." For Bernard of Clairvaux, the guardian of a very different Christian tradition from the one that Abelard, and the Cluniacs, cultivated, all these notions reeked of heresy. Surely, no one could really imagine that Plato could be made over into a Christian, as Abelard had suggested.

Ironically, in our memory of the medieval period, that famous *sic et non* method of argumentation represents the sort of pedantic scholasticism that led to the counting of angels on the head of a pin. While there is some validity to that view—dialectic *is* about details, after all—the foundation of the method was something quite different. It was that vision of the universe precisely reflected in the wonderful name, which is "yes *and* no"— not "or," or "instead of," or "not," or anything else that would suggest that there was a single view, that clear divisions or dichotomies existed because one proposition was self-evidently right or good and the other was to be discarded. For Abelard, and for many of his students, the possibility, perhaps even the necessity, of contradiction clearly existed in God's perplexing and often difficult universe. With his insistence that faith needed to be subject to rigorous rational scrutiny, a novel and threatening idea in his circles at that time, Abelard almost uncannily anticipated the intellectual upheaval that came to dominate Europe a few years later. The Latin Christian Europe, in which Abelard seemed quite unique (*unicus,* "the unique one," is how his learned lover, Heloise, referred to him), could hardly have imagined that in a very few years it would have available the vast Aristotelian corpus in an accurate Latin translation. Moreover, that body of work came with the bonus of nearly a thousand years of close study and notable advancement attached to it, a trove of intellectual effort that ran the gamut from the commentaries of Aristotle's own students to those of more recent Muslim and Jewish Andalusians.

Poor Abelard, whose life he himself called a series of calamities, was still a man of the older universe, no doubt despite himself. The gesture of naming the child Astrolabe was one of endearing optimism for a world whose intellectual riches he did not actually know directly but sensed were there, quite literally around the bend. His discussions, in his wonderful memoirs, of the rigors of philosophy as a way of life were, just a generation later, embarrassing in their extreme old-fashionedness. Abelard's *Dialogue of a Philosopher with a Jew and a Christian*, almost certainly written late in his life, at the height of his struggles with the orthodox authorities, and during the same years Halevi was writing his *Book of the Khazars,* was the near-opposite number of that antiphilosophical Andalusian work. Abelard's hero in this exploration of the ways that faith stands up to rational scrutiny is clearly his philosopher, a character modeled on some rough idea Abelard had of the Arabophone philosophical tradition that had brought revelations such as those of the astrolabe to his universe. And yet, while for Abelard, Seneca was still the master philosopher he actually knew, already Petrus Alfonsi, another contemporary, was condescending to pass on to the clerics of Europe the bits and pieces—"as the Arab philosopher says"—of his perfectly conventional Andalusian education, and he would doubtless have found the notion of Seneca as a master philosopher risible. It would have amused Robert of Ketton as well, who at the time of Abelard's death was sitting amid the golden horde of hard science and Aristotelian splendor beginning to pour out of Toledo.

⚜

Peter's translations included not only the Quran, as it turned out, but a whole bundle of different texts that contained the sayings of Muhammad and the lives of the Prophet and his first successors, among other things, all gathered up by the abbot himself, with the advice of his many Cluniac dependents in Spain. Peter the Venerable made clear from the outset why this project seemed so important to him and, indeed, worth what amounted to a vast investment. To most, it sounded a great deal like the simple maxim of knowing one's enemy, but for a man like Peter, knowing the enemy was not a straightforward proposition, and the political circumstances of the project were complex. The Crusades, which had been launched in France in 1095, loomed large for him, as for many others: they were one of the great causes and great events of Peter and Bernard's generation. Peter's translation of the Quran and the polemical analyses of the failings of Islam that accompany it are often assumed, logically enough, to be part of that same crusading spirit and, in fact, one of the weapons to be used against their Muslim rivals for Jerusalem.

This was a view that Peter himself apparently did not discourage, allowing that sort of facile explanation to circulate to make his efforts seem less suspect. But Peter himself knew better than that. Soldiers taking Jerusalem in the name of Christ scarcely needed a detailed education in the holy books of the enemy, let alone the extra-Quranic niceties of *hadith,* the sayings of the Prophet Muhammad. Part of the problem was precisely that it was widely known that the abbot of Cluny was opposed to the Crusades and very much a man of peace. This attitude reflected his often-bitter enmity with Bernard and the increasingly militant branch of Christian monasticism headed by his Cistercian rival.

The Cistercians, with Bernard as their gifted spokesman, had found their "pilgrimage in arms" in the First Crusade, which was summoned in a famous sermon of 1095 by a fellow Cluniac and predecessor of Peter's, Pope Urban II. The Crusade had actually succeeded in capturing Jerusalem in 1099, and so provided irrefutable grounds for the assertion that the sword should be taken up against the enemies of Christ and Christendom. Bernard, in so many ways Peter's opposite, perhaps most tellingly in the matter of Abelard, not only preached a Second Crusade but became the patron of the Knights Templar, those monks-in-arms vowed to the Christian "liberation" of Palestine and especially of Jerusalem. These behaviors were despised by Peter the Venerable, who saw the Cistercians' faith in the power of arms and violence as all of a piece with their shunning of secular learning, and especially their disdain for the classics, and thus all manner of rational and scientific thought, which came to a head in the charges of heresy brought against Abelard in 1140. Peter's principled defense of Abelard, accomplished at some risk to himself, revealed the stark divisions within the Christian community that are also evident in the purposes and the accomplishments of the abbot's trip to Christian Spain.

Peter's complex attitudes toward both Jews and Muslims were comparable to those of the Andalusian Christians who had lived and worked in the mixed religious communities of most of Spain. Peter, in effect, understood Muslims and Jews to be "Peoples of the Book," and thus amply open to eventually receiving Christ's grace. Though he believed unambiguously in the truth of his own Christian faith, the abbot of Cluny possessed a particularly Andalusian understanding of the special kinship, scriptural and historical, existing among the Children of Abraham. Before his trip to Spain, and probably also sometime during those dangerous and difficult years when he was defending Abelard against charges of heresy, Peter wrote a book about Judaism. In many ways that book was a preview of his later works about Islam. His *Liber adversus Judaeorum inveteratam duritiem* almost certainly took its excellent information about Judaism from Petrus Alfonsi's *Dialogue*, which was widely read

and known by the early 1140s. Unlike earlier anti-Jewish literature, Petrus's polemic had the virtue of direct access to the real
Jewish and Islamic sources. Like the polemical writing about
Islam, and indeed, like Alfonsi's own diatribe, the rhetoric of
Peter's tract ("Against the dug-in stiff-neckedness of the Jews")
can sound exceptionally harsh to our ears. But this should not
obscure how radically at cross-purposes Peter's pioneering work
in translating and studying the Quran was to the sort of attitudes
and behavior advocated and represented by Bernard of Clairvaux
at home and by his Knights Templar abroad.

The abbot of Cluny used the translation of the Quran for
which he paid so dearly to issue a not-too-subtle direct challenge
to his adversary, the abbot of Citeaux. Peter is once again dis-
puting with Bernard on the role of reason, learning, and philosophy in the life and mind of a Christian. He sent Bernard a copy
of the Toledan translation of the Muslim scripture, with the following sly provocation as preface: "My intention in this work
was to follow that custom of the [Church] Fathers by which they
never silently passed by any heresy of their times, not even the
slightest, without resisting it with all the strength of faith and
demonstrating, both through writings and discussions, that it is
detestable." Yes, of course, faith. But also demonstration, writing, discussion, knowledge — and thus translations, reason, and
strength of the intellect. Faith and demonstration, as Abelard
had said, were the backbones of Christianity, "the custom of the
Church Fathers." Yes and no are on the table of the true believer,
who can be an educated and thinking man.

At different moments in the written explanations he sent to
Bernard along with the Latin Quran, Peter laments that
Christians had fallen into such a state of ignorance that they
knew only their own language, and not even that of the Apostles
themselves, let alone a language like Arabic, which was already
the language of access to philosophy. This was an open rebuke to
the Cistercian position on education, which was to oppose

anything that went beyond the Latin necessary to read very lim-
itedly, and safely, in monastic libraries. But Peter's provocations
did not stop there: he was sending these materials to Bernard so
that Bernard himself would be able to write the great refutation
of Islam that surely undergirded his militant posture abroad. Not
surprisingly, Bernard never did any such thing, and when Peter
himself got around to writing his version of the analysis of the
superiority of Christianity to Islam, on the basis of his reading of
the Quran as well as the other materials he had gathered, he
began with the lament that the task had fallen to him, since no
other Christian had come forth to undertake it: "There was not
one who would open his mouth and speak up with zeal for
Christianity." The tone, in this context, was something like
mock regret, or even slightly veiled sarcasm, directed at Bernard,
whose brand of zeal Peter certainly did not endorse.

Peter's trip to the old Muslim centers of Spain was organized and
carried out, at great expense, to procure the information the
abbot coveted, and it revealed to him quite directly the untapped
possibilities of Toledo, a city already well on the way to becoming Europe's center for the massive translation enterprise of the
subsequent centuries. An avid and curious intellect, Peter already had an appealing taste of what the other religions thought
about themselves from the works of Petrus Alfonsi, and especially from his *Dialogue,* with its detailed textual information
about Judaism and Islam. But the abbot of Cluny knew full well
that all sorts of things besides theology would whet others' appetites: from the knowledge of the philosophical tradition of the
Greeks to the technological advances of which the astrolabe was
a dominant symbol. In a sense, the technology, and then the science that lay behind it, was the bait. The complex trap that lay
behind that easy bait—the same attractions Judah Halevi had
recently denounced as inimical to the faith of his fathers—was

the rigorous application of scientific methods, a far more advanced form of Abelard's logic, in sum, the entire armory of pagan philosophy, with its potential to undermine faith itself.

The abbot of Cluny lived his life with a powerful sense that knowledge was not anti-Christian, and that to cultivate it was a very good thing, self-evidently more virtuous than arms. He understood, of course, that the Knights Templar were scarcely about to educate themselves in the details of Islam, let alone study the accurate references to the Quran that Peter's new books from Toledo provided, or to substitute reasoned dialogue about the superiority of Christianity for the sword raised against Islam. Could Peter possibly have imagined that after they spent some time in Palestine a significant number of the Templars would go native? The oldest and most famous of the orders of warriors for Christianity notoriously grew wealthy from a network of business connections they cultivated with Muslim merchants, and eventually they did learn enough Arabic—how ironic, from both Bernard's *and* Peter's perspectives—to have extensive and varied intercourse with the enemy.

During his trip to Toledo, the year after Abelard died, Peter witnessed the shape and challenges of the future for men of faith and learning like himself. There, in that city that was now Christian—indeed, one of the principal sees of the Church, under the control of his own Cluny and now, finally, using the universal Roman rite—men like Robert of Ketton were deeply entrenched, reading everything they could find in Arabic. Who could say how many of those scholars (and there were more every day) might be so fascinated with astronomy and algebra and astrolabes that they might, thus distracted and seduced, lose sight of true Christian faith? At hand, Peter could see, was a battle for the hearts and minds of the next generation of Europe's best intellects.

Gifts

Sicily, 1236

M ICHAEL SCOT WAS ONE OF THE EMPEROR'S FAVORITES, and with good reason. Physician, astrologer, necromancer, and expert translator of Arabic and Hebrew texts, he was the epitome of the intellectual that Frederick II—emperor of Sicily, Holy Roman Emperor, and king of Jerusalem—wanted around him, to help shape his own cultural ambitions and legacy. As his name suggests, Michael was by birth from Scotland, but he had left his homeland as a young man and was a product of the very best school for the craft of translation, the century-old intellectual center of Toledo. In the 1220s, when he arrived in Sicily, where he would live out the rest of his life, he already had a reputation as a magician, but what made him most glamorous at Frederick's court—based in Palermo in principle but a very mobile affair in practice—was his fame as a translator during the early thirteenth century, when translating the vast scientific and philosophical libraries from Arabic into Latin was the intellectual lodestar of the age. Scot found a generous patron in Frederick, who encouraged Michael's ancillary passions in alchemy and necromancy and set the charismatic Scot up with what amounted to his own translation atelier, in the proven Toledan tradition of a cooperative, multi-language, multitranslator process.

Frederick II was one of the most energetic medieval monarchs, and he remains one of the best remembered. His ambitions operated powerfully in the intellectual and cultural spheres as well as in the political, where he spent a lifetime carving out and defending his combined German, Norman, and Sicilian claims, most often against the papacy. He was a Holy Roman Emperor who took the implications and challenges of that title seriously, and in many ways he proved worthy of its grandeur. Not least among these was his underwriting of libraries, as well as founding new centers of learning—he established the University of Naples in 1224—which he understood to be his imperial mark on civilization. Culturally, Frederick was the scion of the "turbaned kings" of Sicily, the Normans who had taken political control of the island kingdom from the Muslims at the time of the great Norman expansion during the last half of the eleventh century. The Normans themselves had then become thoroughly Arabized, and under their rule Sicily shook off a certain provincial stupor it had suffered in the shadow of the brilliant Umayyad caliphate of al-Andalus.

A far more international Sicilian culture had been invigorated by the newly arrived Christian kings, most of all by Roger II, Frederick's grandfather, who put his distinctive cultural stamp on that part of the world during his reign in the first half of the twelfth century. Roger's taifalike court at Palermo was a prosperous and hospitable center for a whole range of intellectual luminaries, and the most important book of geography of this time was called, in Arabic, the *Kitab Rujar* ("Book of

Roger"). This vast work was written by a court favorite named al-Idrisi (sometimes remembered in Latin as Edrisi), a Muslim born in Ceuta but educated in Cordoba and later an immigrant to Norman Sicily, dedicating his famous book to its Christian king. The tradition of translations from Arabic was thus a vital component of the legacy Frederick inherited, with the added richness of Greek as a living language. In Sicily, Greek was part of a living Byzantine layer, unlike in al-Andalus and its cultural dependencies, where Greek was little more than an intellectual memory cultivated lovingly, if opaquely, through Arabic translations.

In 1232, Michael Scot dedicated to his emperor his own translation of an important work of natural history, the tractate *On Animals written* by the Muslim philosopher Ibn Sina (revered in the Latin Christian world as Avicenna). Frederick already possessed Aristotle's multivolumed work of the same title; that, too, had been translated by the indefatigable Scot—begun during his time in Toledo and completed during the years of wandering that led to his settling in Sicily. Both of these translations were invaluable gifts for Frederick, who was enamored of the new sciences of his age and of the possibility of systematic and experimental study of the natural world. These prized books provided foundational theoretical material, as well as inspiration, for Frederick's own most famous work, a treatise on falconry, read and admired to this day. *The Art of Hunting with Birds* was the product of Frederick's own eclectic readings in the sciences and his own passionate dedication to direct observation and minute description. But Michael Scot's translations, and especially his dedication of one of them to Frederick, were more than personal gifts; in fact, Frederick could himself have read the Arabic translations of Aristotle from the Greek, along with Aristotle's many-layered Muslim commentators, of which Avicenna was only one.

The man who had been crowned Holy Roman Emperor a dozen years before, in 1220, spoke and read Arabic, and he was

so familiar with both the philosophical and the religious traditions of the Muslims that he had astonished and perplexed wit-
nesses of his 1229 entry into Jerusalem. In that year the excommunicated Frederick, who was militantly at odds with the pope,
had entered the Holy City. Sovereignty over Jerusalem had been
contested, violently, ever since Christians arrived with the First
Crusade, more than a century before, and Frederick was there to
establish his own complex claims and to be crowned king, which
he managed to do, even while excommunicated, in the Church
of the Holy Sepulcher. He seemed to the local Muslims a rather
different species of Christian from the Franks who preceded
him, and dozens of anecdotes were later recounted about this
leader of a Crusader army whose first deed in the city was to restore the public call to prayer that had been suppressed by previous Christian sovereigns: "When the time came for the midday
prayer and the muezzin's cry rang out, all his [Frederick's] pages
and valets rose, as well as his tutor, a Sicilian with whom he was
reading Aristotle's *Logic* in all its chapters, and they offered the
canonic prayer, for they were all Muslims. . . . It was clear from
what he said that he was a materialist and that his Christianity
was simply a game to him."

But Frederick's own mastery of Arabic, and of some of the
traditions, intellectual and religious, to which the language provided access, did not satisfy his ambitions; he aspired to rival
Andalusian influence in the arts and sciences of the times. If men
of advanced scientific or intellectual achievement appeared anywhere near his extensive orbit, he was likely to draw them in.
Thus, among others, the trader and mathematician Leonardi
Fibonacci, who was revolutionizing Europe's mathematical notation, was courted and received by Frederick; he would make a
gift to the emperor of a copy (second edition, 1228) of his
already-famous *Liber abaci*, first published in 1202. Yet it was
Michael Scot who was the emperor's most vigorous link to the
world of translations that Frederick imagined, correctly, would

reshape the universe in years to come. Scot was himself a sort of translation, and an influential one: from Toledo he brought to Sicily great panache, years of experience working in the most advanced methods of translation, and a taste (which Frederick no doubt to some degree already possessed) for the rational intellectual culture that arose naturally from reading and translating the master works of Greek philosophical tradition. Both directly and indirectly, the man from Toledo, infamous in later years as a master of the black arts, was a pivotal figure in Frederick's considerable efforts to have texts translated from the Arabic as a form of cultural evangelizing.

In the end, the emperor became something of an intellectual philanthropist and made invaluable manuscripts available to institutions beyond Sicily; these texts would include translations of recent controversial works written in Arabic. Most prominent among them, products of Scot's pen (and Frederick's largesse), were the philosophical masterpieces of two near contemporary Andalusians, Averroes and Maimonides. Michael Scot, who would be immortalized by Dante in the *Inferno,* and thus would become the most famous of medieval translators, died in 1236. But the massive translation projects in which he figured so prominently were still alive and well in Toledo, even as Toledo was on the verge of being replaced as the political capital of the ascendant Castillians.

Cordoba, 1236

The translation of texts into Latin from Arabic became a vigorous enterprise just as the Muslim dominions in the Iberian Peninsula diminished. Citizens under the Umayyads—Muslims, Jews, even Christians—were not proselytizers of their own culture, or of the Greek philosophical culture that became their own over the years; they had no reason to care whether the libraries of texts they read and worked with were available to those who could not read Arabic. Until the eleventh century and the large-scale movements of peoples across borders that followed the breakup of the caliphate and the subsequent reign of the taifas, there was little knowledge in the Latin Christian world, on either side of the Pyrenees, of what might even *be* in those libraries, and even less in the way of resources to comprehend their contents. Some important translations did appear before the end of the eleventh century, but they were few and far between.

The situation began to change as Christians from the north moved farther into the south and came directly into contact with the libraries. At the same time, many of the new citizens of the expanding Christian realms were individuals who could make those storehouses of knowledge available to the new rulers. When Alfonso VI took over Toledo in 1085, he simultaneously acquired an immense wealth of books and, the greatest gift of all, whole communities of multilingual Toledans—Mozarabs and Jews prominent among them—who could serve as translators. At the turn of the twelfth century, the hunger for translations was felt even farther afield, and for many reasons. The Latin Christian communities had become increasingly aware of the technological and philosophical riches in the Arabic libraries. That awareness was often aroused by the expansion of monastic centers, Cluny foremost among them, in the newly opened territories farther south of the Pyrenees. The irony, then, was that the intellectual influence of Arabic-based learning and culture—in part Muslim, in part Greek (the latter transmitted via Baghdad in Arabic translations and with Arabic commentaries)—waxed in almost direct proportion to the political waning of what remained of al-Andalus.

In the mid-twelfth century, translation activities in Spain were nowhere near full bloom. In 1142, when Peter the

Venerable had gone there in search of translators for his project, he had been forced to beg, borrow, and in the end offer extortionate fees before he found someone among the mostly unorganized first generation of translators scattered throughout northern Spain who was willing to help him out. The groundwork had earlier been laid by the archbishop Raymond of Toledo during the quarter century of his episcopate, from 1126 to 1151. Raymond was the powerful primate of all of Christian Spain, and he lived and worked in this city full of books crying out to be made readable to Christians. He himself was of French origins, a fitting representative of the ever more diaphanous borders among once isolated parts of Christendom. He was representative, too, of a class of churchmen—such as Abelard and Peter the Venerable—with expanding intellectual horizons, and he was responsible for the initial patronage and organization of the loose body of scholars who made up the Toledo "school of translators." The results of his interest and investments were not much visible until the second half of the century, after his death in 1151, and, critically, after the dramatic change of power in the peninsula's Islamic regions. It was in the transition from one Islamic regime to another that Christian Spain accidentally acquired the manpower it needed to take the translation enterprise to a higher level.

In the aftermath of Alfonso's takeover of Toledo in 1085, the Almoravids had become harsh colonizers of the Andalusians, who chafed both at their loss of independence and at the inimical version of Islam the Almoravids had imported and imposed on them. The Andalusians were never successful in any of their anti-Almoravid uprisings—not even those in alliance with their Christian neighbors, beginning with Alfonso VI himself, the very sovereign whose expansions they had sought to check with Almoravid aid. But the Almoravids eventually suffered an overthrow back in their own North African centers at the hands of another, even more repressive, Berber regime, that of the

Almohads, which ended the Almoravid reign in al-Andalus after little more than fifty unstable years. The new regime was measurably worse: these Islamic fundamentalists imposed dramatic changes on their Andalusian province, none perhaps more transforming than the immediate expulsion of Jews from many of the Andalusian cities.

The fallout from this expatriation of a central part of the Andalusian community was widespread; in one sense, it amounted to a paradoxical series of gifts to other parts of the Muslim world, as well as to the Christian kingdoms to the north. In the northern Christian cities, many of which had not long before been taifas, and before that cities of the caliphate, Jewish immigrants found a society where they were not alone in their Arabized ways, and where they were able to prosper, at least in part because of their familiarity with Muslim culture. In places like Toledo, the Jews continued to be a vital part of a religiously pluralistic and multilingual community, along with the Mozarabs (who were themselves at continuing odds with their non-Arabized Christian brethren) and any number of Mudejars, the Muslims who had never left their home territories when these were annexed by the Christian powers, or those who for other reasons moved into Christian territories. By the middle of the twelfth century there were long-standing communities of Muslims living under Christian sovereignty—despite the strict disapproval of such a situation by many religious authorities, Christian and Muslim alike—and the Mudejars became vital parts of the larger community. These Muslims inevitably became Romanized to some extent, while at the same time they reshaped the Christian world in ways large and small. In architectural terms, "Mudejar" came to be used to describe a broad range of fashions that embody the Islamic aesthetic as it was used within Romance-Christian culture from the eleventh century on.

The Arabized Jews who under Almohad pressure began to resettle in Christian territories became an important link, along

with the Mudejars, to the old Andalusian universe, to its continuation as well as to its transmission. It was at this time that the
translation of thousands of Arabic volumes into Latin began in
earnest, and within fifty years, Latin readers throughout
Christendom had at their disposal such once-unimagined wonders as the full body of Aristotle's works, accompanied by extensive Muslim and Jewish commentaries as well as other study
aids, both ancient and contemporary. In sharp contrast to what
Peter the Venerable had found, a man like Michael Scot could go
to Toledo at the turn of the thirteenth century and find not only
skilled translators but a whole culture of translation. Michael
and many others went to Toledo to learn Arabic and to train in
the special process of collaborative translation developed there.
The common model was for a Jew to translate the Arabic text
aloud into the shared Romance vernacular, Castilian, whereupon
a Christian would take that oral version and write it out in Latin.
Beyond technique, however, what Michael Scot and his contemporaries carried away from that richly polymorphic Toledo during those years was a zeal for unpacking and translating not just
texts but the Andalusian culture that lay behind them. The translators of the Toledo "school," then, were translating more than
individual texts—they were translating a culture. Christian
translators were also increasingly aware that the books they were
working on, even when they were Arabic translations of original
Greek texts, were by then bearers of Andalusian culture, and, inevitably, bearers of the Arabic culture centered in Baghdad.
Translation itself, as well as the texts being translated, played a
vital role for the hundreds of years during which the Muslims
had thought the rational sciences and philosophy indispensable
to their libraries. And it was that culture of translation, perforce
a culture of tolerance, that was now captivating Latin
Christendom.

At the same time, the Almohad-controlled cities and regions of the old al-Andalus began to lose some of what had made

them distinctive, as their ancient Jewish and Christian populations departed into exile, and as their narrow interpretation of
Islam made their scholars far less avid than many Latin readers
of that scientific and philosophical library, the memory palace of
the Abbasids and the Umayyads. Perhaps the most negative effect of Almohad ideology and its practice in Spain was the harshness embodied in the Almohads' stridently monolingual, purist
Muslim regime. It went a long way toward creating a climate of
true Muslim-Christian enmity, something that had been, until
then, quite secondary to other forms of hostility and competition. The political instability and disunity created by this clash
of Muslim ideals and styles coincided with the extraordinarily
heightened papal power and influence of Innocent III during his
years as pontiff, 1198 to 1216. In 1212, with Innocent's encouragement and support, and with the provocations provided by the
Almohads' heightened hostility, the diverse and fractious
Christians of Spain joined with troops from the north to march
against the Muslims, and they routed the Almohads.

The battle that took place in 1212 in Las Navas de Tolosa,
just south of the Sierra Morena, the range that lies between the
two old rival capitals of Toledo and Cordoba, marked the beginning of the last days in the disastrous Almohad chapter, sixty-
four years after it had begun. An almost unremitting series of
Muslim losses and retreats followed that turning point, as one
city after another fell to the armies led by Ferdinand III of
Castile. In 1236, the year of Michael Scot's death in Sicily,
Ferdinand entered Cordoba, the most powerful memory palace
of al-Andalus. The man who would later be known as Saint
Ferdinand (and cousin to another canonized saint, Louis IX of
France) took possession of the legendary old center of Umayyad
splendor, and the next day he prayed to his God in the reconsecrated Great Mosque that the Damascus fugitive Abd al-Rahman
had built as a fitting house of God in a new land.

Granada, 1236

Ferdinand had not taken Cordoba on his own, nor was he aided by Christian forces from abroad. Rather, Ferdinand had subjugated Cordoba in the old-fashioned Andalusian way, in an alliance with a Muslim. After the Almohad defeat of 1212, taifalike rivals sprang up, vying to fill the void left by the widely resented intruders from North Africa. Among these rebellious Andalusians, the most successful was Muhammad ibn Yusuf ibn Nasr, a grandee who prided himself on his old Andalusian bloodline and whose patronymic, Nasr, became the famous eponym of the last Muslim dynasty of Europe, the Nasrids. This first Nasrid, known in his own lifetime as Ibn Ahmar, was able to defeat his Muslim rivals by allying himself with the Christian Ferdinand. The deal struck by the two, somewhere in the vicinity of Granada early in 1236, was relatively simple: Ferdinand would leave the lovely mountain-ringed city of Granada to Ibn Ahmar and his people, and Ibn Ahmar would help Ferdinand take the city the Christian really coveted, the one on the banks of the Guadalquivir, Cordoba. Thanks chiefly to Ferdinand's protection, Ibn Ahmar was able to ensconce himself and, as it turned out, 250 years' worth of his descendants, in the relative seclusion and safety of the Sierra Nevada, in one of the Shangri-las of the West, Granada. Around this city, once known as "Granada of the Jews," was thus crafted the last Islamic kingdom of the European Middle Ages, little more than a miniature jewel-box version of what had once been al-Andalus. Shortly after he moved into Granada, Ibn Ahmar himself understood the perfection of the site at the top of the hill where the old Red Fort had stood, and he began to prepare it to become a palatine city, rebuilding fortified walls and bringing water to it from the mountains. He probably did not live to see much more than these foundations completed, but his son took over the task and under his direction there began to rise the most spectacular of all the memory palaces of Islamic Spain, the Alhambra.

About ten years after Ibn Ahmar settled into Granada, in 1248, Ferdinand took Seville, the last great Andalusian city that remained in Muslim hands—excepting Granada, that is, whose protector he remained. When he entered, the Jews gave him a set of keys to the city, inscribed in Hebrew, Latin, and Castilian. Seville was the lovely city of orange trees that the Almohads had made their capital and in which they had built their mosque with its universally admired minaret. There, too, Ferdinand of Castile reconsecrated the Great Mosque and prayed in it, not only the next day but for the rest of his life. He was the first of many generations of Castilian monarchs who preferred Seville above all other cities as their home. When he died there, in 1252, just two years after Frederick II passed away in Italy, thus vacating the title of Holy Roman Emperor, Ferdinand was buried in a tomb erected inside Seville's enormous old Almohad mosque. The monumental grave was created by his son, Alfonso X, who would become the greatest patron of translations in medieval Europe, and who would spend his life in a futile effort to claim Frederick's prestigious title as successor to Augustus, Constantine, and Charlemagne. Ferdinand's funerary monument was inscribed in the three respectable old languages of the land—Arabic, Hebrew, and Latin—as well as in the upstart vernacular, Castilian, which Alfonso would devote vast effort to making as worthy of inscription on tombs as the others.

Banned in Paris

Paris, 1277

. . . And standing by himself, I saw Saladin.

When I raised my eyes a little higher,
I saw the master of those who know,
Sitting with his philosophic family

Who look his way and pay him honor.
There, nearest him, and before the rest,
I saw Socrates and Plato . . .

I saw Dioscorides, the good taxonomist
Of plants, and I saw Orpheus,
Tully and Linus, and Seneca the moralist;

Euclid the geometer, and Ptolemy,
Hippocrates, Galen, Avicenna,
And Averroes who made the Great Commentary

—Dante, *Inferno*, IV, 129–44

IN 1210, AN EPISCOPAL SYNOD IN PARIS BANNED THE COMMEN-taries on Aristotle written by the Cordoban Averroes. The commentaries were being used at the University of Paris, then scarcely ten years old as a formally constituted institution, and almost a century after Abelard had created a stir with his teachings on the application of logic to faith. Averroes, as Ibn

Rushd was known in the Latin circles where his works enjoyed a wild success (as Dante's homage unambiguously attests), had died barely twelve years earlier, in 1198, in exile from Cordoba. His commentaries on Aristotle, quickly available in Latin translation, had brought to a head in the Christian world the intractable conflicts with normative faith posed by a clear understanding of Aristotle's version of how the world worked. The Church reacted with repeated attempts at prohibitions that reveal the difficulty of controlling the overflowing interest in the new universe these books had opened up. In 1215, just five years after the first ban, the university's new statutes repeated the prohibition on the study of the commentaries and added a further formal ban on teaching Aristotle himself. Explicitly excluded from the university classrooms were the subversive worldview of the *Metaphysics* and the treatises on the natural sciences. Fifteen years later, the pope himself intervened with a specific prohibition of the study of Averroes' texts in Paris.

The "new Aristotle"—the fresh Latin translations wrapped in their learned Muslim and Jewish commentaries—was not so easily dispatched. This Aristotle had made his way to Paris from Cordoba, the city where he had arrived, many generations before, from Baghdad. This was a very different beast from the meager "old Aristotle," which was all there had been in Latin Europe until the mid-twelfth century. The old was the paltry bits and pieces of Aristotle that Abelard knew, little more than the logical treatises of the *Organon,* which had been translated by Boethius. The differences between the new and the old were scintillating: the scant and vague suggestions of the old Latin idea of Aristotle could now be replaced by the detailed, line-by-line, book-by-book, limitless universe of the new Arabic Aristotle. By about 1230, it had become clear that repeated papal prohibitions were having little effect: Paris was becoming a city filled with prominent men publicly teaching Aristotelian thought and Averroes' provocative views. The solution, it seemed, was not going to lie in simply designating certain books forbidden fruit.

A new Aristotle, presumably "purged" of his errors, was being openly and officially taught in Paris by 1255. The genie was out of the bottle, at least for the time being; and a challenge to a certain vision of what constituted the Christian faith was being discreetly tolerated. As a result, for the next twenty-five years or so, Paris was very much the center of the universe, bristling with intense and exciting intellectual life. But it would not last long. In 1270, Stephen Tempier, bishop of Paris and doctrinal authority for the university's clerical faculty, publicly listed thirteen condemned propositions that must no longer be taught. By 1277, the number of prohibited propositions had increased to 219 and included a wide range of ideas about the universe, its workings, and the relationship of the observable world to the invisible universe of God. The speculation represented by these propositions—theories, really—revealed the assimilation of a vast body of rational philosophical thought that had become sufficiently entrenched among the professors and students at the University of Paris to warrant being explicitly condemned as heterodox. This was, in sum, Aristotle as he had been canonized for over four hundred years in the Arabic tradition and, in the culmination of that tradition in the West, as he was understood by Averroes, or rather, as that Andalusian's European proponents and reinterpreters at Paris and elsewhere (the "Averroists," as they were called) wanted to see him understood.

Although it is little remembered, and its cultural setting little understood, this moment of intellectual crisis in Paris was a watershed in Western cultural life. At its heart lay the lifework of an Andalusian thinker, Averroes, as well as the whole intellectual and cultural complex of Islamic Spain. Ironically, by 1277, there was very little left of anything one could properly call "Islamic Spain"—only the embattled corner that was Granada. Yet its intellectual and cultural impact on the rest of Europe was in some ways reaching its peak—perhaps nowhere more than in the rooms where Parisian philosophers and theologians talked about what men thought and how men understood, about what was truth and what was revelation.

At the very heart of this inventory of lapses from an acceptable Christian understanding of the universe were two of Averroes' most uncompromising readings of Aristotle: that matter, and thus the universe, is infinite and eternal; and that individual souls, on the contrary, are not. But even more important, the entire thrust of Averroes' efforts—and this was likewise the core of the work of his countryman and contemporary, Maimonides— was to establish a model for the relationship between philosophy, which meant not just speculative thought but rational and scientific thought, on the one hand, and theology, or faith-bound thought, which accepted the teachings of Scripture and its official interpreters, on the other. The problem of how two such potentially different, even contradictory, modes of understanding the universe could coexist had arisen once Greek philosophy was fully available to Muslim scholars, something that began sometime toward the end of the eighth century. Then the same question presented itself, though not for the first time, in the Jewish community, which had access to the same philosophical library in Arabic. Now, finally, in mid-thirteenth-century Paris, it reappeared in the Latin Christian world.

Judah Halevi, like many others before and since, had taken the easy way out. He simply dismissed philosophy and the very notion of reconciling reason and theology, a view that would later be shared by many men of faith. Of course, for the adherents of pure reason, it is faith that is to be rejected as ultimately irreconcilable with philosophy and reason. But one of the fundamental stories of the medieval West, one where the Latin Christian world and the Arabic Muslim and Arabic Jewish universes are felicitously intertwined, is of the noble effort to produce and maintain a first-rate culture, one that could hold together, at the same time and in the same place, the two contradictory modes of thought and belief.

The first part of the story takes place in Baghdad between the eighth and the tenth centuries, and it is the eastern sequel to the story of the Abbasid revolution in Damascus that sent Abd al-Rahman to the far west, to found al-Andalus. The same revolution had equally earthshaking results to the east, especially in the consequent shift of capitals, from venerable old Damascus in Syria to an upstart Baghdad in Iraq. This pivotal move brought the raw and culturally mixed conditions of Baghdad into the very heart of Islam's playing field. In the fantastic round city created by the cocksure and yet tradition-hungry Abbasids, the caliphs themselves—who were of course the heads of the religious as well as the political community—became the patrons of the most influential translation movement of Western history. For about two hundred years, the translation of ancient Greek scientific and philosophical texts was the focus of extraordinary expenditures of time, effort, and money. This vast cultural enterprise, which absorbed and created vital energy, involved players from nearly all sides, from the Syriac Christians who constituted the principal corps of actual translators, to the Arab caliphs, the "successors of the Prophet" and the aristocratic descendants of the Quraysh of Mecca, and an Andalusian-like mix of others in between.

Scholars are still unraveling the motivations and the conditions that led to this most creative movement of cultural transformation, but the results are clear enough, nothing less than the translation into Arabic of the universe of Greek learning. By the eighth century, that still-dazzling body of knowledge had become fossilized inside its own late-antique environment, and was well on the road to the sort of neglect that in other historical instances has led to the wholesale loss of intellectual traditions. But now, in a different place and in different hands, it acquired a second life, metamorphosed into a vital part of a young and vigorous Arabic universe. With the significant exception of the literary texts, the Greeks were reincarnated as part of the remarkable new Arabic culture of the Abbasids—and from there moved on to other places, some of which would lead to Paris in the thirteenth century. Although the Greeks as we know them eventually arrived into our modern intellectual world via a later, and very different, Renaissance metamorphosis, that version was itself profoundly dependent on the first transmutation.

As was the case with the pre-Islamic, pagan poetry of the Arabs, the vigorous and costly pursuit of this Greek library was part of a fundamental creative freedom within the uncompromisingly monotheistic Islamic world. During those two centuries in Baghdad, a vital model arose and flourished: one of secular intellectual pursuits being carried out in the context of an unambiguously religious dominion. At work there, sometimes consciously and often unconsciously, was the same difficult and long-term effort that, among others, the Jew Philo and the Christian Augustine had already grappled with: how to make the pagan legacy an active and honest participant in the intellectual life of the monotheistic traditions. This massive and systematic undertaking, spanning the eighth through the tenth centuries, was not the sort of mechanical or curatorial effort to "preserve" the Greeks for posterity that some make it out to be.

From virtually every perspective, what is called the translation movement is infinitely more than some sort of autopilot transmission from East to West, both in its immediate intent as well as in its long-term impact. The two-century-long Muslim effort to understand and adapt the Hellenistic intellectual universe reintegrated the vital worldview of the classical world back into a living culture. In all sorts of ways this chapter of cultural "transmission" is a textbook example of how things dying in their native soil can indeed survive, and even flourish, when they are transplanted. In this case, in Baghdad from virtually the time of its founding, the transplant also became a shaping part of its new Islamic home. From that long process a model emerged for Greek texts being transposed not only into a different language — that was only a relatively small part of the problem — but into a monotheistic, faith-bound, and hence reason-resistant, culture. We are thus Baghdad's heirs in ways that far transcend the translations themselves, translations that were eventually replaced altogether when the Greek texts were reintroduced from Byzantium to Europe. Critically, we owe to the long sojourn of those Greeks in Baghdad, which led to an extended residence in Cordoba, the deeply ingrained notion that Greek thought is transcendently valuable — and that it is translatable into and compatible with any language and culture, including the monotheistic ones of the Children of Abraham.

Al-Andalus went through the first stages of the process of translation and absorption along with the rest of the Islamic world, and at first it was one step removed and behind Baghdad. Eventually, in this as in other cultural affairs, Andalusian intellectuals proved to be far more than mere colonials. By the time of the great neo-Platonist Ibn Hazm's death in 1064, it was clear that even in the political chaos that followed the fall of the Cordoban caliphate — perhaps even because of it — al-Andalus in its taifa incarnation remained at the cutting edge in all sorts of cultural endeavors. The political downward spiral that eventually led to increasingly repressive regimes (both Christian and Muslim) after the end of the eleventh century was coupled with an intensification of philosophical activity. As time went by, there was a growing sense of the showdown between faith and reason, to put the matter at its most blunt and simplistic, that was always implicit in the translation movement.

The twelfth- and thirteenth-century Andalusian climax to the story of the translation activities that had begun in Baghdad some five hundred years before was played out in sadly repres-

sive circumstances. Ironically, the descent into states of ideological tyranny began at just about the time that various electrifying
refinements from al-Andalus were beginning to seriously infil-
trate the cultures of the far north and open up previously
unimagined horizons there, with everything from astrolabes to
new musical instruments to the philosophy that would lead to
1277 in Paris. But all the while, the Andalusians themselves were
losing many of the freedoms that had made their vivacious and
unpredictable civilization possible. Above all, the mixed cultures
south of the Pyrenees were starting to doubt the age-old notion
that they could be many things at once — a tradition shaken not
by any single enemy but by a concatenation of voices from all
quarters that began to call for purity. Judah Halevi's rejection of
Jewish Andalusian culture, which he confirmed in his literal
abandonment of Sefarad in 1140, as well as his strident denun-
ciations of philosophy in *The Book of the Khazars,* were omens,
from the inside, of things to come. Whereas Halevi had left vol-
untarily, the Almohad regime that took power but a few years
later would trigger many involuntary exiles from al-Andalus,
and not just of Jews.

In Cordoba, during the last couple of decades of the Almoravid
regime, two extraordinary men were born. Ibn Rushd (Averroes)
in 1126, and Musa ibn Maymun (Maimonides), in 1135. Their
lives and work were shaped by the advent of the Almohads and
the whole range of repressions that gradually became characteristic of Andalusian society; both were victims of a degree of
single-mindedness that their ancestors had not known. The
monumental works of each — curiously, more influential as
philosophers in later Christian Europe than within their own religious cultures — shared a basic vision that can be characterized
as the defense of human freedom. Each focused unflinchingly on
the paradoxes that must be embraced in order for faith and

reason to flourish in their respective domains. Neither faith nor reason was to have precedence (this would necessarily lead to a tyranny of one over the other), but rather each was to have a generous and uncompromised place at a table where both could share in the banquet of truth.

Averroes' line-by-line commentaries on Aristotle's works and Maimonides' provocative and hermetic *Guide for the Perplexed* are enduringly great books, and their merits and broad impact far transcend their immediate historical circumstances. But these circumstances nevertheless shed light on the tenor and perhaps even the motivations of their work, and the works themselves are eloquent memory palaces of sorts. These two men of God and philosophy were constructing heroic defenses of a vision of the world that they were born into and which they were educated to take for granted, but which for them, in the course of their very lifetimes, had in fact disappeared. These men were raised in the intellectual aristocracies of their communities: Averroes was the grandson and son of distinguished Cordoban judges; Maimonides was the son of a rabbi. Both were supremely educated and heirs to the long tradition of Andalusian intellectual freedoms. They were also both deeply attached, sentimentally, to al-Andalus and died in exiles tinged with bitterness: Averroes in 1198 in Marrakech (although his body was returned to Cordoba for burial), Maimonides in 1204 in Alexandria, where he had lived for many years.

The story of the Maymun family is a somewhat perplexing one. They were among the many who fled Cordoba in the wake of the transition from Almoravid to Almohad governments in 1148. But instead of fleeing to the Christian north, as many Jews did, they headed south, farther into the heart of Almohad territory. From Cordoba they went first to Almeria, and then, in about 1160, to the great city of Fez. This chapter in the family's exile has always provoked a certain consternation among Jewish scholars, since it seems quite possible that during their years in

Morocco, the heartland of the Almohads, who were so intolerant of Jews—and indeed believed that the Andalusian Muslims' tolerance of Jews was itself something to persecute—the Maymun family might have converted to Islam. A conversion of convenience would certainly have facilitated their emigration farther east, and perhaps an emigration in those years would not even have been possible without it.

The Maymuns did eventually leave the Maghrib, migrating first to Palestine and later back to Egypt. There, the prodigious and brilliant son of the family, Musa (in Hebrew, Moses), lived out his life, earning his living as the celebrity physician to his Muslim sovereigns. Because Maimonides went on to become not only a leader of the Jewish community but a figure so revered in later Jewish history that he can be referred to as "the second Moses," the perceived ignominy of a family history that involved conversion is considerable, even if it was forced, and even if it was only temporary. Yet a fundamental part of Maimonides' public makeup and profile was his attack against the concept of Jewish martyrs. Many religious leaders encouraged voluntary martyrdom as preferable to conversion, but Maimonides vehemently disagreed and mounted an open defense of dissembled conversion in order for Jews to survive during times of religious persecution. Maimonides' views of identity did not make much room for any sort of imposed unity or trivial consistency in the life or the intellect. He was, for starters, far too Andalusian, and far too mixed in his own cultural and intellectual identity (and, unlike Halevi, happily so) to advocate deadly simplicities. It is too often forgotten that his entire corpus of writing was in Arabic, with the sole exception of his *Second Law,* or *Mishneh Torah,* his encyclopedic and practical systemization of Jewish law.

Maimonides carried on very much in the tradition of the Andalusian intellectuals who preceded him but who, until Halevi, had not much imagined that one would have to choose between being Jewish or being Arabized and secularized, or even being a philosopher. Indeed, one of the ways of understanding the Maymun family's decision to make the perilous trip into the heart of Almohad darkness in Fez, in preference to the easier trip north into Christian territory, is to accept their move as revealing a profound insight that their generation had about the "Arab world." For educated Andalusians, the Arabized world was that of civilization and light; it was the culture in which one read Aristotle, as the young "second Moses" had been brought up to do; and it was the home territory of the language of civilized Jews in recent memory. Islam itself could be many things: for Jews it could be sheltering or persecuting; and that range of possibilities existed for Muslims as well.

The writer of the difficult *Guide for the Perplexed,* patently a work intended only for the intellectual elite, has nearly everything in common with the Muslim who was his fellow Cordoban and fellow Aristotelian. Averroes' principal philosophical treatise was also self-consciously for the elite, the wickedly titled *Incoherence of the Incoherence.* This masterwork of Averroes' was a refutation of the work of one of the luminaries of eleventh-century Islamic theology: the *Incoherence of Philosophy,* by al-Ghazali. Like other Muslims well read in Christian circles, al-Ghazali had acquired a Latin name, Algazel. He taught in Baghdad and died in 1111. Algazel's work, to which Averroes was responding, was itself a response to Ibn Sina, another Muslim philosopher and physician, known by the Latin name Avicenna. Born in 980, Avicenna had been the preeminent philosopher of the Islamic world, a man as cosmopolitan in his travels and outlook as he was prolific in his work. In many ways he was the most important product of the several centuries of assimilation of the Greek scientific and philosophical curriculum, and in the Latin West he was revered as an original and penetrating philosopher as well as the author of the *Canon,* which became one of Europe's chief medical texts.

Avicenna had made famous claims about the possibility of scientific thought producing independent truths that could be compatible with revelation. These propositions, these Aristotelian defenses of the validity of scientific thought, were what Algazel refuted in his own work. Algazel articulated the uncompromising stance that the God of the philosophers was not the God of Islam—thus the "incoherence" of philosophy for a Muslim. Algazel's work was a frontal attack on philosophy per se, which he saw as being intractably at odds with the fundamental revelations of the Quran. Averroes, then, was the third and, for all intents and purposes, the last in a sequence of writers carrying on an acerbic dialogue across time and space, across the astonishingly broad expanses of the Islamic world. His vigorous defense of Avicenna and his attack on Algazel's "incoherence" made him a hero to many of the Parisians who struggled throughout the thirteenth century to be able to use him and his Aristotelian commentaries in their classrooms.

But at home, and inside his own culture, Averroes received a markedly different reception. He died in Marrakech under suspicious circumstances, but almost certainly while under some form of house arrest by the Almohads. This was in many ways a symbolic end to one aspect of al-Andalus. Averroes and Maimonides caused the stir they did among the Parisian intellectual elite (most of them also part of the Church hierarchy) because their works—the commentaries, the various refutations of the notion that faith had unique access to truth—profoundly reflected the four-century-long Aristotelian heritage within the Arabic tradition. Their understanding and insights were all based on an unrivaled and, for northern European Christians, barely imaginable authority rooted in centuries of intense and fruitful study. Theirs was a last flowering of a tradition that had begun in the Baghdad of Harun al-Rashid in the eighth century and had in many ways reached its apogee at that inhospitable moment in Andalusian history.

Averroes' fate in the historical memory of the self-consciously devout segment of the Islamic community has been largely benign. In that context, the suspicions and deadly persecutions that Averroes encountered at the end of his life from the Almohads are often handled with sleight of hand and dissimulation. Indeed, one of the ironies of the larger story, the one that leads back to Paris and the bans on his work there in the latter part of the thirteenth century, is that Averroes' impact on intellectual life among those who read him in Latin would be far greater than for those who could read him in his own language. And this was a fate shared by Maimonides, the Arabic-writing philosopher, although it certainly was not the fate of the second Moses, the lawgiver of the Jews of latter-day Egypt, whose *Mishneh Torah* could be studied by the devout in Hebrew, and without much difficulty to the reader's faith. Among some of the devout, however, even this Maimonides became suspect because of the extraordinary hubris, verging on heresy, involved in writing a "second" Torah.

By the mid-thirteenth century, Paris had become the center of the intellectual life of Europe that Abelard's career had foreshadowed. The city and the university saw the comings and goings of the great intellectuals of the times, including the Englishman Roger Bacon, who was, on multiple occasions, "confined" for heretical writing, and the rest of the time in spiritual retreat as a good Franciscan; the extraordinary Albert "the Great," who was really the first to grasp fully the notion that for Christianity to maintain a certain integrity, it would have to come to terms with the entire Aristotelian canon; and Albert's student, Thomas, the aristocrat from Aquino and the most influential of all. Aquinas had emerged from his studies with Albert understanding that just putting out lists of what was wrongheaded in the Averroists' view was insufficient. Just how, after all, *was* Aristotle to be squared with the God of Abraham?

Although Aquinas's great work of Aristotelian synthesis, the *Summa theologica,* seems the height of orthodoxy from our safe distance, it was not always judged so. In places, it flirted perilously with heterodoxy, at least until he began to be read through the always thicker layers of orthodox commentary. Thomas was treading on dangerous ground, as were a number of his counterparts, Maimonides and Averroes prominent among them. But Aquinas had certain advantages. Before he arrived on the Parisian scene, he had the benefit of an education shaped by Frederick II's Andalusian-like culture in southern Italy, where he had been able to read a Latin translation of Maimonides' *Guide for the Perplexed,* reputedly a favorite of Frederick's. The book had previously been translated from Arabic into Hebrew by the Toledan Judah al-Harizi, and at Frederick's court Michael Scot had been a key member of the group that translated it from Hebrew into Latin. Aquinas eventually had other resources as well. Starting in 1260, and likely at the urging of Aquinas himself, a Flemish Dominican who had been active in Latin-Greek Church relations undertook a series of new, literal, and very accurate translations from the Greek of Aristotle and his commentators, which allowed Thomas to effectively break away from his Muslim and Jewish informants on the philosopher. Nevertheless, numerous Thomist propositions appear to be included in the list of 219 banned by Bishop Tempier in 1277, and much of Aquinas's writing was in fact proscribed until 1325, shortly before he was canonized.

What was happening in thirteenth-century Paris was not unlike what had occurred in the Arabic-speaking world of the tenth and eleventh centuries, with the obvious and directly related difference that the Christians of the still-Latinate world did not have to do the complete range of translations and development for themselves; they could and did take advantage of the full library of Greek great books that came to them via al-Andalus. Albertus Magnus and Avicenna both did what one might regard as the first step of "adaptation" by providing the necessary structural paraphrases, while building their own theological reputations, so that suspicions of heterodoxy could be avoided. Both projects accomplished something like the same end: scholars beyond reproach had by indirection, and under the cover of their own good names, smuggled into their own religious cultures the principal Hellenic modes of reasoning and seeing the world, and Aristotle, who had been walked in by a back door, could no longer be ignored. In the end the theologians would of course respond: Algazel and Aquinas, who assumed the task of defending the faith, were themselves trained as Aristotelians and could do something far more compelling than issue simple lists of ideas that should not be thought. The theologians eventually walked the theology right back in, but with the powerful language and intellectual heft that their philosophical training had given them.

Visions of Other Worlds

Avila, 1305

IN THE HEART OF CASTILE A WOMAN WAITED FOR HER HUSBAND to return home. For the past fifteen years they had made their home here, in the walled-in city of Avila, where the cathedral's walls were part of the city's massive ramparts. For many years before that they had lived in Guadalajara, about sixty miles to the east, still in Castile but close to Aragon, and halfway toward Catalonia. During all the years in Guadalajara, the woman's husband had been an upstanding member of the venerable Castilian Jewish community, a respected scholar, the author of many books. But then he had become something of a peddler, out on the road more often than not, and she worried he was half-mad. He had taken to selling those pamphlets he wrote, in a language that looked like their sacred language, Hebrew, but wasn't that at all; it was some other language only the other rabbis could understand. He told everyone that what he was selling were bits of wisdom copied out of an old holy book, but she knew there was no book he was copying from, except maybe in his head. Once, when she had asked why he claimed he was only a copyist and not the author of those pamphlets he sold more and more of every day, and on every road trip, he answered her: "If I told people that I am the author, they would pay no attention nor spend a farthing on the book. They would say that these are but the workings of my own imagination. But now that they hear that I am copying from the book *Zohar* which Simeon ben Yohai wrote under the inspiration of the Holy Spirit, they are paying a high price for it, as you know."

For years Moses of Leon had been wandering through both Old Castile to the northwest, toward Leon, the land of his ancestors, and across New Castile, to the south and the east, in places where most of the Jews still spoke Arabic. That day in 1305, his wife waited in vain for him to return to Avila from his trip out hawking his amazing goods, with whatever sums he had made from the sales of those little books. This particular excursion had been to the north, to Valladolid, where the kings of Castile were sometimes in residence, and it was his last: Moses of Leon had died on the way home. Soon thereafter, his widow received a visit from one of the wealthiest Jews of Avila, who offered his son's hand in marriage to Moses' daughter in return for a singular dowry: the manuscript of the *Zohar* from which the rabbi Moses had spent those last fifteen years transcribing the teachings of the second-century rabbi Simeon ben Yohai of the Galilee. But his widow and his daughter had to explain that there was no such book—who knows whether in shame, despair, or amusement.

Moses' *Zohar* is a voluminous book, or, more accurately, a huge collection of booklets that Moses had laid out serially, and it is the very heart and soul of the Jewish mystical tradition called Kabbalah, which itself means nothing more than "tradition"—what is handed down. What was "handed down" was a great body of esoteric learning and practice, some of it transparently Greek, other parts detached from deep within an ancient tradition of magic that had been quietly circulating in rabbinic circles for centuries. Although the *Zohar* is now understood to have been the product of the genius and imagination of this Castilian Jew who lived and wrote at the end of the thirteenth century, Moses' pious fiction was that he was merely a transcriber and that the real author was the revered Simeon ben Yohai. This story of the book's provenance was embraced from the time the text began to be widely read at the end of the fifteenth century (some two hundred years after Moses had released it) until the late nineteenth and twentieth centuries, when modern scholarship identified its true author. Just why did Moses need to claim the sort of authority that he felt he himself as the author could not have possessed but which was fully granted to a remote historical rabbi? What was it about this book that made it so revered among Jews, the only post-Talmudic book to acquire canonical status and be read along with the Bible and the Talmud as one of Judaism's sacred texts until well into the nineteenth century? If it is not, after all, a reflection of the culture of a learned Jew in second-century Palestine but instead that of a thirteenth-century Castilian Jew, how are we to imagine the world of Moses of Leon, the world out of which the *Zohar* was conjured?

Like Judah Halevi some 250 years before him, Moses rebelled against much of the Arabized rationalism of many of the members of the Jewish communities around him, and, like Halevi, he took leave of his old-fashioned Andalusian-based education. He, too, had begun his intellectual life as a student of the "Greek religion," but he came to see the philosophical pursuit of knowledge as spiritually sterile and the Jews of Sefarad as too worldly, too successful, and thus spiritually lazy. Yet Moses was no more satisfied with the conventional pieties (and pietists) and was at least as scornful of Jewish traditionalists who never went beyond the positivist Mishna and the legalist Talmud, the body of canonical law and canonized commentary that governed Jewish life from the third century down to his own day. For Moses, these seemingly opposing visions of the universe, the philosophical and the normatively religious, were alike in that neither could lead to any real understanding of the true complexities of God and existence.

Unlike Halevi, Moses did not abandon his culture or his homeland, nor did he withdraw from society and human intercourse, in the manner of many other mystically inclined individuals, in order to achieve personal communion with his God. Instead, Moses became an unusual hybrid, a poetic and mystical proselytizer, a teacher with a method and a text that appealed to the imagination more than systematic analysis or the elaborate rules the Jews call *halakah*. He spread the message not all at once but over time, in bits and pieces, and then only through the voice of an ancient sage, through the putative recordings of a second-century rabbi's discussions with his disciples and with some of the characters of the Bible itself. This, Moses was sure, was the light-filled way for all to approach God and the Torah, and he called it *The Book of Splendor, Sefer ha-zohar.*

This sprawling book, which has been variously described as the Bible of the Kabbalah or a mystical midrash, and even an esoteric novel, was written by Moses (whose own languages were Hebrew, Castilian, and Arabic) in a creative pseudo-Aramaic studded with Hebraisms, Castilianisms, and Arabisms. The use of Aramaic, the language of ancient and far-off Galilee, was obviously meant to bolster Moses' claims that he had a real second-century text in front of him. But the insidiously counter-traditional claims of the *Zohar* and its scandalous bid to replace the Mishna as the canonical Jewish commentary on the Bible are revealed in its very structure: the book is made up of five books of exegesis intended to correspond to the five books of the Torah

(Genesis, Exodus, Leviticus, Numbers, and Deuteronomy). Moses needed the cover of a far older authority, a once lost but now found authoritative text from the period when Judaism was still adding to its textual canon, to present a vision that, in his own voice, that of a thirteenth-century Castilian, would have been problematic.

Most radical in the *Zohar* was precisely what Moses sought to obscure by his serial distribution—namely, that there was a full text here to replace the traditional legal approach to interpretation of the Talmud. This was not an isolated different interpretation or a piecemeal penetration of the text, but a wholly distinct vision, a gnostic opening onto the Scripture, a mystical and poetic approach to oppose and rival the Mishna's approach. The powerful aspect of Moses' book lay not in the absolute originality of the approach as such but in something like the codification—if such a word can be used for anything so inherently resistant to codification—of the strong kabbalistic tradition that had flourished among the Jewish communities of Moses' ancestors and his neighbors. This Moses, too, was a codifier, a latter-day poetic lawgiver, scion of both the visionary and the rational cultures of his time.

Both before and during Moses of Leon's lifetime, a rich mystical tradition thrived among the communities of Jews who lived on either side of the Pyrenees and who shared the vernacular often referred to as Provençal. During the eleventh and twelfth centuries, this land, with its intimate ties to the still-Arabized Christian courts of Catalonia and Aragon, had been the breeding ground of a whole stable of institutional misfits. This was the native land of the first generation of poets who attempted to replace Latin as a literary language with the vernacular that within a few years would be poetically dubbed *langue d'oc,* "the language of yes," by Dante Alighieri in not-so-far-off Florence, and it was also the seat of the Jewish mystics and esotericists we call kabbalists. Culturally they were much like their Andalusian brethren, but spiritually they were at odds with the Andalusians' intellectual and philosophical visions of faith. This "land of yes" seemed to specialize in nay-saying, and it was also the breeding ground of the Cathar, or Albigensian, heresy, the resolutely Manichean "Church of the Purified" that Rome began to come down on heavily by the mid-twelfth century. The Cathars in their fortified Languedoc towns were the object of an all-out, papally sanctioned Crusade at almost the exact moment that the pan-Christian armies were helping the Christians of Spain destroy the Almoravids.

Both before and after the battle against the Muslims was being fought at Las Navas de Tolosa in 1212, this other war was being waged with equal ferocity by Innocent III and his Dominican shock troops against the enemy within Christendom. Although the fascinating political and religious details of the Albigensian Crusade are not of direct relevance to this story, its effects, which reverberated throughout the first half of the thirteenth century, are. The once prosperous and independent courts of Languedoc were devastated and came under the political control of the French to the north—which meant that the roads south were soon filled with refugees from the social and religious persecutions that followed, including those of the papal Inquisition established in 1233 to eradicate the heresies associated with the Cathars. Prominent among those who emigrated to the more congenial atmosphere of adjacent Oc-speaking Catalonia, whose vernacular tongue was barely distinguishable from that spoken just to the north of the Pyrenees, were Jews among whom Kabbalah had been cultivated for years, alongside Cathars and troubadours alike. In places like Gerona, a town no more than 120 miles from major Cathar strongholds such as Toulouse, and much closer to many smaller towns—all left ravaged in the last years of the Albigensian Crusade—prosperous

enclaves of Jewish immigrants succeeded in reestablishing themselves out of the war zone.

Inevitably these refugee communities began to commingle
and combine with the older Iberian Jewish settlements in the
adjacent areas of Aragon and Castile. Moses of Leon was thus
born into a world where the mystical beliefs of Kabbalah were
part of the cultural heritage and practices of the Occitan (or
Oc-speaking) side of the community, which included such
revered rabbis as Nahmanides of Gerona.* He thus had access,
before he composed his own *Zohar,* to the principal kabbalistic
text of his time, the *Sefer ha-bahir,* or "The Book of Brightness,"
which came from somewhere in those Oc-speaking territories,
perhaps from Gerona itself. But what is also visible in the *Zohar,*
in its ultimately successful attempt to systematize what its predecessors had not imagined systematizable, is that other side
of Moses. He was very much part of an old Castilian Jewish
world that proudly cultivated its highly rational, philosophical,
and scientific Andalusian heritage, one that still remembered
Maimonides, especially the Maimonides of the *Guide for the
Perplexed,* as one of its own, and that remained a vital component of the vibrant intellectual scene of Alfonso X, known as
"the Learned," centered in Toledo, home to the grandest of the
Jewish communities.

One of the earliest attestations of Moses of Leon's whereabouts
and interests is his purchase, in 1264, of a copy of the Hebrew

---

*Nahmanides, or Moses ben Nahman as he was actually known, was one of the most em-
inent medieval rabbis. He famously defended Judaism at a public disputation convoked
by King James of Aragon in Barcelona in 1263, a debate very much in the tradition of the
dialogues between representatives of the different religions (including philosophy) that
produced Petrus's *Dialogue,* Halevi's *Book of the Khazars,* and a host of others. There are
also reports of these public debates taking place at the Abbasid courts as far back as the
time of the caliph Harun al-Rashid.

translation of Maimonides' *Guide for the Perplexed*. This was not a particularly early translation of the book that was already dramatically affecting religious thought among both Jews and Christians in the West, since the *Guide* had been translated from Maimonides' native Arabic into Hebrew much earlier in the century, and then rendered from the Hebrew into Latin by a group of translators at the court of Frederick II working under the direction of Michael Scot. By 1264, the year that this Hebrew version was being copied for Moses of Leon, it had already been studied in Latin by Thomas Aquinas at Frederick's university in Naples. But Moses' 1264 Hebrew copy was in its own way emblematic of the local culture of Christian Spain, this one dominated by the complex historical figure of Alfonso X, who had ascended the throne of Castile in 1252, at the death of his father, Ferdinand III.

Early in his reign, Alfonso had attempted to establish a new center of Arabic and Latin studies in Seville, the old Almohad capital that was the last city taken by the Castilians and which they made very much their own, the city where the sainted Ferdinand was buried in the emblematic tomb inscribed in the four languages of the realm. But Alfonso, who for all his learning proved to be a politically inept ruler, failed in this attempt to set up what may have been perceived as a rival to the internationally prominent center of translations in Toledo, the much older seat of Castilian assimilation of Arabic and Hebrew learning. Alfonso was thus thwarted in his attempt to set up a Sevillian school bearing his imprint and under his control, and so he had ample incentive to try to upstage the old Toledo school, which for about 150 years had been principally supported by the city's archbishops. Far beyond any personal animus and rivalry with the church, however, Alfonso grasped that already in his lifetime, in the mid-thirteenth century, there was little cultural novelty left in the ongoing task of translating the still-considerable Arabic scientific and philosophical library into Latin. The work needed to continue, but it was no longer itself the essence of the avant-garde.

Alfonso's brilliant gambit was to abandon Latin, as a language no longer adequate for a modern society and its empire. Alfonso had a visionary grasp of the fundamental importance of having a society's vernacular serve as the vehicle of more than the mostly oral lyric and epic poetry that was the entertainment of the moment. The model closest at hand, of course, was the one the just vanquished Islamic empire had provided, with its near-universal use of Arabic. Over four hundred years after Alvarus had railed against the abandonment of Latin by the Christians of Cordoba, Castilian, a kissing cousin of the Mozarabic the Cordobans spoke, began its road to dominance among the competing children of Latin. Under Alfonso's direct patronage and intense personal involvement, and in Toledo itself, Castilian began to be made over from the rough-and-tumble spoken language of the mostly illiterate population into a written language that could serve the institutions of a civilized and modern society: to record its history and laws, extend science and education, and become the appropriate vehicle of literary and even religious texts—and not just those of the Christians.

In the period of Alfonso's reign, from his accession in 1252 to his death in 1284, Toledo thus became the first laboratory in Europe dedicated to forging a modern language, a vernacular that would replace Latin in all its functions save the purely ecclesiastical and liturgical. The old Toledan process of translation involved multireligious teams whose common language had always been the mother tongue, the local Castilian vernacular. Jews and Muslims were usually the core members, providing direct access to the Arabic texts. Their oral translations into Castilian were then, in a second step, rendered into written Latin by the Christian members of the team. Embedded in this traditional Toledan practice was the foundation for the revolution at hand. Latin was set aside as the antiquated and extraneous final step, to be replaced by the transformation of Castilian from the merely instrumental—the mother tongue in which men had perforce to speak to each other, the true lingua franca of the interfaith community—into a noble written language.

Alfonso's canny perception of the inherent precariousness of such a venture, and of the multiple difficulties to be encountered in the laborious process of forging a new written language, led him to engineer it as a multipronged attack. Alongside the translations from Arabic that now began to appear in Castilian (rather than in Latin) were brand-new texts in this vernacular that was being rapidly elevated and expanded in status. These texts were not direct translations from Arabic but part of the broader cultural translation of one civilization's perceived sources of legitimacy into another's: extensive works of world history (meaning to lead up to the Castilian ascent to power), collections of legal statutes, and scientific tracts that took the basics of the old tradition a few steps further. Finally, among the new translations and adaptations into the Castilian vernacular were works from the other realm that had rarely, if ever, seemed appropriate to translate into Latin: works of imaginative fiction. The first classics of Castilian fiction appeared out of this grab bag, fresh versions of the sort of story collection that Petrus Alfonsi had once contrived to pass off as a work of instruction for the clergy. All of these were drawn from the eclectic treasure troves of tales that the Islamic empire had accumulated from the eighth century on, from the Indian cycles of animal fables to the Persian-based and Baghdad-adapted master text of the tradition we call *The Thousand and One Nights*.

This metamorphosis was not altogether unlike the one that Hebrew had undergone several hundred years before, in this same land, when it had been reborn as a language that could be written and sung outside the synagogue as well as read inside. Alfonso's patronage of the Castilian dialect was decisive. He transformed it from just one of the peninsula's many competing

Romance vernaculars into a legitimate language of authority and history by making it the official written language into which Arabic texts and Islamic literary forms were translated. The learned king was quite purposefully crafting a new Latin, the contemporary and living version of Latin that could speak the language of the new empire he thought he would be able to lead. In both the Jewish and the Christian instances, the linguistic breakthrough was a rivalrous response to Arabic and everything that could be written in it, accompanied by a profound appreciation of the lesson that had been absorbed: that a great people in a historically central civilization has to speak a language intelligible not only to God but to history itself. When Alfonso had histories, scientific treatises, and legal codices written in Castilian, not to mention the many astronomical and astrological writings and the star charts that would be something like bestsellers throughout the rest of Europe, what was being replaced, in the most immediate sense, was Latin. Yet what was being replaced in the broader cultural sense — in accord with the historical vision cultivated by the monarch himself — was clearly Arabic, the still-living language of the older empire that Alfonso wanted to displace. Alfonso failed miserably in his political aspirations; he died abandoned by his political allies, embattled and estranged from his family, never even coming close to attaining the title Holy Roman Emperor. But his audacious vision of the languages of the future prevailed.

Among the dozens of scandalous books that came out of Alfonso's workshops, perhaps none has remained as provocative as the one called the *Book of the Ladder*, the *Miraj* in its original Arabic. It can be dated exactly to 1264, the same year as the translation of Maimonides' *Guide* that was made for Moses of Leon, and they were produced almost within shouting distance of each other, one in Toledo, the other in the vicinity of

Guadalajara, some seventy-five miles to the northeast. The Alfonsine translation of the *Book of the Ladder* into Castilian, by one "Abraham of Toledo, a Jew," has been lost. But at least two other translations were made, provoked by the unusual interest in this apocryphal and highly literary recounting of the Prophet Muhammad's famous "night journey" from Mecca to Jerusalem, followed by his ascent (up the "ladder" of the title) to the nine circles of heaven and his descent to hell, the whole of the trip under the guidance of the archangel Gabriel, narrated by Muhammad himself in the first person.

Both surviving translations, one in French and one in Latin, both from 1264, were made directly from the written Castilian translation rather than from the Arabic original, revealing the not-so-subtle ways in which Alfonso had managed to displace Latin as the primary language of written texts. Also revealed were the severe limitations of that displacement—and of national, as opposed to international languages, although Castilian would eventually serve as the language of an empire in the sixteenth century—since the Castilian text proved of limited or no use beyond the boundaries of Alfonso's own kingdom, where either another vernacular (French, in this case) or Latin itself would be necessary for any sort of reading public. The French translation and probably also the Latin were executed by a man named Bonaventura, from the prominent Tuscan city of Siena. Bonaventura was one of the more visible Italian diplomats and translators at Alfonso's court, many of whom were refugees from the ferocious civil wars—between Guelphs and Ghibellines and later between Blacks and Whites—that since the time of Frederick II had pitted the papacy against those in favor of a relatively autonomous empire, and in which Alfonso was indirectly involved, given his claims to succeed Frederick as emperor.

Among the other prominent Tuscans at Alfonso's court, none was better remembered than a Florentine named Brunetto Latini. In 1267, three years after the translations of the *Book of the Ladder,* Brunetto was inspired by the magic of Toledo and the linguistic metamorphoses and creations at hand to write a book called the *Treasure.* This was a cross between an encyclopedia and a rhetoric manual for yet another of the new vernaculars, this one the dialect of northern France (the *langue d'oïl*), where he went after his time in Toledo, exiled there for some years by the continuing civil wars of Florence. Brunetto Latini was not subsequently remembered so much for his own seminal book, however, but for his role in the most transcendentally important vernacular work of the period, the *Divine Comedy,* which Dante Alighieri began to write just about the time that Moses of Leon died, still peddling parts of his *Zohar* in Castile. A few years into what would be a lifelong exile, Dante left unfinished his theoretical defense of the use of the vernaculars for literature, *On Eloquence in the Vernaculars,* the work in which he divided the Romance world into three parts, according to their way of saying "yes." He began, instead, writing the poem that narrates his journey into hell, purgatory, and heaven. Dante, who was born in 1265, while Brunetto was in Toledo, immortalized his fellow Florentine as a revered teacher, a benevolent father figure, and a visionary influence, even though in the *Inferno* he damned him to the circle of the Sodomites, a literary act which has long puzzled scholars. But no question has more scandalized and provoked students of Dante than whether, among the many treasures the world traveler Brunetto revealed to the young Dante, was included the book that had been all the rage at Alfonso's court and had been translated by another fellow Tuscan, the amazing vision of the other world narrated by Muhammad himself, the story of his guided tour of heaven and hell.

Foreign Dignitaries at the Courts of Castile

Seville, 1364

O NE DAY IN 1364, A YOUNG DIPLOMAT APPEARED AT THE COURT
of Peter of Castile (remembered as Peter the Cruel by
those who wrote the histories of his rivals and their descendants). The young man, named Ibn Khaldun, had arrived
from Granada to see Peter in Seville, the monarch's favorite
among his various royal cities, and where he was in fact just fin-
ishing work on a new Alcazar. The old Arabic word for palace,
al-qasr, was what the Castilians called their splendid new royal
homes. The elaborate plasterwork that decorated nearly every
inch of the Alcazar's interior walls was barely dry, and the
Muslim emissary from Granada found himself in rooms that in
every way echoed the freshly finished palaces of the Islamic city
he had just left. Peter, a son of Alfonso XI and the heir to his
great-great-grandfather Alfonso X (the Learned), who had died
in this city, was justifiably proud of this example of his wealth,

taste, and vision. All three were on display in this Sevillian tribute to the very latest architectural style of Spain. Ibn Khaldun
could hardly have avoided the realization that Peter's new
palaces, with their multilobed latticework arches and their pure-
white arabesque ornamentation on every spare surface, were an
unstinting homage to the style of the Nasrids, whose envoy he
was. There, on the open and sunny plain, sitting next to the giant
old Almohad mosque in Seville—the mosque had been reconsecrated more than a hundred years before and was the cathedral
of the Christian capital—was an unabashed evocation of the
fortlike palaces at the top of the rocky mountain retreat of
Granada, the last and lonely Islamic state on the Iberian
Peninsula.

Ibn Khaldun was not an Andalusian, although he was of
very old Andalusian stock—Arabic names ending in -un were
said to be characteristically those of the earliest converts to Islam
on the peninsula. His prominent and wealthy family had fled the
region of Seville, their original home, during the turbulent last
years of the Almohads, settling in Tunis. The up-and-coming Ibn
Khaldun had been visiting Granada when he was tapped to go to
Seville. We can only imagine the effect of these trips on the brilliant young historian-in-the-making, who knew the histories of
al-Andalus both from his readings and from family accounts. He
arrived in his ancestral land more than a century after the nearly
complete triumph of the Christian states, under Castilian leadership, over the Almohads and over all the old great cities of al-
Andalus but one: the craggy retreat of Granada, where Ibn
Ahmar, in cahoots with Ferdinand III—whom he helped take
Cordoba from the Almohads—had set himself up as king. The
sights that Ibn Khaldun saw in Seville were most likely not what
he expected, and probably not at all consistent with what he was
taught in his native Tunis. In Granada, in relative seclusion and
safety, Ibn Ahmar's descendants, the Nasrids, had had the time,
money, and inclination to create a heartstoppingly beautiful

home at the top of their mountain, pearly-white palaces on the inside, a wall of red clay on the outside. This was their triumph in their *Iliad*-like siege, the Alhambra, a serendipitous echo of the alternating reds and whites of the Great Mosque of Cordoba, a testament to their own vision of their loneliness as the last Islamic polity in all of what had once been the great Umayyad caliphate. In the former Almohad capital of Seville, Peter's Alcazar sat next to the old Almohad mosque-turned-cathedral, the place where Saint Ferdinand's tomb sat, and that of his son Alfonso, who had also died there.

The ruins of once great empires have famously provoked grand historical visions and moved men to contemplate the question of history itself. Edward Gibbon records his own moment of epiphany and transformation, in poetic terms: "It was at Rome, on the 15th of October 1764, as I sat musing amid the ruins of the Capitol, while the barefooted friars were singing vespers in the temple of Jupiter, that the idea of writing the decline and fall of the city first started to my mind." What was moved in the heart and spirit of this other historian, whose family had been part of the glories of al-Andalus? What did he see in the half-ruins of al-Andalus in the mid-fourteenth century, when friars were singing their vespers in mosques, ruins as evocative as the Piranesi visions that dotted the Roman landscape in Gibbon's time and spawned the writing of *The Decline and Fall of the Roman Empire*?

Ibn Khaldun did not leave behind any single description of a dramatic moment of transformation such as Gibbon's, but there can be little doubt that his 1364–65 sojourn in what had been al-Andalus helped shape the extraordinary historical sensibilities of the most influential philosopher of history who wrote in Arabic. The man who would write eloquently of the historian's task as that of understanding not just the facts but the shape of history and politics directly observed the multiple layers of the tragic, unrelenting civil wars that were everywhere around him, some just finished, others soon to begin. Unlike Rome in Gibbon's set piece, the ruined al-Andalus that Ibn Khaldun saw was not only a place dotted with abandoned temples overtaken by barefoot friars; it was also a place filled with brand-new temples that honored the defeated old civilization, unexpected places like the Alcazar of Seville. What would a man already contemplating the problems of the cycles of history have made of that? And what did the young Ibn Khaldun come away with from his sojourn in his ancestors' once glorious and now abandoned land? What moment of history, what images of the past and the future, did this visionary glimpse in Granada, and then in Seville, in the mid-fourteenth century?

Ibn Khaldun had found refuge in Granada when, after a few missteps in his politically byzantine home of Fez, he fell out of favor there. He had ended up in Granada, thanks to the equally byzantine and dangerous politics of the Nasrid house. Muhammad V, the young ruler of Granada, had met the impetuous young intellectual just a few years before, in Fez, when Muhammad's half brother deposed him and sent him packing into exile in North Africa. Muhammad's entourage included his vizier, a man named Ibn al-Khatib who was already an intellectual heavyweight renowned throughout the Arabic-speaking world. Ibn al-Khatib met and took a liking to the young Ibn Khaldun. The Granadans were eventually able to return home, redeemed from that exile thanks mostly to Peter the Cruel. (The two princes, the Muslim and the Christian, much like Peter's ancestor Ferdinand and Muhammad's ancestor Ibn Ahmar, had an alliance of mutual defense—and convenience—and Peter had come to Muhammad's rescue in his moment of severe difficulty.)

Back in Granada, Muhammad, as well as his vizier Ibn al-Khatib, remembered Ibn Khaldun and a few years later offered him a safe haven from the political upheavals in Fez. Ibn

Khaldun found himself in congenial exile in Granada: the rightful Nasrid sat once again on the throne, his insurgent half brother efficiently dispatched by Peter; and the intellectual life of the court was vibrant under the influence of Ibn al-Khatib, the dazzling polymath of a vizier. Ibn Khaldun was a great success all around, and it looked for a while that he might stay on in his ancestors' homeland. In 1364, Muhammad sent Ibn Khaldun to visit his old benefactor, Peter, who, like Muhammad himself a few years before, was involved in an increasingly bitter and dangerous rivalry for the Castilian throne with his own half brother, Henry of Trastamara, child of a mistress of Peter's father, Alfonso XI.

In Seville, too, Ibn Khaldun was triumphant as a visitor. He fit naturally into the realpolitik of the moment, and he seemed so vital a part of the landscape of lavish cultural fraternization that Peter decided he wanted him to stay on. The Christian monarch offered to restore to him his ancestral properties in the environs of Seville if he would grace his court and his kingdom, to be his adviser, diplomat, and house philosopher—his vizier, in effect. Ibn Khaldun declined and returned to Muhammad V's court in Granada. In fact, as it turned out, Ibn Khaldun's ambition was to be all those things—not for the Castilian king, but for the still malleable young Nasrid prince. That job, however, was already taken, by Ibn al-Khatib, the Nasrids' counselor, teacher, and political sage of some years. The grand old man is remembered in the history of Arabic letters as one of its most eminent and prolific writers and was himself the inspiration for the essential source on the history of Islamic Spain.* Ibn al-Khatib was still very active in the court, and Ibn Khaldun's

---

*The most important historian of Islamic Spain, al-Maqqari, wrote his indispensable chronicles of the rulers of Spain as an almost accidental effect of his abiding interest in the vizier of Nasrid Granada in the fourteenth century. Al-Maqqari's history of the Andalusian rulers, written in Damascus between 1628 and 1630, was meant merely as an introduction to his central project, a comprehensive biography of Ibn al-Khatib.

interest in the vizierate of Granada displeased him. Although the powerful minister had originally welcomed the ambitious young man—indeed, had been the one to offer the invitation of refuge in Granada—something clearly changed after Ibn Khaldun returned from his trip to Peter's Seville.

Eventually Ibn Khaldun was encouraged to abandon Granada and his ambitions there, and he returned to North Africa. Were there days, during the next decade, when Ibn Khaldun rued his choice, when he wondered how the course of history might have gone differently had he become adviser to the king of Castile and Leon? In the midst of an ill-advised military campaign in 1369, just a few years later, Peter was murdered by his illegitimate half brother, Henry. A few years after that, in 1375, Ibn Khaldun's rival for the ear of the Nasrid king, Ibn al-Khatib, was himself exiled to North Africa, a victim of the complex politics of the Nasrid court and Muhammad's increasing despotism. The Maghrib, however, was no safe haven for the grand old man of Andalusian letters: tragically, he was accused of heresy, the burden of the accusation being his tolerance of Sufis and his delight in philosophy. He was murdered in prison while awaiting an official decision on his fate.

There is some evidence that Ibn Khaldun had second thoughts and that, in despair over the madness of the cycles of political violence in North Africa, he did try to return to his ancestors' homeland, where he had been an honored presence not so many years before. But it was too late. Peter was dead by then, and Christian Spain was in the hands of a monarch of a very different temperament. Muhammad V was no longer a tractable young man but a middle-aged tyrant who had countenanced (or worse) the murder of his old teacher and adviser. He did not make Ibn Khaldun welcome in Granada, and so the historian crossed the strait for the last time and left the Maghrib altogether. He settled permanently in the East, where he wrote his great *Muqaddimah* (translated as the "Prolegomenon," or

"Introduction to History"), read today alongside the comparable works of writers such as Vico and Gibbon. This famous meditation on the new science of history deals with its implacable cycles, the rise, decline, and fall of societies, and then the whole thing starting up all over again, in some different and yet resonant version. The book was written far from al-Andalus, in time and in space, but its author had surely never forgotten the sights, smells, and flavor of Seville at the time of Peter the Cruel.

> *Of Pedro, King of Spain*
> *Noble and honoured Pedro, glory of Spain,*
> *Whom Fortune held so high in majesty,*
> *It is your pitiful death we must bemoan,*
> *Your brother drove you out of your country,*
> *And later, at a siege, by treachery*
> *You were betrayed, and brought to his pavilion*
> *There to be killed by his own hand; when he*
> *Succeeded to your revenues and kingdom.*
>
> —Geoffrey Chaucer, *The Canterbury Tales*

In Seville, in 1364, Peter had welcomed the envoy from Granada in the reception halls of the new Alcazar, built on the foundations of the fortified palaces the Almohads had left when they abandoned their capital a century before, in 1248. For the last hundred years the Castilians had loved Seville and made it their own. They had made the imposing Great Mosque, built by the Almohads in the last part of the twelfth century, their own cathedral, and prayed in it. Just as his Muslim predecessors had done, Peter could take the private passageway in the Alcazar, where he worked and lived, straight to his prayers in the House of God. Did Ibn Khaldun accompany the royal entourage through that private passageway into the cathedral? Or did he instead go in through the public entrance, the charming enclosed grove of orange trees with the Visigothic, or possibly even Roman, fountain for ablutions at its center? Either way, the Muslim visitor would have observed that mosque now being used, naturally, as a Christian sanctuary.

For the past century—in some places even two centuries—the policy and practice of the Castilian monarchs had been not to destroy the monuments of the Islamic past but to appropriate them and write over them lightly. The mosque of the Almohads of Seville was now Peter's church, just as the one in Cordoba had been made over into the cathedral of Alfonso X. In Cordoba, in the last half of the thirteenth century, Alfonso had hired the best Mudejar craftsmen that money could buy. These Muslims who had stayed on in Christian Cordoba had built him a small, aesthetically harmonious altar and a crypt within the Great Mosque, the greatest of the Islamic world's Great Mosques and itself a brilliant testimony to the various cultures it was replacing. This aspect of the Islamic past for these Christians was a bed to build on, to be layered, continued, reinterpreted. There is a telling, if perhaps apocryphal, anecdote about the Castilians who took control of so much of the peninsula during the thirteenth century, the people who were Peter's ancestors, both literally as well as in their cultural vision. According to the story, Alfonso X, not yet king in his own right but leading armies for his father Ferdinand III, heard that the panicked and outraged Muslims of Seville, those who stayed when the Almohads decamped, were threatening to pull down the minaret rather than let the Christians have it. Alfonso was said to have prevented this by threatening to put the good Muslim citizens of Seville to death if they attempted any such thing. So the Great Mosque of Seville survived, minaret and all, and it was there that Peter worshiped. (It was almost certainly where Alfonso had heard his last mass, since he had died besieged in Seville.) The imposing mosque occupied the same extensive space as the current cathedral, which is the largest Gothic cathedral in the world, built on the mosque's foundations after it was torn down in the fifteenth century. But, as if still cowed by Alfonso's threat, the Sevillians never tore down—although they did alter and add to—the famous minaret, now called "la Giralda," which survives as the bell tower of the cathedral and one of the city's premier tourist sites.*

Many of the old palaces the Almohads had abandoned more than a hundred years before were sufficiently in disrepair that Peter rebuilt them, salvaging bits here and there and building on the older foundations and outer walls. But Peter rebuilt much of the complex from scratch, and in a style different from both the Almohad style dominant in Seville and the older Umayyad style of the cathedral of Cordoba. The new palaces Ibn Khaldun saw and worked in during his stay in Seville had been built to Peter's own taste, in the image he had of himself and of his stature and legacy. Peter's new palaces smelled of the fresh plaster of the Nasrids because he had brought in workmen and craftsmen from Granada. For several generations these craftsmen had been at work on the extravagantly ornamented buildings in the palatine city called the Alhambra. Now visitors to Peter's court, from Ibn Khaldun's appearance on, could marvel at the plasterwork, exquisitely laid on the walls and ceilings and then carved out like stalactites. Even there, in the Christian capital, the surfaces were written over with the language of the God of the Quran, as it was throughout the Alhambra.

The new vogue in architecture was marked by a relentless use of what we now call arabesques. Ibn Khaldun must have been struck by the bittersweet irony of the poor Nasrids having become the ultimate arbiters of the new styles of Christian Spain.

---

*The twin of this magnificent example of Almohad architecture is a minaret called the Kutubiyya, built in Marrakech at about the end of the twelfth century, at about the same time as the Great Mosque of Seville was built.

The Nasrids, Ibn Khaldun understood, were for several generations now turned back onto themselves and their solitude, lonely
in their knowledge that where once there had been a vast and
much visited caliphate, an ornament for all the world to admire,
there now remained only them, alone and cornered.
Exceptionally in the Islamic history of the peninsula, Nasrid
Granada was almost entirely Muslim, devoid of dhimmi communities, no Christians, a handful of Jews. In stark consciousness of their belatedness, the Nasrids made ornament and ornamentation their last will and testament. Walls plastered in Arabic
spoke the language of God himself. Everywhere one looks, there
is writing on the walls in the Alhambra, speaking out from the
past and to the future. The walls are covered with the incanta-
tion "There is no victor but God," obsessively repeated, and with
the words of the Quran, but one can also read there the poetry
of the Nasrid courts, so that the last chapter of Arabic poetry in
Spain is literally written into the walls of this memory palace.

It was this look, this aesthetic, that was coveted and then
re-created by the powerful Castilian monarch of Spain, this
brand-new style born out of a mentality of siege; and that is what
his Alcazar in Seville looks like, down to and including the
Arabic *Wa la ghalib ill Allah*—"There is no victor but God"—
adorning the walls. And if he had gone to Toledo, another of
Peter's cities, Ibn Khaldun would have seen similar Christian
memory palaces. Toledo was, after all, the place where ersatz
Arabic writing had been used to decorate the Church of San
Roman, at the top of the highest hill, a hundred years or more
after Peter's ancestor Alfonso had taken it as the new Christian
capital.

Toledo, 1364

In the fourteenth century, not only the Christians loved the Alhambra style, the look that began by covering every possible surface with decoration and the writing that had become decoration itself. The Jews of Christian Spain, especially the Jews of Christian Toledo, also admired it. Peter himself preferred Seville as his home, but Toledo too was an ancestral and much loved home for the Castilian monarchs. Its thriving Jewish community was so wealthy and so culturally in the avant-garde that they were the first outside Granada to put up a building in the new Nasrid style. Since there is no record of Peter's having been to see the Alhambra in person, it is quite possible that it was that building in Toledo, constructed by Peter's own treasurer and adviser, that opened his eyes to the expressive power of the style.

In 1360, Samuel Halevi Abulafia had built a synagogue in the Nasrid look for himself and his community, filled and over-filled with that otherworldly stucco relief and, of course, with writing intricately, brilliantly, carved into the sparkling white plaster. Some of the writing in this synagogue is in Hebrew. But some of it, surprisingly, is in the Arabic that was still the nostalgically beloved language of the cultured Jews in Castile and still their everyday language, a mother tongue alongside Castilian. It had been many years since Jews had lived in the sort of cultural and political well-being afforded by the Umayyads and then by most of the taifas. But the vivid memory of that heritage was inscribed onto the walls of this expensive and ambitious synagogue, whose Arabic writing includes verses from the Quran.

Abulafia's new Toledan synagogue was miles away, in its lavish ornamentation, from the severe thirteenth-century synagogue just a stone's throw down the street. Santa Maria la Blanca (as it eventually would be rechristened and thereafter known) had been built in the comparatively puritanical style of the

Almohads, the same repressive Muslim regime that had expelled the Jews from many Andalusian cities and driven many of them to cities in the Christian north, such as Toledo. The Jews seemed to regard the Almohads as mere avatars of the real culture that had made their community prosperous and that had shaped its aesthetic sensibilities. But this new synagogue, Abulafia's, was in the style of Granada, a legendary memory palace for the Jews too. The Nasrid palaces that were the inspiration had themselves been built at the top of a hill that had first been laid out as a fortified citadel by the Jewish nagid Samuel and his son Joseph. By the middle of the fourteenth century, the memory of a Jewish vizier and the poetry he wrote in the new Hebrew was a deeply buried layer in Granada itself, which had become a sadly insular Islamic polity devoid of either Jewish or Christian citizens. But the memory among the Jews was still vivid, so much so that when the wealthy and well-connected Samuel Halevi Abulafia decided to build a sumptuous new synagogue in the heart of the extensive Jewish quarter of Toledo, he wanted it to speak the languages the Jews had once shared with Andalusian Islam.

In building his synagogue so that it spoke the new language of the Nasrids loudly and clearly, Abulafia was not only adding forcefully to the Jews' nostalgia for Sefarad—a nostalgia that would grow as the years went by, and which remains strong even in the modern world. Although he could not know it, this impressive synagogue was also a last testament, both his own and for the Toledan Jews. The irascible Peter, for whom Abulafia worked, soon became convinced that the vast expenditures on the synagogue had been embezzled from the royal treasury and had him executed; a few years after that, Peter's successor (and half brother) fomented the severe anti-Jewish riots that nearly overnight decimated Toledo's venerable Jewish community. But when Abulafia built the synagogue he was also being stylish—and thus very Castilian, very Toledan, since a sense of the importance of style had been at the heart of the Castilian tradition since 1085. The Jewish community had been centrally involved with the Castilians in every question of style, in the development, cultivation, and translation of all its languages, old and new. The community that would pray in Abulafia's synagogue understood, both as Castilians and as Jews, that style was a marriage of intellectual and artistic languages and had no respect for the narrow dialects of religious ideology. During the previous century, Alfonso X had shaped Toledo so that its citizens could see themselves as the most stylish of Andalusians, or at least the most able to claim as their heritage the traditions of advanced learning and cultural brilliance that had belonged to the Muslim Andalusians before them. Those were the traditions that had startled Latin Christendom, from the time that Gerbert of Aurillac had first taken news of the astrolabe from the precincts of the Umayyad caliphate north, beyond the Pyrenees. Remarkably, at the time that Abulafia built his synagogue in the 1360s, there were still brilliant men from the north writing books about astrolabes.

Ibn Khaldun was not, of course, the only visitor from abroad to see Christians worshiping in old mosques and to smell the still-fresh plaster of the brand-new palaces built to store the complex memories of al-Andalus. Many of these foreign visitors came not from North Africa, as he did, but from the northern precincts of Europe. At that time, those northern states were often intricately involved with the kingdoms south of the Pyrenees through marriage and other political ties. Neither the marriage bonds nor the byzantine politics of the time respected national borders or divisions as we know and imagine them. Many of those northern visitors would gladly have spent time in Peter's Toledo, drawn there by the smell not of the wet plaster from Abulafia's synagogue but of books, some old and some new, the smell of the most valuable library of half-hidden wisdom, science, and magic in Europe.

The intellectual descendants of the eleventh-century pioneers who had first made the arduous trip to Toledo to beg, steal, or borrow enough Arabic for translations of the first treatises on mathematics and astrolabes could now stay in Paris or London and buy many of those same books at home, and many in modernized versions. But even so, a trip to the original library, to Toledo itself, would have been a rare treat. This would have been especially so for a man who already knew and loved the books that had come from there, most of all the astronomy books and star charts that had poured out of the Toledo of Alfonso the Learned, a man who would himself eventually write a book on the astrolabe. Geoffrey Chaucer began his *Treatise on the Astrolabe* in 1391 but left it unfinished, with only two of its projected five parts completed. His sense of the culture of the astrolabe was, like that of Peter the Venerable, not acquired only from books: he had traveled into the territories of Peter the Cruel in 1366, two years after Ibn Khaldun had been there, and three years before Peter was murdered by Henry of Trastamara.

Chaucer was there because of the terrible civil wars between Peter and Henry, because the English were strong allies of Peter against the Trastamara pretender, and because of the extraordinarily tangled web of relations between the Castilian monarch and the two strongest men in Chaucer's life. First, there was Edward, the "Black Prince," who was perhaps Peter's most important ally, and who was himself in and out of Spain throughout his brilliant military career. It was often in Edward's service that Chaucer traveled throughout Europe, and in 1366 it was once again to do his diplomatic work. But, beyond that, Chaucer had a far more intimate connection to Peter the Cruel through his own brother-in-law, John of Gaunt, duke of Lancaster, hero of Shakespeare's plays on the early years of English history. Not many years after Peter's death, John himself became the ferocious and bitter rival to the Trastamara claims to the Castilian throne, through his marriage to Peter's daughter, Constance. Chaucer's alliances with the Castilian Peter—whom he called "noble and honoured," not "cruel"—and with Peter's line were thus eventually intimate and familiar as well as political and diplomatic.

In *The Canterbury Tales,* in the Monk's Tale, we find the great English writer's tribute to this man whose political fortunes Chaucer was aware of at every turn and even directly involved with from time to time. Alas, the rest of the story of Chaucer's trip to Spain is deeply shrouded, and the cause of Peter of Castile lost too, although there are some enduring emblems of the ties that linked the beauties of Granada of the Nasrids to the English, through their common ally, Peter: one of Peter's gifts to the Black Prince, a ruby later described by Elizabeth I as being as large as a tennis ball, and which Peter himself had received as a gift from the grateful Nasrid prince Muhammad, ended up in the English crown. But the beauties Chaucer may have seen are not so directly on display, and we don't even know in which of Peter's cities Chaucer met with him, so we don't know which of his palaces he might have seen and slept in. But virtually everywhere in Peter's kingdom was the musty smell of old books that Chaucer already knew well, the books of the old Arabic libraries translated into languages men like Chaucer could read, as well as the fresh smell of new stucco, carved out in arabesques and in Arabic.

In the Alhambra

Granada, 1492

Their highnesses and their successors will ever afterwards allow [the Granadans] to live in their own religion, and not permit their mosques to be taken from them, nor their minarets nor their muezzins, nor will they interfere with the pious foundations or endowments which they have for such purposes, nor will they disturb the uses and customs which they observe.

—from chapter 6 of the Agreements of
Capitulation of the City of Granada

O N JANUARY 2, 1492, THE RULERS OF SPAIN, WHO WOULD EVER after be known by papal decree as the Catholic Monarchs, walked up the steep and heavily shaded hills that led to the palatine city of the Alhambra. It was an arduous climb to the top, and the palaces that overlooked the valley below were heavily fortified. But the king and queen of Castile and Aragon—distant cousins descended from the rival half brothers Peter the Cruel and Henry of Trastamara, she Peter's great-great-granddaughter, he Henry's great-great-grandson— faced no opposition. This taking of the Muslim stronghold was purely ceremonial, since the grounds were already in the hands of the Castilian military. Dressed in their finest clothes, their

Moorish garb, as the chroniclers described it, the Castilian queen
and her Aragonese consort walked into the overwrought rooms
the Nasrids had crafted and proclaimed this place their new *casa
real,* the royal residence of the monarchs of Spain. In playing out
that scene, dressed in their Arab finery and moving into palaces
they treated as if they had owned them forever, Isabella and
Ferdinand revealed just how thoroughly they were the cultural
heirs to so much of what that place represented. Isabella had
been crowned queen in Seville, and she knew the Alcazar, her
family's ancestral home, well; when she saw the Alhambra for the
first time, it was through eyes that recognized the powerful orig-
inals of her own palaces, and with an aesthetic sensibility that
was intimately familiar with the look of the rooms and the sound
of the courtyard fountains. The guarantees of religious freedom
offered by these victorious Christian monarchs to the Muslim inhabitants of Granada may have seemed as reasonable as the fact
that the monarchs were outfitted in the fashion of the
Granadans. Isabella had yet to open the closets in the Alhambra,
her new home, but her ancestors had been rummaging through
Andalusian chests for hundreds of years, and in many ways she
knew how to dress the part. There were reasons to be suspicious
of the protections offered to Muslims, of course. But there were
also reasons to have hope.

The Agreements of Capitulation that were the terms of surrender of this city that had been a Muslim stronghold for the
previous 250 years had been agreed to several months before, in
the fall of 1491, in a secret arrangement between the last of the
Nasrids, named Muhammad XI but known as Boabdil, and the
Catholic Monarchs. There was no bloodshed in the city and no
damage done to the precious palaces. The well-known expression "the Moor's last sigh" refers to Boabdil's own grief on leaving Granada, city of the Nasrids for nearly three centuries. The
little anecdote recounted over the years finds Boabdil sighing
with regret on his way out of Granada, only to be chastised by

his mother, who observes tartly that he should not cry like a woman for a place he would not defend like a man. But it is not a simple matter whether, at that historical moment, Boabdil should have fought on "like a man." By then the cards were so stacked against Granada—and against Boabdil himself, whose own son was a hostage—that surrender was inevitable.

Boabdil handed over the keys to the Alhambra, his ancestral home, to Ferdinand and Isabella in the January 2 ceremony. Who can fathom what he really believed would happen to those he left behind, to the many thousands of Muslims of Granada? What was not inevitable, despite our own historical perspective, was the series of events that followed Isabella and Ferdinand's triumphal march up the hill. Within a fairly short period, the Catholic Monarchs abrogated the Agreements of Capitulation that they and Boabdil had signed. The terms of surrender of the city, and thus the kingdom, had conspicuously included the provision that Muslims would be allowed to practice their faith openly and without harassment in the new Christian state, of which the agreements proclaimed they were full citizens. This was hardly a revolutionary notion; Muslims had been living in newly Christian states in this same land for hundreds of years, as the political landscape had shifted in its complex ways. Iberian Christians had by and large absorbed the principles of the dhimma the Umayyads had brought to Iberia, and in places like Toledo—the heart of the Church of Spain and one of the capitals of the Castilian monarchs—both Jewish and Mudejar communities had not only carried on but were vital parts of the cultural makeup. Of course, problems had arisen from those circumstances, and Mudejars had been ill treated, or worse; crises were often precipitated by their rebellions. The religious authorities on both sides regularly decreed it unacceptable and unholy for Muslims to live under Christian sovereignty. But the sometimes fragile arrangements had nonetheless endured as a deeply ingrained part of the complex culture of the time and place. The Muslims played vital social, economic, and cultural roles in the Christian polities that few except the uncompromisingly ideological imagined could be done without, and there are all sorts of indications that Christian Spaniards across the political spectrum considered the Muslims of their own territories to be Spaniards like themselves. Over the nearly five centuries since the Umayyad caliphate had broken apart, the Mudejars had become part of the peninsula's social and cultural landscape, as visible and common as the buildings they had helped build throughout Christian Spain. But for most Granadans, the northern lands may as well have been thousands of miles away instead of just beyond the snowcapped mountains they looked out on every day. For these Muslims, Boabdil knew, the changes required would be difficult, since they, unlike their antecedents under the Umayyads and during the times of the taifas, had scarcely ever lived with Christians, or even Jews.

Once they took the keys to the palatine city from Boabdil, the Christians for a time behaved as their medieval heritage, especially their Castilian heritage, had taught them. They not only moved into the Nasrid palaces, but the pious Isabella had the mosque consecrated and began to worship there. These were acts of open-armed embrace of their patrimony, unthinking acceptance of the familiarity, and not the foreignness, of places where Arabic was written on every wall, and of a culture where a ritual wave of the hand could make a mosque into a perfectly fitting church. Their royal patronage, and that of most of the Spanish Christian monarchs who followed them, kept the lavish memory palaces of the Nasrids relatively well protected over the years, and they survive as the best-preserved examples of Islamic palaces from the Middle Ages anywhere in the Islamic world. But the repudiation of the agreement and the harsh persecution of the Muslims that followed meant that within a short time the gorgeous language that covered nearly every inch of that royal house became a forbidden language—and those who could read it were decreed not real Spaniards. The Muslims were forced into conversions and called Moriscos; the reading of books in Arabic was prohibited and many of the books themselves were burned.

The edict expelling the Jews from Christian Spain was signed by the new inhabitants of the Alhambra just three months after the capitulation of Granada. Did the Catholic Monarchs know that the Nasrid palaces had themselves been built on foundations laid by the prosperous Jewish community of the tenth and eleventh centuries, when the vizier to the Islamic taifa, and the leader of its armies, was the great poet Samuel the Nagid? The signing of the Edict of Expulsion on March 31, 1492, caused great consternation and despair within every segment of the Jewish community, and the obvious shock it created belies the many versions of the story that proclaim that this, too, was a long time coming. Nowhere was this event seen more apocalyptically than among the best-informed circles, where Jews and New Christians — the latter the name for those who had converted from Judaism to Christianity — were still working at the highest levels of the Christian government, as they had for centuries. Long-term and often intimate advisers to Isabella and Ferdinand suddenly found themselves in the extraordinary situation of having to plead for the right simply to remain in their own country, let alone to be able to serve at court as trusted counselors.

The most eloquent and persuasive of the Jews with direct access to the monarchs, Isaac Abravanel, managed all that could be managed. In his near cosmic dismay at this imminent tragedy, the loss of a homeland where Jews had prospered as nowhere else, Abravanel found refuge in liturgical symbolism. He was able to negotiate a small and clearly iconic postponement of the final day for the Jews to leave Spain, from July 31, the original date set (four months after the proclamation was issued), to August 2. The second of August happened to correspond, in

1492, to the ninth of Ab in the Jewish calendar, the anniversary of the destruction of the Temple in Jerusalem and thus the beginning of the first diaspora. Although some later historians have disputed Abravanel's own account of this crucial realignment of dates, the truth is that Abravanel—and certainly not he alone—understood the scope of the tragedy as one unparalleled in Jewish history since the destruction of the Temple. Since he was unable to persuade Isabella and Ferdinand to rescind the expulsion, this most influential of the Jews at court engineered it so that at least history would understand the depth and breadth of the loss, by recalling the date of this second diaspora when commemorating the first. Abravanel wanted it to remain forever clear that the expulsion from Spain, called Sefarad, marked the cataclysmic end of a long sojourn in a promised land.

On the other side of the ninth of Ab, the Sephardim, the Jews of Spain, were scattered far and wide, and they took what little they could gather in the four short months allotted them to pack and leave. Among their most precious possessions carried into the diaspora were those most purely symbolic of their deep attachments: the keys to their houses, and the fifteenth-century Castilian they spoke. Those who left included men of the stature of Abravanel, who would later understand the tragedy in apocalyptic terms and begin predicting the imminent coming of the Messiah. There is something especially poignant about his laments on the terrible exile of the Jews, written from Safed, in northern Palestine. Because of the exodus from Spain, Safed became a famous kabbalist center, a city on whose streets the Romance vernacular spoken by the Jewish exiles was heard, what they called Ladino, meaning Latin—that is to say, not Hebrew, not Arabic—and what we recognize as a form of old Spanish. But the sound of the language of the lost land was nowhere near an adequate comfort for Abravanel and others of that first generation expelled from Spain. For them, Palestine itself, with its crown of Jerusalem, was far from what they felt was their true promised land, Sefarad. That was the fate of those who chose this most painful of exiles: to never again see the houses to which they kept the keys, memory palaces that could be held in the palm of the hand. But there was a practiced alternative in the conversions of convenience, something Maimonides himself had defended, and many chose that path in 1492 and in the years following. It was a path opened wide to them, since the stipulations of the expulsion specifically exempted converted Jews, called either Conversos, converts, or (more disparagingly, from a vulgar word for "hog") Marranos. There are no clear or undisputed numbers here. Some say most left, some say most stayed, converting, or pretending to convert—and these last, and their descendants, and their complex adaptations to necessarily half-secret lives, became parts of the fabric of Spanish Christian society, both in Spain and in places not yet dreamed of in the first months of 1492.

Luis de Torres left the port of Palos on August 3, 1492. The weeks and days leading to August 2, the Hebrew ninth of Ab, had been dolorous and chaotic, with thousands of Jews desperately doing what they could to pull their material affairs together enough to be able to leave. Thousands of others were just as frantically being baptized: the decree issued in Granada had stipulated that the Jews' conversion to Christianity was its objective, and so baptized Jews were entitled to remain. As with the guarantees of religious tolerance for the Muslims, this promise, too, would prove illusory, since nearly all New Christians were eventually suspected of bad faith in their forced conversions and then persecuted for that. But on August 3, the last of those whose choice had been to keep their faith openly but abandon their homeland were leaving, on this first day of the second diaspora, and every port was still overflowing.

Luis de Torres left along with one of the men who had

actually been present at the signing of the Edict of Expulsion. They were together on one of three ships that left that morning from Palos, a port downriver from Seville but not nearly as big and convenient as that of Cadiz, eighty miles east along the coast. But beggars, on such a day, could not be choosers, and so Christopher Columbus left with his three ships, and his Jewish translator, perhaps officially baptized so that he could accompany the Spanish expedition, perhaps not. In either case, Torres was taken along to speak the language that Columbus expected would be understood where he thought he was going: surely the lingua franca of the Indies would be Arabic, as it was in the rest of the infidel but civilized world. One scarcely knows whether to laugh or cry at the layers of irony in the scene that resulted from these tragicomic circumstances and assumptions. Arriving, eventually, on a large island that showed some signs and promise of being the place he hoped to find, and hearing the people encountered speaking of a "Cubanacan," Columbus took that to be their referring to the "Gran Can" (or Great Khan) he was looking for, and sent Torres on the first official diplomatic visit between the Europeans and the peoples of the American New World. In the hinterlands of that island, Torres found not the lord of the Mongols but a tribal chief of Cuba. The two men, the Taino chief and the Arabic-speaking Jew, struck up some sort of conversation.

The conversations on the other side of the great divide that is 1492 would all take place, sooner or later, in a universe where translators were a dim and dangerous memory, where Castilian had been rechristened "Old Christian," or just plain Cristiano, where it was *the* language, not *a* language. During the summer of that extraordinary year, while Columbus and thousands of Jews were packing their bags for places they could only imagine, the first grammar book of one of the languages of modern Europe was published. The *Gramatica de la lengua castellana* ("Grammar of the Castilian Language") was dedicated to Queen Isabella by its author, Antonio de Nebrija, who saw his work not as an old-fashioned palace, and certainly not as a memory palace, but as a very modern edifice. The old age of translators was at an end; at hand was the new age of a new empire, with a new language to replace all the old ones. The old wars had been won, Nebrija wrote in the preface to his famous book, the old religions put aside, and the old languages translated. "The only thing left to cultivate is peace."

Somewhere in La Mancha

1605

*T*HE STREETS OF TOLEDO ARE DESOLATE, GHOSTS OF WHAT THEY
had once been. A man has come in from the country-
side, looking for a book, a book whose name he doesn't
yet know but which he is sure will have a lost history in it. He
has roamed the narrow and winding streets of this once library
like city, perhaps as far as this hilly city's highest point, and perhaps he has snooped around the Church of San Roman, at the
crown of this now abandoned old capital. But in the end he
knows the best place to hunt such things down is in the former
Jewish quarter, although no Jews have lived there for a hundred
years. Or at least no Jews admitting to being Jews, a very different thing. Sometimes it's just the trick of saying you are one
thing when others say you are something else. When people
want to say something is a windmill but you know perfectly well
it is a giant, who is to say otherwise?

The old Jewish quarter is full of such tricks, this man knows. You walk down the street and see the Convent of Santa Maria la Blanca. They say that inside it looks like a mosque and that, like the Church of San Roman, it seems to be held up by rows of horseshoe-shaped arches. Everyone who has been as far south as Cordoba has seen how they hold up the cathedral there, the endless rows. But everyone in that part of town says it was really once a synagogue, back in the days when Jews could pray there openly as Jews, when there were a dozen synagogues crowded into that part of town. And then there is the magnificent Church of the Transito, with its carved white walls, farther down the same broad main street that runs along the walls at the edge of the mountainside. All the good Christians, old and new, who pray there now—mostly the rich ones, for this is a sumptuous place—say it looks like the royal palaces in Granada, and everyone recognizes, although they pretend not to notice, the handwriting all over the walls. And they say that this is where the rich Jews once prayed, the ones who used to know how to read the writing all over the walls, both kinds of writing.

The man is wandering down these streets because it is now the neighborhood of the rag sellers. The old neighborhood of books and the men who wrote books and translated books for the world has become a place where the books no one is supposed to read anymore are turned into pulp. The man sees a boy with a pile of papers he is trying to sell to an old silk merchant, and he can tell they are written in Arabic. It is a dangerous language to know how to read; no one understands it anymore except the Old Muslims who, like the Old Jews, go around saying they aren't that at all, that they are New Christians. But who is to believe that? Who in this world ever says that he is what he seems to be? And who seems to be what he no doubt really is?

Something about that pile of papers has caught the man's

attention. Could that really be it, the book he has been searching for, about to be sold to be made into rags? Since he can't read it himself, or at least would not want to be seen out on those mean streets reading it, he needs to find what he calls a *morisco aljamiado,* one of those New Christians who can still read that old language. Moriscos ("little Moors") is what they call the Old Muslims, all those who were supposed to have changed themselves; they are still all over Spain, just like the Old Jews. But everyone knows, or everyone thinks they know, what people really are and aren't, everyone really knows, at the end of the day, the difference between giants and windmills. And those Moriscos aren't really Christian at all, which is why they can still read the language they call Aljamiado, whatever that means. Why not just call it Arabic and have done with it?

The man has to do little more than turn around in this neighborhood—it is called the Alcana, and everyone says that in the old days the name was a word in one of those languages that aren't supposed to exist anymore—and he finds one of these Moriscos. The man seems to be winking at us because, as he says, it isn't really hard at all to find a translator for that language in this place. "Even if I had wanted one for a better and older language I would have found one," he confides. Everyone knows, don't they, that the old Jews can still read Hebrew, just like the Old Muslims can still read Arabic. It just goes to show how people say they are one thing when really they are another—who can tell the difference?

The man asks the Morisco he has found to begin translating for him. It's a risky thing, to be standing out there in the middle of the street reading that forbidden language, but both the man in search of his book and the Morisco seem momentarily oblivious, in the excitement of a possible discovery. Let us listen to the man himself tell the rest of the story. It is his story, after all, and no one has ever told it better. We pick up where he has handed the book to the Morisco, out there on the street:

He opened it in the middle, and after reading a little began to laugh. I asked him to tell me what he was laughing at, and he answered that it was something written in the margin of the book by way of a note. I asked him to tell me what it was and, still laughing, he answered: "This is what is written in the margin: 'They say that Dulcinea del Toboso, so often mentioned in this history, was the best hand at salting pork of any woman in all La Mancha.'"

When I heard the name of Dulcinea del Toboso I was surprised and astonished, for I immediately surmised that these books must contain the story of Don Quixote. With this idea I pressed him to read the beginning, and when he did so, making an extempore translation from the Arabic into Castilian, he said that the heading was: History of Don Quixote de la Mancha, written by Cide Hamete Benengeli, Arabic historian. I needed great caution to conceal the joy I felt when the title of the book reached my ears. Running to the silk merchant, I bought all the lad's parchments and papers for half a *real*, but if he had had any sense and known how much I wanted them, he might very well have demanded and got more than six *reals* from the sale. I then went off with the Morisco into the cloister of the cathedral, and asked him to translate for me into Castilian everything in those books that dealt with Don Quixote, adding nothing and omitting nothing; and I offered to pay him whatever he asked.

Miguel de Cervantes published the first part of what is arguably the most canonical of all novels, *Don Quixote de la Mancha,* in 1605. Almost immediately the novel became a phenomenal bestseller. Its second part appeared in 1615, on the heels of a spurious sequel that had appeared to take advantage of the extraordinary popularity, and thus the sales, of the original novel. The opening of Cervantes' own continuation of his characters' adventures, his own part two, begins with a half-ironic denunciation of the pretender to the authorship of a Quixote that is not, of course, authentic. It is a historical prank worthy of the great Spanish novelist, and some have been tempted to note that if Avellaneda and his rogue sequel had not existed, Cervantes might have had to make them up. Thanks to this intervening impostor, Cervantes ended up pondering more openly than ever the problem of fiction's relationship to reality that had driven the original novel and made it such a runaway bestseller in Spain and abroad, especially in the thriving colonies of the New World.

Among the other ironies that the second part of *Don Quixote* rather painfully puts before us, perhaps none is as acute as the strictly historical one that reflects back on this novel's original conceit, the conceit recounted in that early chapter when our narrator has looked for and then found the story of Don Quixote de la Mancha. Cervantes' complex fiction is that the novel is actually the work of an Arab historian, Cide Hamete Benengeli, that the book that contains the true story of Don Quixote de la Mancha was written in Arabic, that it was once lost but then found in Toledo's now bedraggled old Jewish quarter, among the piles of rags about to be recycled into new paper, and that it was then translated for him by a Morisco who happened to be wandering the streets of Toledo and could still read the old language. But in 1615 there were no Moriscos left in Spain. Between 1605, when the novel *Don Quixote de la Mancha* first appeared, and 1615, when Cervantes published his sequel, the Spanish government had expelled the Moriscos, or New Christians, thus ending a century of forced conversions of the Muslims who in 1492 had been guaranteed religious freedom. The Quixote-like irony of the political events lay in the government's declaration that those conversions, which had been required by the authorities when they abrogated the dhimma-like guarantees of religious freedom in the Capitulation Agreements of 1492, were not good enough.

Cervantes' 1605 *Quixote*, which is part one of the complete novel, was written in full historical consciousness of the broad and complex tragedy represented by the Toledan scene. There, the glory of Toledo's—and Spain's—past as the great center of interfaith confluence and as the nonpareil center of translation for all of Europe is alluded to through its ruin, which was the all-too-visible reality by the turn of the seventeenth century. The manuscripts and books that had once been the heart and soul of Toledo's vast riches were so devalued that, if they turned up on the streets, it was so they could be turned into rags. And those were the relatively few that had survived the fires. The book-burning that had begun at the turn of the previous century, after the capitulation of Granada, is reenacted in another highly allu-sive and famous scene of Cervantes' exceptional novel, in chap-ter 5, the famous "Inquisition of the Books." It was not just the books, of course, but the knowledge of the languages of those books, Arabic and Hebrew, that had disappeared in Cervantes' time—the very skills that had once made knowledge and the transmission of knowledge and learning possible, and that had made Toledo the center of the universe for many civilized peo-ple. These were precisely the skills one would need, inside the brilliant universe of Cervantes' novel, to be able to read the only surviving manuscript of that very same novel.

Cervantes' stage was crowded with versions of the question of whether things could ever be what they appear to be, what they claim to be, what we want them to be, what others may need them to be. This theme, so intricately explored throughout the novel, is also neatly summarized in the persona of the trans-lator of the Arabic manuscript that contains the "true history" of Don Quixote. The anonymous *morisco aljamiado* was the near perfect historical embodiment of the proposition that a mutual shaping of reality and fiction lies at the heart of this novel. The Moriscos were the descendants of the last freely practicing Muslims of what became a unified Christian Spain in 1492. By 1499, the guarantees of religious freedom of the Capitulation

Accords signed by Ferdinand and Isabella in Granada had been violently rescinded. Spain's cultural landscape, as a result, was radically redrawn by the forced conversions of the Muslims and the public burning of books written in Arabic, all throughout the following century. This was also the century during which the New World was being explored, and then colonized, by colonists overwhelmingly from the southern provinces that had once been the heartland of al-Andalus. During the subsequent hundred years (a century whose name the great Spanish intellectual Americo Castro thought ought to be *La Edad conflictiva,* "the Conflictive Age," instead of the more conventional "Golden Age" used by Hispanists), the Moriscos both were and were not Muslims, just like the Conversos, their Jewish counterparts.

Many Spaniards, of every stripe and every background, were thus caught up living in a world of fun-house mirrors created by a whole series of edicts requiring that people profess transparent falsenesses, a state of self-destructive madness worthy of Cervantes' creative literary genius. The claims of New Christian identity that were required of the Muslims, forced on them under pain of death or expulsion, were subsequently suspected of being false, and punished accordingly. Their once sacred language was now prohibited and its books burned, and thus slowly but surely lost and replaced with this other thing we find in the pivotal chapter 9 of *Quixote,* when the narrator finds the Morisco he describes as *aljamiado.* In the sixteenth century, this was the last vestige of the language that had once been the marker, in medieval Spain, of culture itself. Even though it looks like Arabic to those who cannot read it—and because of that it was often called Arabic in a universe in which people could no longer read it—Aljamiado was not really Arabic at all, but the Arabic script used for writing the Romance vernacular that had become the native and often only language of these Spaniards.

Aljamiado is another Quixote-like twist, not unlike the ersatz Arabic decor of the Church of San Roman, at the top of

Toledo—although it was born of something quite removed from the Christian admiration for its beauty that made Arabic writing the fitting ornament for a new Christian church in the twelfth century. Much like the Ladino spoken by the Spanish Jews living in permanent exile from Sefarad, Aljamiado was Castilian, with its admixture of Arabic expressions and words (just as Ladino has its Hebrewisms), but Castilian nonetheless, dressed up, disguised as Arabic and written in the beautiful Arabic script that evoked something that was no longer real. This was the native language of the poor Moriscos, many of whom were indeed crypto-Muslims, trying hard to remain Muslims and keep their Arabic but obviously unable to do so very successfully in a universe where the language of books, and even people, ended up in bonfires. Aljamiado, like the Moriscos themselves, is part of the Cervantine repertoire of tragic identity tricks. Cervantes did not have to invent this one, however, because, as with Avellaneda and his rogue "part two," historical reality provided it for him. It is only the appearance of Arabic, but no less a danger than the real thing. That the Moriscos proudly and tenaciously hung on to their pretend Arabic was an act of quixotic faith—or madness. They risked being caught reading and writing what could well be taken to be Arabic and so might have had mortal consequences, even though beneath that dress-up, that layer of play-acting, the language was what they called *cristiano,* after all. Poignantly, the exiled Sephardim spoke their *cristiano* or "Latin" too, and Ladino, their own fifteenth-century Spanish, has been spoken in the Sephardic diaspora ever since.

The very foundations of the modern novel and the sort of complex literary questions that will be played out by *Quixote*'s progeny—from Emma Bovary to the magician-storytellers of what we call magic realism—are carefully crafted as one of the very last memory palaces of medieval Spain. The anonymous translator of the Arabic book, the lost and found "true history" that Cervantes was looking for, is one of the novel's most exemplary characters because he is the most unvarnished historical figure in it. He comes straight out of the universe that Cervantes tells us is the crux of fiction, harder to read than any fantasy: history itself. Who is that translator, after all, but a crypto-Muslim beneath a Christian veneer, decipherer of a language that is crypto-Castilian underneath an Arabic veneer? Ironically, prophetically, tragically, or all of these, by the time Cervantes publishes the second part of *Quixote,* the Moriscos with their Aljamiado writings, the pseudo-Arabic in which they wrote apocalyptic stories about the end of history, survive only inside the singular work of fiction that is Cervantes' novel.

Don Quixote is mostly remembered as someone whose relationship to reality is mediated to the point of a certain kind of madness by his apparent belief in literary texts. But Cervantes portrays a universe in which literature is not a refuge from the demands of political engagement but the most powerful weapon against certain realities, most of all against tyranny in its most extreme forms. Cervantes was, inevitably, shaped by his own history, in a time and place where book-burnings were not just literary tropes but a vivid reality. His masterpiece, which has permeated every nook and cranny of the Western canon, has given us a vision of the life-altering powers of fiction. But it is no less a vision saturated with historical reality and deeply involved with the problem of how to deal with tragic realities. *Don Quixote* has largely been read as a book obsessed with the history and functions of literature "itself," with literature as the giants that replace the "realities" of windmills, a book that somehow escapes history and the contingencies of its moment. But isn't it a Cervantes-like delusion to imagine we can read the novel outside its complex and tragic historical setting, a setting that does not have to be detailed in *Don Quixote* itself precisely because it is the everyday fare of its author and its readers, and which perhaps cannot be detailed on pain of being burned?

The problem with the Middle Ages, from the point of view

of the brave new world of the sixteenth century, was that religion *was* merely belief, not some intrinsic separation. Who can tell the difference between a Jew and a Muslim and a Christian when they're dressed the same? Among the many diabolical ingredients that went into the making of the infamous "purity of the blood" notions of Inquisitorial Spain and the New World was precisely the fact there were no visible racial differences. If Jews and Muslims didn't look different and yet their differences were crucial, then the reality of it had to be—as Don Quixote never tires of telling us—in a place where it was not visible; it was, no doubt (we can hear Quixote saying so), the work of malicious magicians, in the blood. There were quirks of behavior, of course, but those could be faked, as everyone knew. If you were a crypto-Jew, you would make an art of eating forbidden foods in public, knowing full well that not to do so would give you away and land you in the Inquisitorial fires. The highly advanced Converso and Morisco art of being able to fake eating like Christians led, eventually, to a Spanish society obsessed with the public and ritualized eating of ham as a display of Christian authenticity.

It is Cervantes' lucid and ironic understanding of this particular sleight of hand about identities and realities rampant in his society that makes the Morisco laugh out loud when he begins to read the manuscript that the narrator has found and handed to him to translate. The Morisco bursts out laughing when he arrives at the annotation about Dulcinea. The homely peasant woman, whom the wonderfully deluded Quixote has reimagined to be a lady, is, in fact—as some anonymous and perhaps denouncing hand notes in the margins of the manuscript—the "best hand at salting pork of any woman in all La Mancha." She is of good Converso stock, in other words. In sixteenth-century Spain, and thus in that masterwork of fiction that looks back on the "true history" with more or less equal measures of despair and bemusement, things are often upside down and down a rabbit hole: the more conspicuously she did all those Christian things, the more likely she was to be merely pretending to be a Christian. Or, more insidiously, and in the end more tragically, that her parents or her grandparents had pretended to be Christians, to survive. And she, well, who knows what she might be, after a while; after one generation, or after a century, or perhaps more, you forget why you lit those candles on Friday night so secretly; she can't remember whether eating all that salted pork is part of what she was supposed to be or what she was not supposed to be.

After 1492, the religions of a significant portion of Spain's population were ferociously repressed, and eventually extinguished. Forged in the bonfires of ideas, of books, and of people was the illusory conceit that there could be a pure national and religious identity, and yet this became the ultimate religion everyone had to live with. Even though the famous scene of the burning of Don Quixote's library is often discussed as if it were no more than a self-referential literary conceit, can we really forget it was written at a moment when not only books, the most flammable of the memory palaces, but also people were being burned? *Don Quixote* is thus in part a postscript to the history of a first-rate place, the most poignant lament over the loss of that universe, its last chapter, allusive, ironic, bittersweet, quixotic. It is perhaps the last, the best, the most subtle of the Spanish memory palaces. Its incomparable Castilian is the direct descendant of the Castilian first forged out of the little groups of Muslims, Christians, and Jews who worked together, in Toledo, to translate that magnificent Arabic library first into Latin and then into Castilian, which was the mother tongue of all of them and which they all spoke to each other. Aljamiado and Ladino, the forms of native Castilian spoken by the descendants of the Toledan translators, were quixotically defiant memory palaces in their own right, the languages of exile and persecution that spoke to the "Spanishness" of the Muslims and Jews.

The story of sixteenth-century Spain, which is usually told as the story of its remarkable American empire, or the story of the explosion of a modern literary aesthetic in texts that rival Shakespeare's, is no less the tragic story of the forced extinction of the two other religious cultures that had once made up Spain. But this tragic story—the story of forgetting a past in Toledo where there is a church with an homage to Arabic writing on its walls, and where there is a sumptuous fourteenth-century syna-gogue built to look like Granada's Alhambra, and where Europe's richest libraries and most industrious translators of philosophi-cal and scientific texts once sat—is inseparable from the other stories of the age that culminates with *Don Quixote de la Mancha* and the expulsions of the Moriscos. Cervantes' novel is framed, laid out for us, as the child—the stepchild—of that history, grotesquely transformed: Arabic books are now rags being ped-dled to the poor merchant in the streets of a Jewish quarter where no Jews can live; and these books will be translated by the barest remnants of a Muslim, a man who must pretend to be a Christian and who, tragically, cannot really read Arabic. The hid-den stories, and their necessarily slippery relationship to the outer stories, lie at the heart of that modern literary aesthetic of the invention of the modern novel. In equally complex and even more hidden ways, this half-garbled and half-hidden medieval world enters into the story of the American empire, first ex-plored and peopled by untold numbers of first-generation immi-grants from all the old provinces of al-Andalus. The trunks taken to the New World were filled, necessarily, with what those Andalusians were—and what they wore and what they ate and what they assumed buildings should look like. This is, of course, why the courtyards in Cuba and southern California look much like the courtyards of Cordoba, themselves complex echoes of Abd al-Rahman's homesickness: turned inward and tiled in blue and white, and if a palm tree can be managed among the lush flowers that surround the water basin, so much the better. The

Americans of the Spanish New World are descendants of all manner of good Andalusians.

Cervantes' novel is a masterpiece in part because it can be read outside the historical circumstances that shaped it, and we can understand its author's struggle to deal with the existential problem of the individual against the "real" world. It is the story of every individual, in every historical moment, to face, perhaps through and with the consolations of literature and the play of texts, the ugly realities with which he must live, and the story of what happens to ideals when they run into the brute force of disillusion. Idealism—what we call quixotic idealism, so vividly is it depicted by Cervantes—is an act of the imagination, and perhaps a doomed one, and the question on the table becomes whether this is a good thing or a bad thing. At stake is the ethical and aesthetic question of how we deal with the reality and the history around us. The modern novel is forged out of very real Inquisitorial fires, out of a historical calamity that can only be alluded to covertly, and it asks us, among other things, to contemplate the ways in which fiction can be a refuge, not only in the sense of an escape from reality but in the sense of a hiding place. As readers, we are in the end faced with the choice embedded in the novel itself: Do we use this great story to forget history or to remember it?

Epilogue: Andalusian Shards

WHAT HAPPENED? HOW AND WHY DOES A CULTURE OF tolerance fall apart? How did a people come to abandon a culture rooted in an ethic of yes and no, so readily able to love and embrace the architecture or the poetry of political enemies or religious rivals, so willing to read good books regardless of the library they came from? All the answers are themselves bundles of contradictions. The deed was both very easily done, it seems, and yet it was accomplished only with great difficulty. The outcome was all too predictable from very early on, yet it was also sudden, from one day to the next, and quite unimaginable at the time. Events could well have turned out quite differently indeed. Perhaps all that can be said with any conviction is that in the combination of spectacular successes and failures presented by this history lie tales of both warning and encouragement.

It is telling that the first significant instances of cultural puritanism in the Iberian Peninsula were imported from places with little of the Andalusian experience. The Berber Muslims of North Africa never quite understood the Andalusian application of the dhimma, and they mostly disapproved of the syncretic culture that resulted from it. From the Berber sack of Cordoba at the beginning of the eleventh century on, a variety of "reform" movements swarming northward from across the Strait of Gibraltar always threatened to remake Andalusian politics and culture in their own image of Islam. At the same time, the Berber obtuseness was mirrored by the incomprehension with which the peninsula's Christians were viewed by their coreligionists north of the Pyrenees. This was especially evident after Castile began to expand into territories that had been under Islamic rule for three and four centuries, and to incorporate their thoroughly Arabized populations, Muslims, Jews, and Mozarab Christians alike. An often stark difference in worldview separated the Roman Church as it had evolved outside the peninsula from the Christian communities within it. And these differences grew more profound in the decades and centuries that followed the Christian expansion southward. New Castile, as the conquered lands came to be called, was shaped by the relatively easy accommodation of Jewish and Muslim communities in cities like Toledo, and by the conspicuous cultivation of the flourishing Mudejar architectural style and the translation movement.

During the second half of the twelfth century and the beginning of the thirteenth, more puritanical visions of these cultures converged in Iberia. The determinedly crusading forces from Latin Christendom and the equally fanatic Berber Almohads became influential parts of the landscape and inevitably met, head-on, on the plains between New Castile and old al-Andalus, at Las Navas de Tolosa in 1212, with disastrous results for the Almohads. The effects of the long-term presence of two expansive religious ideologies, each originally foreign to the Andalusian ethic, transformed the nature of the conflicts at hand. They made religious-ideological warfare a reality, cultural orthodoxy a real possibility, and monochromatic identity a realizable ideal. And yet it must be said that neither Castilian Christians nor the Nasrid Muslims of Granada were ever vociferous advocates of these notions, although certainly both societies moved toward far more conspicuous levels of religious segregation and intolerance. They nevertheless continued to deal with each other in a universe characterized by realpolitik and by a cultural openness of the sort that led to the building of Seville's Alcazar in the middle of the fourteenth century.

A very different kind of external force may also have played a decisive negative role. The devastating Black Death, the bubonic plague that swept through Europe and decimated its populations in the middle of the fourteenth century, provides the most solid conventional explanation of the rise of religious intolerance in the Iberian Peninsula—as well as throughout the rest of medieval Europe. The nearly unimaginable upheavals and despair triggered by the sudden death of upwards of twenty percent of the overall population were most vividly described by the contemporary Italian writer Giovanni Boccaccio. *The Decameron,* his masterpiece, which was written shortly after the height of the plague, in 1348, begins with a description of the horrors of the plague. The physical ravages were terrible enough, but far more telling was the utter destruction of the social mores and civic standards that were (and are) the backbones of any civilization, the devastated communal and familial structures that followed from the fast-spreading illness. Bodies were thrown into the streets and most people died alone, abandoned by terrified and helpless family and friends. This catastrophic and wholesale undermining of the social and religious order resulted, among other things, in the scapegoating of certain minority communities—the Jews conspicuously so—as well as in the scapegoating of tolerance itself. In answering the question of why God would countenance the near-destruction of His people, it was easy enough for certain voices to claim, echoing Scripture itself, that society was surely being punished for its lack of true belief, as well as for the toleration of nonbelievers in its midst.

The "yes" of the Black Death explanation is a relatively clear one, since it was true everywhere in Europe, including Spain, that societies were significantly restructured in the aftermath of the plague, during the second half of the fourteenth century. And what rose from the ashes, by and large, were the structures of religious intolerance, as well as a notion of cultural purity that would be the hallmark of the postmedieval period. We can see clearly in retrospect that the end of the long period of prosperous Jewish life in old Spain began in the *annus terribilis* of 1391: widespread anti-Jewish rioting throughout Iberia, and especially in Castile, decimated the Jewish communities. Those who were not killed (and it is estimated that some 100,000 may have perished) either converted or fled to Muslim lands. The transformation of Toledo, not long before still called the "Jerusalem of the West," is revealing: where there had been close to a dozen prosperous synagogues, including the Alhambra-like beauty built by Abulafia scarcely thirty years before, there remained but a handful after 1391, and soon enough there were only the two that survive today. At about the same time, we see the beginnings of what would be deadly changes in attitudes toward the Islamic past of the Christian kingdoms and the Arabic heritage of Christian culture. Not long after the turn of the century, the reconsecrated Great Mosque of Seville, in which the Castilian kings had long worshiped, and in which Ferdinand III's tomb lay, was torn down to make room for a very different style of cathedral.

But there is also a "no" to be registered here. The plague had not created religious intolerance, let alone the sort of purist attitudes about cultural intermingling that had produced Alvarus of Cordoba in the middle of the ninth century, or Judah Halevi's tortured rejection of Arabized poetics and Greek philosophy at the beginning of the twelfth, or the Almohads' disrespect for Islam's own dhimma principles shortly thereafter. The plague, and everything it brought in terms of scapegoating and social upheavals, did not manage to eradicate the virtues of tolerance in one fell swoop, and perhaps ought not to be made a scapegoat for behavior for which people and societies are, in the end, responsible. The turn of events at any given moment reveals that individuals and their values play crucial roles, no matter what the broader forces at work may be. Peter the Cruel lived and ruled, after all, during the years of the plague, and his own Alcazar, as well as his financier's synagogue in Toledo, was built after 1348. And if the same Peter had Abulafia executed, it was because he suspected him of embezzling the funds for his sumptuous synagogue and not because he was Jewish. The anti-Jewish riots of just a few years later were fomented by individuals close to and protected by Peter's murderer and successor, his illegitimate half brother, Henry of Trastamara, whose attitudes about the Jews of Castile, as well as Islamic style in Christian buildings, were poles apart from those of Peter.

But most telling of all is how many of the values of medieval Spain were still alive a century later, and how easily events might have gone in a very different direction. The descendants of Peter and Henry, Isabella of Castile and Ferdinand of Aragon, marched up the hill to the Alhambra to take formal possession of Granada dressed in their Arab finery, and it was in the company of some of their many Jewish counselors and advisers that they signed a treaty granting dhimma-like rights to the Muslims. A very cynical view of this scene would perhaps regard it all as posturing and deceit, conspiracy and duplicity. Perhaps. But it seems more plausible to see in this scene what can be glimpsed in all of the stories here: the possibility for religious and cultural tolerance was there. Sometimes it triumphed and at other times it was squandered. The Catholic Monarchs could just as well have ignored and overridden the advice coming to them from the Church (however much their own attitudes coincided with such advice) that led them to expel the Jews from their lands and abrogate the treaties they had signed with their Muslim subjects. Christian Spain might thus have moved into the modern era with an exemplary working definition of religious tolerance and with a cultural politics that would have followed the traditions of their Castilian forebears, as far back as Alfonso VI.

The fact that Ferdinand and Isabella did not choose the path of tolerance is seen as an example of the intractability and inevitability of intolerance, especially in the premodern era. But their actions may be far better understood as the failure to make the more difficult decision, to have the courage to cultivate a society that can live with its own flagrant contradictions. They chose instead to go down the modern path, the one defined by an ethic of unity and harmony, and which is largely intolerant of contradiction. The watershed at hand was certainly the rise of single-language and single-religion nations, a transformation that conventionally stands at the beginning of the modern period and leads quite directly to our own. But not only could the Catholic Monarchs have made other decisions; as it turned out, it was no easy task to eradicate many of the deepseated attitudes that they themselves had seemed to personify, from the love of Arab baths and clothes to the reliance on Jewish physicians.

The Spanish Inquisition was set up to cure the perceived ills created by five hundred years of a society that did tolerate contradictions of all sorts. It turned out, however, not to be so easy. Despite the commonplace notions that Spain's intolerance was especially authentic and ferocious among those of premodern Europe, and that the events of 1492 were the triumphant culmination of hundreds of years of "Reconquest" and virulent anti-Semitism, something like the opposite was true. So deeply rooted were the old Andalusian habits that it was only with great violence over more than a century, with the burning of thousands of libraries and with the insistent propagation of even-then risible notions of the racial purity of Christians, that the Spaniards were finally cured of their deeply entrenched "medievalness."

A couple of snapshots from the royal family album tell bits and pieces of the tale. It was in the sixteenth century, during the reign of Charles V, Ferdinand and Isabella's grandson, that the lethal combination of Renaissance aesthetics and nationalist political ideology led to the tearing down of parts of the Alhambra in order to permit a disciple of Michelangelo's to build the neoclassical palace that now sits so awkwardly at the main entrance of the old Islamic palatine complex. It was also during those same decades of the mid-sixteenth century that a partial destruction took place of the interior of the Great Mosque in Cordoba. The mosque had originally been Christianized in a Mudejar style that harmonized with the Umayyad masterpiece, and this by medieval Christians who admired and even loved Islamic styles, and for whom Arabic was a language to be neither feared nor despised, even when the Muslims were political foes or religious rivals.

Some of the Christians of the new age at hand, however, hewed to their principles of political correctness and felt they could no longer pray surrounded by the languages of a religion they opposed. They thus made for themselves a sheltered and pure space in the center of the venerable old church, for by then it had been the Christian cathedral for nearly three centuries. They altered the whole in a dissonant and peremptory chord, with the building of the soaring and intrusive Italianate chapel that sits in its midst. Even Charles himself, it was said, was appalled by the result. The monarch who would eventually preside over the most repressive period of the Inquisition, during which, among other things, books written in Arabic were burned on a regular basis, was himself, much like his pious grandmother, not impervious to the charms of the old-fashioned Arabic style. When he was crowned Holy Roman Emperor in 1519, Charles was dressed for the ceremony in the royal gowns of his imperial predecessor, Frederick II, robes very much in the Islamic fashion that Frederick had so loved, a cape with a vast encircling hem embroidered in Arabic, no doubt with invocations to the One True God.

In 1991, Salman Rushdie published his first book of fiction after the notorious fatwa issued in 1989 by the Ayatollah Khomeini. That decree convicted the writer of blasphemy in his novel *The Satanic Verses*, condemning him, in effect, to death. The fatwa was described, with dreary predictability, as medieval: that is, as antimodern, backward, and unenlightened. The much anticipated post-fatwa book was entitled *Haroun and the Sea of Stories*, and it was generally understood to be an escape into fantasy or children's literature. A book dedicated to Rushdie's own son, whom he had not seen since he had gone underground in fear for his life, *Haroun* presumably allowed Rushdie to take a break, in the world of relatively harmless entertainment, from the harsh and dangerous political universe into which his *Satanic Verses* had cast him. Occasionally a reviewer mentioned the self-evident connection with the medieval classic *The Thousand and One Nights*, but this observation seemed to bear little significance within the political context that defined the furor over *The Satanic Verses*, nor was much made of the possibility that this purposeful link suggested ways in which *Haroun*, far from being an escapist work, might be something more like a statement of historical hope.

    Haroun's eponymous hero is himself named for the Abbasid caliph who was one of the greatest patrons of the translation movement that carried Greek philosophy into Arabic, as well as for a character from *The Thousand and One Nights*, a book that acquired much of its modern form in Baghdad, during the rule of the historical Harun al-Rashid. But Rushdie's diffuse allusions are at the same time an evocation of the culture that made so much provocative philosophy and literature a part of the Western tradition. Petrus Alfonsi (who, like Rushdie, interestingly, lived as an immigrant in England) was the first to bring the framed-tale tradition to Latin Europe, and he was followed by dozens of others, most of them anonymous Andalusian collectors and translators. By the middle of the thirteenth century, translations of those Arabic stories into both Latin and the vernaculars had become some of the bestsellers of Europe, and these in turn laid the groundwork for some of the seminal works of early European fiction. If the frames of these works characteristically present some sort of tyranny—direct or indirect echoes of Scheherazade's plight—the tales told within them embody the hope that stories can bring, since by their very nature they resist clear-cut interpretations and are likely to reveal the different ways in which truths and realities can be perceived. In its insistence that the point of stories, of literature, is to pose difficult questions rather than to propose easy answers or facile morals, this tradition is a central part of the Andalusian legacy to subsequent European culture.

One of the most distinguished descendants of that tradition, and one of *Haroun's* noblest predecessors, is Boccaccio's *Decameron,* that masterpiece about the saving power of stories and storytelling in the face of death. This fourteenth-century Italian work's brutal description of the Black Death serves as the prelude for a hundred stories about life itself, many of which speak to the happy complexities of the religious and cultural admixtures of the medieval world. One senses Boccaccio knew that much of that world, with its relish of contradictions, was on the verge of perishing in the plague, along with countless people. Among his stories, none is more iconic than "The Three Rings," in which Saladin asks a Jew at his court which of the three religions of the Children of Abraham is the true one. In the tradition of the framed-tale collections, the Jew answers Saladin with a story that can be interpreted in any number of ways: Once there was a king who had three sons he loved equally, and because he could not bring himself to give only one of them the ring that had marked the inheritance of the kingdom, generation after generation, he had a brilliant goldsmith make two rings identical to the first. All three sons thus inherited his divided kingdom, and thereafter no one was ever able to tell the original from the copies. The reader understands that Saladin's question itself springs from a universe used to the difficulty of such questions and not from any simpleminded or monochromatic orthodoxy.

Rushdie, too, believes in the jewel-like nature of the Andalusian Middle Ages and puts himself there through much of his own writing. Sometimes with as little as the title of a novel (*The Moor's Last Sigh*), sometimes elaborately explored in the space of a short story ("Christopher Columbus and Queen Isabella of Spain Consummate Their Relationship, Santa Fe, January, 1492"), Rushdie displays any number of attachments to medieval Islam, and especially to al-Andalus—the icon for him, a victim of fundamentalism, of a lost version of that religion and a Golden Age of Islamic civilization. Rushdie is far from alone in holding the Andalusian experience of Islam up as a model. In a superb scene in the movie *Lawrence of Arabia,* we see an eloquent reflection of the pervasive memorialization of al-Andalus as a unique moment in the history of the Arabs. Prince Faisal accuses Lawrence of being one of those "desert-loving Englishmen," whereas the Arabs instead love fountains and gardens—and the epitome of such love, and a grandeur that once shamed what was a dimly lit northern Europe, comes soon enough in the conversation when the embattled prince, weary of war, evokes the memory of the "vanished gardens of Cordoba." These are the ruins of Madinat al-Zahra, of course, which in

Arabic poetry have for centuries been a complex trope for both the heights of cultural achievement and centrality, as well as for the commensurate depths of tragic loss.

There are any number of shards of the Andalusian world that can be glimpsed in our own, and some of these have palpable connections to the unique cultural achievements that once adorned their world, our world. The Andalusian Hebrew poets have been the heroes of many of their preeminent twentieth-century successors, those pioneers in our own age in crafting Hebrew, once again, into a language that could begin to speak, as it did in David's time and then in Sefarad, as a vernacular as well as a liturgical language. The complex fraternity with the Andalusians, whom the contemporary Israeli poets understand to be their ancestors, just as David was for the Andalusians, often lies just beneath the surface of the poetic language. The links are perhaps visible only to those who know the complexities of linguistic history, but at times they are transparent to almost anyone, and especially striking when an Israeli poet like the late Yehuda Amichai, Israel's preeminent master of the new poetic language, crafted poems in which men like Judah Halevi and Samuel the Nagid mingle effortlessly with Amichai's other poetic personae.

Along with manifest connections such as these echo more complex resonances between our present and the Andalusian past, where the historic parallel may come with ironic twists. In the shadow of the new Hebrew poets, and scattered throughout the landscape of the mixed cultural identities of Israel, we can see Andalusian situations by the fistful. That legacy is alive and well in a host of instances, from the emergence of a generation of Palestinian-Israeli writers who have adopted Hebrew—either in place of or alongside Arabic—as their own literary language, with invigorating literary effects and vexing ideological consequences, to the controversial award of the Israel Prize in 1986 to Emile Habibi for his remarkable Arabic novel so suggestively titled *The Pessoptimist*. Even when political and ideological circumstances are characterized by strife, artistic and intellectual life prospers and reinvents itself in spaces created by cultural tolerance. And once a cultural intertwining follows from that tolerance, who can say that there will not be a better way to find solutions for seemingly intractable ideological and political differences? The Andalusian story reveals the inevitable tensions between our desire for cultural coherence, on the one hand, and the excitement and vitality of contradictions in ourselves and in our midst, on the other.

The Andalusian moral, in that sense, is that there are Judah Halevis within each of us, and thus within our communities. Halevi turned against his own and others' poetic triumphs because he believed in an ideology that shunned the languages of a foreign God, and for us it may as easily be the architecture of a tyrannical state, or the statues of pagans, or the novels of an oppressive culture that make us uneasy. Does poetry — or language or philosophy or music or architecture, even that of our temples — really need to dance to the same tune as our political beliefs or our religious convictions? Is the strict harmony of our cultural identities a virtue to be valued above others that may come from the accommodation of contradictions? The Andalusian stories allow us to glimpse one long and extraordinary chapter of our history in which the three major monotheistic faiths struggled, successfully and unsuccessfully, with the question of tolerance of one another. Just as important, certainly, is the kindred question, for those three faiths so dominant in our culture, of tolerance within themselves and their always variegated communities of believers; and this, too, was a question asked insistently in al-Andalus. Other questions echo endlessly: Can Muslims be successfully integrated into contemporary and secular European nations? Should fundamentalist Christians have to expose their children to the teachings of reason as well as those of faith, to evolutionary theories as well as scriptural truth? Can Catholic Croatians, Orthodox Serbs, and Muslim Bosnians coexist in the Balkans? How can tolerance and intolerance coexist?

On August 25, 1992, the Serbian army began shelling the National Library in Sarajevo. On purpose. Over a million books and more than a hundred thousand manuscripts were deliberately destroyed. Three months earlier, the same army had attacked the Oriental Institute in that city, with its magnificent collection of Islamic and Jewish manuscripts, and over five thousand of these were burned. Why? Since when are libraries strategic military targets? But wars are, of course, fought on many fronts, and the attack on those Sarajevan palaces of memory took place for reasons not unlike those that led to the burning of so many books in sixteenth-century Spain, and to the destruction or mutilation of any number of the memory palaces of al-Andalus. Books, like buildings, like works of art, like songs and sometimes even like the languages of prayers, often tell stories about the complexities of tolerance and cultural identity, complexities that ideological purists deny, both as an immediate reality and as a future possibility. Books—and the kindred fruits of the human imagination—often reveal that beneath the façades of even the most strident official tyranny, social and cultural intercourse will surely try to carry on. The artifacts, the books and the buildings that manage to survive, are themselves the acts of tolerance and resistance, or at least their best concrete measure.

A handful of treasures were saved from the terrible destruction of 1992, which fell, uncannily, on the five-hundredth anniversary of the capitulation of Granada and the expulsion of the Jews. Little survived in the ruins of the whole of the magnificent library and museum of Sarajevo, but among the most precious of the items that did is a famous manuscript called the

Sarajevo Haggadah. A Haggadah is a book of prayers and stories: tales to be told and prayers to be said on Passover, in remembrance of the Exodus. Despite the name, this gorgeous illuminated manuscript, considered the best of its kind anywhere in the world, is not "Sarajevan" at all but, like the two surviving synagogues of Toledo, a child of the mixed marriage that was the politically Christian but culturally neo-Islamic world of the Middle Ages in Spain. The book was made somewhere in the Christian territories in the late thirteenth or early fourteenth century—who knows, perhaps in some small town through which Moses of Leon passed, peddling his *Zohar.*

The book's first rescue from the bonfires of oblivion was when it was taken out of Spain in the Exodus of 1492 by Sephardic Jews who then settled in the Ottoman empire. There the Haggadah was cherished and protected, for nearly five hundred years. But then the precious book had to be rescued a second time during World War II. It was well known in intellectual circles that a certain Muslim curator in the library in Sarajevo had saved that Sephardic Haggadah from the atrocities of the Nazis, who were also inclined to burn it. For several years, whenever I spoke on this subject, I would note, at the end of the story, that the Muslim—whose name I did not know, and who I assumed was unknown—had saved that beautiful book no doubt in part because he knew its provenance. Like many Muslims to this day, he would certainly have had a special place in his heart, and in his memory, for what was once al-Andalus. I liked to suggest that he was obviously a quixotic type, an honorary descendant of that anonymous Morisco whom Cervantes had run into one day in Toledo, the one who had translated that true history, written in one of those mixed languages of Spain, the book with the story of Don Quixote in it, about to be destroyed, turned into pulp.

On May 2, 1999, I discovered that he was not, after all, anonymous. Some seven years after the book had been saved from the violence in Sarajevo, the front page of the *New York Times* ran a remarkable piece of true history that Cervantes himself would not have been embarrassed to tell. One of the thousands of "ethnic Albanians," a commonplace euphemism for those European Muslims who were herded out of Kosovo in early April of 1999, was a woman who, like most others, was able to take with her only a handful of belongings when she fled. As refugees are wont to do, what she chose to take into exile were tokens of purely sentimental value, among which the most precious, since she kept it on her person rather than in one of her two bags, was a piece of paper in a language that, as Cervantes would say, she could recognize but not read. All she knew, vaguely, was that it was some sort of prize that her father had once received and had cherished greatly. On the other side of the Macedonian border, after a harrowing trip, the woman thought to show her precious paper to the members of the local Jewish community, a group involved in the relief efforts for the Kosovars. She took the piece of paper to them because she knew it was Hebrew and she sensed it might well be the key to some story worth translating at that trying moment.

Indeed it was. The document was as precious, for her, as the discovery for Cervantes' narrator that the Aljamiado manuscript was the lost story of Don Quixote. The paper was the commendation her father had received from the Israeli government for saving not only the Sarajevo Haggadah but, as it turned out, Yugoslavian Jews from the Nazis. The Muslim librarian, who was a hero in book circles for having rescued that token of hundreds of years of medieval tolerance from the depredations of twentieth-century barbarism, had also hidden fellow Sarajevans, Jews, in his apartment during World War II. What was revealed in May of 1999 was that he was the father of one frightened and desperate woman, one of the victims among the thousands of such victims, in camps created by yet more twentieth-century barbarism. The daughter, who had known little about just what her father had done, was grateful for the special refuge she and her family instantly received at that hour of their greatest need. She was taken out of the camps and out of the war zone in Eastern Europe to Israel. She was met at the Tel Aviv airport and taken home by a man who greeted her as a long-lost relative, since he is the grown child of a woman among those saved by the good librarian, along with the great book of Passover prayers. "My father did what he did with all his heart, not to get anything in return. Fifty years later it returns somehow. It's a kind of circle."* The circle goes back further in both time and space than the librarian's daughter perhaps imagines, and it is intricately intertwined with any number of the stories that can be found inside our half-excavated Andalusian palace. There, in both the ruins and in the surviving beauties of that edifice, in books destroyed and in books saved, lie so many layers of our own cultural memories and possibilities.

---

*"An Indebted Israel Shelters Family of Kosovo Albanians," *New York Times*, May 2, 1999.

Postscript

On September 11, 2001, unimaginable violence came quite literally flying out of the blue and into the center of American life. Although a relative handful of analysts have claimed otherwise, it was soon enough clear that the attacks on New York and Washington, D.C., were the fruit of the sort of uncompromising religious intolerance that most Americans, myself included, would have said played little part in their daily lives. How wrong we all were. And how irrevocably has that universe of ours been changed by the appearance at our own front door, one beautiful early fall day, of a ferocious version of Islam.

I had some weeks before finished writing this book, an account of and tribute to the culture of tolerance brought to Europe by the Umayyads. But the book is also necessarily an account of the forces of intolerance that were always present and that ultimately triumphed. Just as our clichés about interreligious enmities blind us to the long and influential dominance of that culture of tolerance and its many unique material and intellectual achievements, they keep us from perceiving the deep divisions within each of the religions. The complex problem at the heart of the cultural history of medieval Europe was first and foremost how the great monotheistic religions of the Children of Abraham—faiths that all have powerful strains of ferocity within them—struggled to define what they were and what they might become. When they managed to find it within themselves to be truly first-rate, admirable achievements followed, and men like Samuel the Nagid rode the land and churches like San Roman were built and philosophers like Ibd Rushd were honored. But when, instead, the centers of such tolerance did not hold, irreparable destruction often followed, from the eleventh-century sacking of Madinat al-Zahra by fundamentalist Berber troops to the fifteenth-century tearing down of the old Almohad mosque that had served for so long as the cathedral of the Castilian monarchs in Seville.

And after the events of September 11, which make us read and hear everything somewhat differently—most of all, of course, anything having to do with Islam and with its relationship to other religions and cultures—it seems impossible to understand the history of what was once, indeed, an ornament of the world without seeing reflections of that history right at our own front door. Every reader will take away different lessons from the tales told in this book—and there is plenty of warning and encouragement in them all—but no one, including myself, is likely to see any of the morals as detached from us, as we might have before our own universe was devastated.

I have resisted the strong impulse to alter any part of the book, to fill it with pointers to the newly discovered morals of the story, as I see them. If the stories are well told and if the morals are clear enough, then these new meanings will seem obvious to the reader. And if some of the stories are now tinged with painful irony, so be it.

Paris
November 2001

Other Readings

Primary Sources and Their Interpreters

PAGE 32:

The brilliant ornament of the world shone in the west, a noble city newly known . . .

For translations of Hroswitha's works, see Katharina Wilson, *Hrotsvit of Gandersheim: A Florilegium of Her Works* (D. S. Brewer, 1998), readily available now in paperback.

PAGE 61:

A palm tree stands in the middle of Rusafa / Born in the West, far from the land of palms . . .

This translation of the much-quoted poem of Abd al-Rahman is by D. F. Ruggles, to whom I am also indebted for her brilliant work on the gardens and agriculture of al-Andalus, all now available in *Gardens, Landscape, and Vision in the Palaces of Islamic Spain* (Pennsylvania State University Press, 2000).

The pre-Islamic odes can be read in the volume of powerful translations by Michael Sells, *Desert Tracings* (Wesleyan University Press, 1989), which includes an excellent introduction to pre-Islamic poetry. More recently, Sells has also made available to English speakers eloquent versions of the early suras of the Quran in *Approaching the Qur'an: The Early Revelations* (White Cloud Press, 1999), a volume accompanied by a CD recording of Quranic recitations. His brilliant renderings of the luminous poetry of the Andalusian Sufi Ibn Arabi may be found in his *Stations of Desire: Love Elegies from Ibn 'Arabi and New Poems* (Ibis Books, 2000). Both volumes include introductions of value for both the uninitiated and the expert. I am also grateful to Michael for his translation of the part of the ring song quoted in my chapter "Love and Its Songs," and for the decade of friendship, and readings of Arabic poetry, that lie behind it.

PAGE 66:

The Christians love to read the poems and romances of the Arabs; they study the Arab theologians and philosophers, not to refute them but to form a correct and elegant Arabic . . .

This translation of the famous passage from Alvarus is taken from the masterful work of Jerrilyn Dodds, *Architecture and Ideology in Early Medieval Spain* (Pennsylvania State University Press, 1990). Not only from this book, which is the indispensable source for the complex web of relations between Mozarabs and Muslims, but from all her varied work, as well as from her generous friendship, I have learned almost everything I know about the culture of the arts, and the architecture, of Islamic Spain.

PAGE 79:

Let it be known to you, my lord, that our land is called Sefarad in the Holy Tongue, while the Ishmaelite citizens call it al-Andalus, and the kingdom is called Cordoba.

My thanks to Tali Farhadian for her translations from Hasdai's letter to the King of the Khazars.

PAGE 102:

My friend, for me in my straits / the Rock rose up, / therefore I offer these praises, / my poem to the Lord . . .

This and all other translations of the poetry of Samuel the Nagid are from Peter Cole, *Selected Poems of Shmuel Ha-Nagid* (Princeton University Press, 1996), with gratitude to the translator for his ongoing and generous interest in this project. Cole has also now published a second volume of translations of the great poets of the new Hebrew poetry of Islamic Spain in *Selected Poems of Solomon Ibn Gabirol* (Princeton University Press, 2000), this with an inspiring introductory essay.

PAGE 112:

Love, may God honor you, is a serious illness, one whose treatment must be in proportion to the affliction . . .

Translations from Ibn Hazm are newly done by H. D. Miller, with special thanks. The *Tauq al-Hamama*, this most famous work of the classical Arabic tradition of Spain, was influentially translated into Spanish as *El collar de la paloma*, by Emilio Garcia Gomez, but it has no worthy English translation.

PAGE 158:

Anxious or secure, my soul is Yours, / submissively and gratefully. / I roam, I wander, filled with joy in You / and thanking You in all my wanderings. . . .

This and other poems of Judah Halevi are the translations of Raymond Scheindlin, to whom I am grateful for these and many other translations over the years, and especially for the friendship and happy collaboration they represent. Scheindlin's two anthological volumes of translations of the Andalusian Hebrew poetic tradition, *Wine, Women and Death* and *The Gazelle*, seminal books from which so many first learned about this extraordinary body of poetry, are now available in paperback (Oxford University Press, 1999).

PAGE 164:

[The reason for the delay in my writing is] the long and difficult exile in which fate has tossed me, in a faraway land in the end of my days. . . .

Thanks to Samuel Rascoff for his translation and his many insights, all from his extraordinary Harvard senior essay, "Cosmopolitan Critic: A Cultural Profile of Moshe Ibn Ezra" (1998).

PAGE 170:

His eyes, grievously weeping, / he turned his head and looked back upon them . . .

From W. S. Merwin's translation of the *Cantar de mio Cid*, based on the edition by Ramon Menendez Pidal. Although Merwin translates the title as *Poem of the Cid*, Menendez Pidal's famous version of the epic work is pointedly titled *"cantar"* rather than *"poema"* to underline the editor's strong belief in the oral-formulaic nature of the poem and its performed nature. Among the versions currently available in paperback, the best for the uninitiated is the prose translation *The Poem of the Cid* (Viking, 1985) by Ian Michael, Rita Hamilton, and Janet Perry.

PAGE 174:

Fulfil then, my brother or rather, my lord, what you promised to your sister, or I should say, to your servant . . .

From *The Letters of Abelard and Heloise* (Penguin, 1998), translated and with an introduction by Betty Radice.

PAGE 201:

. . . *And standing by himself, I saw Saladin.*

Translation of *Inferno*, IV, by Mark Strand from *Dante's Inferno: Translations by Twenty Contemporary Poets*, ed. Daniel Halpern (Ecco Press, 1993).

PAGE 217:

If I told people that I am the author, they would pay no attention nor spend a farthing on the book. . . .

Text and translation from Gershom Scholem's fundamental work on the *Zohar* and the Kabbalah, *Major Trends in Jewish Mysticism*, available in paperback (Schocken, 1995). This book of Scholem's, originally a series of lectures, is still the most useful book for the relative beginner in this dauntingly complex subject. Another reliable introduction, with an extensive selection of translations from the *Zohar* itself is *Zohar: The Book of Enlightenment*, translation and introduction by Daniel Chanan Matt (Paulist Press, 1983) in the useful series Classics of Western Spirituality.

PAGE 235:

Of Pedro, King of Spain / Noble and honoured Pedro, glory of Spain . . .

Chaucer's description of Peter the Cruel is in "The Monk's Tale," here taken from the verse translation of *The Canterbury Tales* into modern English by David Wright in the World's Classics Series (Oxford University Press, 1986), as is his description of the new "Toledan Tables," which appears in "The Franklin's Tale."

PAGE 244:

Their highnesses and their successors will ever afterwards allow [the Granadans] to live in their own religion, and not permit their mosques to be taken from them . . .

The translation of the excerpt from the Agreements of Capitulation of the city of Granada is by L. P. Harvey. The entire agreement appears as an appendix in his excellent *Islamic Spain: 1250–1500* (University of Chicago Press, 1992), which, although written principally for scholars, is accessible to others as well, and in paperback.

PAGE 256:

He opened it in the middle, and after reading a little began to laugh.

Passage from *Don Quixote de la Mancha* by Miguel de Cervantes, from the translation by J. M. Cohen in the Penguin Classics edition (Penguin, 1998).

Other Readings in Literature

For those interested in reading further in Arabic literature:

The Arabian Nights is available in two paperback volumes, in a fine new translation by Husain Haddawy (Norton, 1990 and 1995). Robert Irwin's *The Arabian Nights: A Companion* (Penguin, 1994) is an outstanding study that places this quintessential medieval text in its many contexts. Irwin has more recently published an equally useful anthology of classical Arabic literature called *Night and Horses and the Desert* (Penguin, 1999). He precedes his selections with clear introductions that make this far more than the average anthology, and more like a concise literary history. An older but still useful volume is James Kritzeck's *Anthology of Islamic Literature from the Rise of*

Islam to Modern Times (Penguin, 1964), no longer in print but sometimes seen in used-book stores. Both have generous selections from Andalusian authors, located in the larger context of Islamic literature. As a supplement to the various volumes of Michael Sells's translations of poetry, the interested reader can find additional material in Cola Franzen, *Poems of Arab Andalusia* (City Lights, 1989).

In addition to the series of volumes of translations mentioned in the first section, there are several other excellent studies of the Hebrew poetry of Islamic Spain. Dan Pagis, himself a brilliant Israeli poet, delivered a series of highly accessible lectures later published as *Hebrew Poetry of the Middle Ages and Renaissance* (University of California Press, 1991). More scholarly but still readable, and a source of further bibliography, is Ross Brann's *The Compunctious Poet: Cultural Ambiguity and Hebrew Poetry in Muslim Spain* (Johns Hopkins Press, 1991).

Among contemporary writers, several are notable for the use they make of Andalusian characters and themes in their fictions. Jorge Luis Borges wrote essays on the *Thousand and One Nights* (a title he prefers to "The Arabian Nights") as well as a number of short stories intertwined with medieval Spain, among them most prominently "Averroes' Search." The recent publication of Borges' *Collected Fictions* (Penguin, 1999) and *Selected Non-Fictions* (Penguin, 2000) makes these readily available. Salman Rushdie's body of fiction is filled with appreciations of the medieval Islamic world from the outset, with ties especially to Islamic Spain in his more recent, post-fatwa, years. The story "Christopher Columbus and Queen Isabella of Spain Consummate Their Relationship, Santa Fe, January, 1492" is available in the collection *East, West* (Pantheon, 1994). *The Moor's Last Sigh* (Pantheon, 1997) takes the expression descriptive of Boabdil for its title, although the novel itself is only very indirectly involved with al-Andalus. Finally, among the historical novels concerned with medieval and Islamic Spain (almost all of which deal with the events surrounding 1492), the most distinguished is certainly that by the great Israeli novelist A. B. Yehoshua, whose *Journey to the End of the Millennium* (Harcourt Brace, 2000) takes several Andalusians from the time of the Cordoban caliphate on a journey to the environs of Paris.

Other Histories

The pioneering works of history and historiography by Ibn Khaldun and Edward Gibbon are readily available in paperback: Franz Rosenthal's translation of *The Muqaddimah: An Introduction to History* is available in an abridged one-volume format (Princeton University Press, 1969) in the Bollingen Series; an abridged, one-volume *The Decline and Fall of the Roman Empire* is available as the "Portable Gibbon" (Viking Press, 1970). Also still available and eminently worth reading is the classic *The Renaissance of the Twelfth Century* by Charles Homer Haskins (Harvard University Press, 1979), in which a scholar first took on the widespread prejudice (among scholars as well as laymen) about the "darkness" of the Middle Ages.

A wide-ranging selection of primary historical texts and documents from medieval Spain is provided in usefully annotated form in *Medieval Iberia: Readings from Christian, Muslim, and Jewish Sources,* edited by Olivia Remie Constable (University of Pennsylvania Press, 1997). No scholar has had greater impact on a field than Americo Castro in the area of medieval and early modern Spanish history and historiography. Castro's work on the interaction of the three religions in what he famously called a state of *convivencia,* or "living together," provoked considerable controversy, especially in Spain. Over the course of a distinguished career as a professor in the United States, regarding his vision of medieval Spain, and Spain's culture afterward, Castro wrote a number of seminal studies, and the 1971 translation of much of his work, entitled *The Spaniards: An Introduction to Their History,* captures a great deal of his thought.

The larger contexts in which the history of Islamic Spain unfolds is masterfully laid out by Albert Hourani, *A History of the Arab Peoples* (Harvard University Press, 1991). In addition to the treatment of Islamic Spain from 1250 on by L. P. Harvey, there are several useful narratives of al-Andalus in the broader medieval Iberian context. Bernard F. Reilley, *The Medieval Spains* (Cambridge University Press, 1993), interweaves the parallel histories of the Christian and Muslim dominions. Richard Fletcher, *Moorish Spain* (University of California Press, 1992), focuses more narrowly on al-Andalus, while Fletcher's *The Quest for El Cid* (Knopf, 1990) delves into the complex of Christian and Muslim relations during the taifa period. A very detailed political history can be found in Hugh Kennedy's *Muslim Spain and Portugal: A Political History of al-Andalus* (Longman, 1996). Among the recent histories of the Jewish communities of Islamic and Christian Spain, I find most useful, and readable, Jane Gerber's *The Jews of Spain: A History of the Sephardic Experience* (The Free Press, 1992).

It is worth mentioning two specialized books of extraordinary usefulness and particular interest, both out of print but both worth finding in research libraries for those interested in the topics: *Peter the Venerable and Islam* (Princeton University Press, 1964) by James Kritzeck and *The Matter of Araby in Medieval England* by Dorothee Metlitzki (Yale University Press, 1977).

Reference Books

The catalogues from two important museum exhibitions offer not only outstanding illustrations of a range of art and architectural monuments but many informative articles as well. The magisterial *Al-Andalus, The Art of Islamic Spain* edited by Jerrilyn Dodds (Metropolitan Museum of Art, 1992) is out of print, unfortunately, but well worth either the search for a secondhand copy or a special trip to a library. Still available is the less lavish but still beautiful *Convivencia: Jews, Muslims, and Christians in Medieval Spain* (George Braziller and the Jewish Museum, 1992), edited by Vivian Mann, Thomas Glick, and Jerrilyn Dodds. Both these books, as well as many others of a commemorative nature, were published in 1992, the quincentenary of the fall of Granada and of the expulsion of the Jews.

None of these commemorative volumes, however, approaches the encyclopedic scope of *The Legacy of Muslim Spain,* edited by Salma Khadra Jayyusi (Brill, 1992), which stands out with articles on virtually every aspect of al-Andalus' history, intellectual history, literature, and a host of miscellaneous and usually fascinating topics, from Andalusian culinary culture to the role of Muslim traders in the Mediterranean. Finally, in the series The Cambridge History of Arabic Literature, *The Literature of al-Andalus* has recently appeared, edited by M. R. Menocal, Raymond Scheindlin, and Michael Sells. Articles on conventional literary topics and authors are complemented by articles in important ancillary areas (such as "Language" and "Music").

In this volume, "Arabic" is defined broadly to mean literary phenomena inside the Andalusian orbit, and thus includes a series of Jewish and Christian authors not conventionally covered in such histories. Both this and the Jayyusi volume offer abundant bibliographies in every area they cover.

Thanks

This book was born as the vaguest of notions: that I might be able to transform the world I had for so long inhabited as a scholar into one that nonspecialists could enter. In the spring of 1998 I was invited by the Yale Alumni Association to be one of the speakers at that year's reunion weekends, when faculty give general-interest rather than scholarly talks on their research and teaching. In preparing and delivering the lecture, I realized explicitly something I had long suspected, that the world I was used to looking at mostly microscopically, the multireligious and multilinguistic world of medieval Spain, was ready-made for much broader exposure in our own time. The subtitle I used for the talk, "Medieval Europe and Authentic Multiculturalism," pointed in the direction of the self-evidently relevant aspects of the material, but beyond that it was the treasure trove of mostly unknown and unheard of stories and characters that seemed to be begging to be let out of the small scholarly precincts they mostly inhabit and into the wider world.

I suspect, however, I would have done very little or nothing with this insight after the alumni talks, and this book would be a vague notion still, were it not for the serendipity that on the afternoon of one of those talks, Jeanne Bloom happened to ride on the same train, on our much-traveled line between New York and New Haven. Jeanne's lively intellect and open-hearted friendship are among the finer pleasures of life for those of us lucky enough to be a part of her universe. And that afternoon she brought those qualities to bear, and it was her own insistence, when she read the typescript of that talk, that this was material for a nonacademic book, that transformed a vague idea into an active project. I am grateful for Harold's intense interest in the project—and his taking the time and trouble to write a foreword for the book is but a small part of it—but I owe Jeanne the most fundamental thanks, because it was she who set everything into motion. In the nearly four years that followed that fortuitous train ride, especially at discouraging moments when I doubted I could really write this kind of book, I could and did buoy myself with the vivid recollection of Jeanne's face when she read what turned out to be the first installment.

My other fundamental thanks go to Yale University, where I have taught and learned and thrived since the fall of 1986. This book would not exist without the many luxuries that institution lavishes on its faculty: years that can be devoted to specialized research, reading, and writing; the company and the example and the provocations of fellow scholars of every intellectual stripe; a library with incomparable resources; generous funds for travel and research assistance; and, perhaps most of all, the dozens of courses to be taught to the most appreciative and shaping of audiences, the Yale undergraduates. Paradoxically, more than any other book I have written, this one is the fruit of the rich life I have led at Yale. No list of the hundreds of individuals who have played roles in this life and no attempts at evocation of the dozens of occasions that have gone into shaping the stories and the arguments of the book, could even begin to do the matter justice. I leave it, then, to this rather impersonal expression of gratitude at the life I have been able to lead and the people I have been able to know, and love, and argue with—and I hope that many will understand who they are and know what roles they have played.

A handful of individuals, however, have been of such direct and significant help in the preparation of the book that they simply cannot go unnamed. Three students, Abigail Krasner, Howard Miller, and Ryan Szpiech, have provided invaluable help at different stages of preparing the manuscript: double- and triple-checking facts and years and names, hunting down seemingly unfindable books in the libraries, making suggestions for illustrations—and in the case of both Howard and Abby actually photographing sites in Spain for which it was otherwise nearly impossible to find good images. Kim Hastings, who was my student a number of years ago and who has since then become a coveted manuscript editor for many university presses, dropped all sorts of things in her life and work when I asked her to help with this book. This is now the second book that Kim has helped make possible with her loving attention to every detail of a manuscript and with that uncanny way she has of remembering that some verb used in one chapter early on appears again much later in all too similar a sentence. For all that, and more, not least of which is the sweetness and good humor that make working with her a delight, I thank her.

Perhaps the greatest pleasure comes from being able to recognize two people who have been indispensable to my life during these past several years of intense writing, because they are the most modest and least likely to understand their importance if they are not named out loud. Jane Levin and Norma Thompson, with whom I have the great luck to teach and work, have routinely lightened my various loads and given me shelters from all sorts of storms and made my peripatetic life in New Haven an easy part of their own, day in and day out. That unflinching generosity of spirit that characterizes each of them is at the very heart of what makes life at Yale so many of the good things that it is for me.

Alice Martell and I met as many mothers of a certain sort do — sitting watching our boys play ice hockey, at an indoor rink in the dead heat of August in New York, preparing for the season just ahead. I was a veteran and I could tell a mile away Alice was a rookie, and I was overcome with pity, and introduced myself, when I overheard her say that she hoped her son's playing hockey wasn't going to interfere too much with her family's weekends in the country that winter. Did I have news for her! I even had, I told her, a little piece I had written, mostly to amuse myself, on what it was like to have a child play hockey, every harsh winter weekend morning, at the dilapidated rink at the northern end of Central Park, where really tough hockey was played — and only really tough parents survived. I figured, with some amusement, that this beautifully dressed woman with her nice briefcase didn't have a clue and didn't stand a chance, but of course Alice was destined to become a far tougher hockey mom than I had ever been. My little essay on the subject might have failed at scaring her away from ice hockey, but it accomplished something infinitely more important: it made us friends, and it made her my agent even though at that time I had nothing much to sell. But Alice loved the little bits and pieces of nonacademic writing I had done and mostly kept in a drawer, and I loved her instantly for loving what I wrote and for saying it with that radiance and intensity of hers that could make whole skating rinks melt. She insisted I should be writing other things, and when the time eventually came that I was ready to do this book she brought every ounce of her boundless energy and intelligence to bear, walked me through a half-dozen versions of the proposal with unflagging enthusiasm, and then found me the world's best editor for the book-to-be. Alice is a life force, and the ideal agent a writer might dare to invent in a story about an improbable writer meeting an agent she wasn't even looking for—and the worthiest of hockey moms, besides.

It seems to me that for as long as I have read about books and writers I have heard the clichéd lament that editors are not what they used to be: they used to read every word an author wrote, or even thought about writing; they used to take a book from an idea through every draft, no matter how many, and then copyedit the last one for good measure; they used to care about books and writings as good things in and of themselves, and so on, every sentimental bit of it. Bill Phillips comes straight out of that universe of old-fashioned editing that has, by all accounts, nearly disappeared, and his work honors those traditions and keeps them alive. From our first phone conversations, when the book was little more than an idea and an outline, all the way through to our last discussion about the last adverb he had slashed and the last comma he had added, Bill was always as involved in the book as I was, some days more so. He has endless gifts and endless willingness to use them for his writer, and I still don't know how he managed to tell me I had to throw away the whole first draft and start all over again without provoking utter despair, or how he was able to read the very last draft, which he practically knew by heart at that point, with the fresh intelligence few would have had for the first. I suspect that his kind of editing was always a rare thing, even in the most golden age of bookmaking, and I thank Alice and my lucky stars for having thrown me his way. And Bill for never despairing of me.

And George Calhoun can still come up with the single perfect sentence to hand me, just when I need it. A small miracle, this, and all it stands for, and all some thirty years since he first took me down the road to those places where Arabic is the language of God and of love poetry. For all of which I am always grateful.

Books have an uncanny way, sometimes, of bringing to a close chapters in one's life, and this one does so for me. I write these thanks surrounded by boxes of my books, and many of my other things, packed up and waiting to go into storage, not really knowing where it is they will be unpacked, in half a year's time. It is a bittersweet task, at such a moment, to give the final thanks to the person whose unconditional love nourished me over the better part of the last five years, and especially so during the making of a book that, in a thousand and one ways, is as much his as mine. Public acknowledgment is not part of the deal, but this book is itself a witness and a tribute to that vivid life we somehow managed to lead during those years.

New York City
August 2001

Index

❀

DATE DUE

MAY 1 5 2008			
GAYLORD			PRINTED IN U.S.A.